THE
SUBTERRANEAN
RAILWAY

THE
SUBTERRANEAN
RAILWAY

How the London Underground
was built and how it changed
the city forever

CHRISTIAN WOLMAR

Atlantic Books
London

Published in Great Britain in 2004 by Atlantic Books,
an imprint of Grove Atlantic Ltd.

9 8 7 6 5 4 3 2 1

A CIP catalogue record for this book is available from the British Library.

ISBN 1 84354 022 3

Designed by www.carrstudio.co.uk
Printed and bound in Great Britain by Creative Print & Design,
Ebbw Vale, Wales

Atlantic Books
An imprint of Grove Atlantic Ltd
Ormond House
26 – 27 Boswell Street
London WC1N 3JZ

www.christianwolmar.co.uk

In memory of Eric Mattocks, squatter extraordinaire
and rail enthusiast, whose library I have gratefully inherited.

CONTENTS

ILLUSTRATIONS

Traffic chaos on the streets, print by Gustave Doré

The 'Great Victorian Way' by Sir Joseph Paxton (Copyright © TfL reproduced courtesy of London Transport Museum)

The pneumatic railway at Crystal Palace (TfL)

Charles Pearson (TfL)

'Cut and cover' at Parliament Square

Notting Hill Gate station (TfL)

Sir Edward Watkin (TfL)

James Staats Forbes (TfL)

A Circle line train approaches Aldgate (TfL)

Station advertising on the underground railways (TfL)

First-class travel

Earls Court station (TfL)

Inhospitable carriages on the first tube trains

Boat race day at Baker Street station

The Big Wheel at Earls Court (TfL)

Central London Railway locomotive (TfL)

Building a station using the Greathead shield (TfL)

A 1908 map of the Underground

A 1932 map of the Underground

A modern-day version of Harry Beck's map of the Underground (TfL)

A 1905 poster advertising the 'Twopenny Tube' (TfL)

Down Street station, Mayfair (TfL)

Charles Yerkes (TfL)

ACKNOWLEDGEMENTS

The staff of the London Transport Museum and, in particular, the library have been extremely helpful in meeting my requests for information and allowing me to visit the Acton Depot several times. Thanks also to the staff of the British Library, a wonderful but greatly undervalued resource.

Thanks are also due to: my agent, Andrew Lownie; my researcher, Gully Cragg, who found many of the gems; John Fowler and Mike Horne for reading the text and picking up errors; and Scarlett MccGwire who not only read the text but also made many helpful suggestions.

AUTHOR'S NOTE

In this book, I have used 'tube' normally to refer to the deep-level lines and 'Underground' for the whole system even before the name was in current use; the Metropolitan District is referred to as the District to avoid confusion; and, to make the book more easily readable, I have avoided acronyms as much as possible.

THE

PHANTOM RAILWAY

When I was a child, I used to be haunted by the sound of ghostly horns echoing through the night near Campden Hill where I lived. I wouldn't learn the source of this ghoulish noise until much later, but it was the Underground which used to keep me awake. On a hot night when the windows were open, the sound felt so close and threatening that, for a while, I demanded that my poor mother sat on a chair outside my room in our little flat while I fell asleep. It was not until I started researching this book that I made the connection between my troubled nights and the railway which I used to take to school every day.

It seemed inconceivable that the source of my childhood terror should be the Underground which, surely, as its name suggests, was safely buried under the ground. But the Victorians who built it were always trying to cut corners, not least because they were beholden to shareholders who wanted to see a profit out of their enterprise. The Circle Line passes under Campden Hill between Kensington and Notting Hill Gate but the builders left the ground open above the line wherever they could in order to save the cost of covering all their excavation. Moreover, this is an early section of the Underground, built by the Metropolitan Railway in 1868 when the line was operated by steam engines and therefore these open sections provided much-needed ventilation. Because these gaps were surrounded with walls for obvious safety reasons, they act as echo chambers and when the trains passing late at night sounded their horns to warn workers on the line, the noise reverberated far and wide, even to our flat several hundred yards away from the nearest hole.

My sleepless nights were a legacy of decisions made by the Victorian designers of the Underground. So much of Londoners' daily lives is affected by similar considerations. My daily journey to school, too, was heavily influenced by the way in which the Underground lines had been set out by the Victorian builders of the system. Virtually every day when my Circle line train pulled out of Kensington High Street towards South Kensington, two stops down the line, it would grind to a halt in the tunnel. Why? Because the District line trains from Earls Court would be cutting across our path on a level junction and we would have to wait. Such a junction on a crowded railway would never be built today – instead there would be a flyover or tunnel – but the Victorians were constrained by the fact that they had to build their railways in the cheapest possible manner in order to have any chance of recouping their money. That junction, which was then under the West London Air Terminal being built at the time, remains one of the bottlenecks of the network today, still causing grief and hassle to thousands of people every day.

But, despite the daily delays endured while crammed into crowded carriages, like many children of my generation I fell in love with the Underground at an early age. It represented freedom and adventure, a seemingly limitless network of stations with wonderfully exotic names such as Cockfosters and Burnt Oak. There were no automatic gates in those days and for a couple of pence thrust hurriedly into the hands of the ticket collector together with a mumbled mention of the previous station, I had the freedom of the system for a day. There were even stations, like nearby Holland Park, where you could exit the system for free provided you were prepared to walk up the stairs rather than use the decrepit lifts. Trips to the end of the line were particularly exciting, passing places like Totteridge or Theydon Bois that still, in the 1960s, had the feel of a distant village rather than being so easily connected to what claimed to be at the time the world's biggest metropolis. I never quite dared to venture out on the far reaches of the Metropolitan, which, I feared wrongly, had ticket collectors on the train since the distances were so great and the fares so high.

Returning to the site of my childhood adventures today, it is remarkable how little has changed on the older parts of the system since then, but a returning Victorian would be deeply disappointed at the lack of recognition of the fantastic achievement in creating this remarkable system. Indeed, most Londoners are oblivious to this history, taking the Underground for granted and, when complaining about its inadequacies, failing to recognize the reason for them.

Taking a trip along the oldest section of line, from Paddington to Farringdon, which opened in 1863 (see Chapter 2), it becomes clear why there is so little knowledge among today's travellers. There is precious little to show that this section of line, now shared by the District, Metropolitan and Circle lines, has such a historic significance. The original stations, built in simple Italianate stone style, have all been replaced, and though some of their successors still have 'Metropolitan Railway' just below the roof, invisible to most passers-by, none show the original date when the system first opened.

At Paddington, I searched in vain for any recognition of the history in the tacky station entrance while the only clue inside was the fact that the platforms are in an airy space far more generously proportioned than their more recent equivalents. At Edgware Road, again much more spacious than normal stations, a large display is given over to the staff's success in London Transport garden competitions, but, again, there is nothing about the fact that this is part of the route of the world's first underground line.

Only at Baker Street has there been a real effort to honour the history and not just with Sherlock Holmes kitsch. There are plaques telling the story of the early days of the line and the station was refurbished in 1983 to create much of the original atmosphere, except, of course, the clean electric trains could never recreate the smoky fug of their steam forebears. Much of the original sandstone brickwork has been uncovered and freed of advertising, but the high alcoves were unfortunately covered with ghastly white tiles, out of keeping with the Victorian interior.

At Great Portland Street, originally Portland Road, the station is in an island of traffic and as I supped a cup of tea in the small friendly café, and again I searched in vain for any recognition of the history. The absence of any such signs is illustrative of the way that London and Londoners take the Underground for granted, with so little homage to its historical significance. Indeed, some of the traces of history left on this original section of line is misleading. At Farringdon, the old name, unnoticed by the rush of commuters because it is high above the newspaper and flower sellers, is given as Farringdon & High Holborn, a rather inaccurate appellation – since High Holborn is nowhere near the station – that was only used between 1922 and 1936. Today, Farringdon is a busy through station for the Underground, and for Thameslink trains which run on two parallel lines that were, as we shall see in Chapter 3, built within five years of the opening of the Metropolitan to cope with the huge number of trains seeking to use this new underground railway. There is no trace of the fact that Farringdon was the original terminus where the banquet was held to celebrate the opening of the Metropolitan in 1863.

London, in fact, pioneered two different types of underground railway, both of which were unique world firsts – those built using the 'cut and cover' method like the Metropolitan (now known prosaically as the sub-surface lines) and the deep tube lines drilled out of the London clay deep below the surface in order to avoid the clutter of drains, sewers and utilities which had already built up in Victorian times. There is even less recognition of this colossal achievement. The first of these deep lines (see Chapter 7), the City & South London, ran between a now defunct station, King William Street (near the present

Monument), and Stockwell and was completed in 1890, but there is little left at those stations today to indicate this was another brilliant first by the Underground's pioneers.

Another reason for the lack of knowledge is that the London Underground has so often been ignored. It is amazing how little has been written about the effect of the Underground on London. There are countless tomes about its construction, a truly miraculous undertaking, largely, but not entirely, funded by private entrepreneurs. There has, too, been much on how the construction of the main line railways affected Britain by dramatically reducing the time taken to travel around the country. However, scant attention has been paid to the fundamental role played by the Underground in the life of Britain's premier city.

Oddly, even many biographies of London pay little attention to the system hidden anything from thirty to 250 feet beneath its surface.[1] Of course there are many books which concentrate on the engineering achievements of the railway and its haphazard construction. The spectacular feat of building a railway underneath a built-up area, a concept so brave and revolutionary that it took nearly forty years for any other country to imitate it, should not be underestimated. The people who devised and developed the concept were visionaries, ready to risk ridicule and bankruptcy to push forward their ideas. This book explains how they did it, but the achievements of the Underground go way beyond its mere construction. Its role in the development of London and its institutions is probably greater than that of any other invention apart, possibly, from the telephone. Without the Underground London would just not be, well, London. Oddly, that is recognized more often abroad where the famous roundel, the 'logo' of the system created long before that word was ever in common parlance, is the emblematic image of the English capital. Here, with our usual disdain for engineering and our inability to recognize our own achievements, we have tended to ignore the magnificent organism living permanently under our feet.

Most fundamentally, the Underground allows Londoners to traverse the city in a way which would be impossible by any form of surface transport. Yes, more people use buses every day – but many of those journeys are in the suburbs. In central London, the Underground is the way to get around town, as demonstrated by the fact that it is used both by besuited City gents and by their cleaning ladies. There is something remarkably egalitarian about the Underground, and that was true right from the beginning when it attracted both the bowler hat and the cloth cap brigades; though, of course, there were separate classes for them until the advent of the deep tubes where such niceties were not possible.

But apart from uniting the capital in an unprecedented way and enabling journeys which had hitherto been impossible or incredibly lengthy, the creation of the Underground stimulated development of the city itself. This is most famously illustrated through the expression 'Metroland' (Chapter 12), the area of north-west London which was built and indeed marketed as a direct result of rapid access to the centre of London via the Metropolitan line. But in fact, right from the start, those who conceived of a railway under London realized that it would create the opportunity to build new developments around stations. More than that, the poor would be able to afford decent housing thanks to the cheaper land available outside the centre of London. It did not quite work out like that, but then that is very much part of the Underground story, with plans and projects not always turning out as expected.

Probably the next greatest impact of the Underground on London is the design and architecture. The purity of the design is encapsulated most famously in Harry Beck's map of the system, but also given expression in the architecture of numerous stations and the consistency of the use of the typeface, Johnston, devised specifically for the Underground. There is barely a streetscape in the centre of the city or in most high streets served by a station which is not made recognizably and demonstrably London by a design feature initiated by London Transport. That, of course, goes beyond the Underground, as it includes the humble bus stop with its characteristic roundel and the majestic Routemaster, a bus that manages to look modern forty years after it first rolled on London's streets. All this is deliberate and most of it can be attributed to the meticulous requirements of Frank Pick who, with Lord Ashfield, did more than anyone to integrate London's transport. It is no exaggeration to say they created a brilliant system of transport management which, in the 1930s, became a world class model, envied and studied around the world (see Chapter 13).

Another breathtaking legacy of the Underground is the wealth of posters commissioned by London Transport which are of a remarkably high and, most important, consistent standard. They cover a breadth of subjects ranging from simple information on ticket offers or destinations to excursions or warnings of danger, and the designs manage to reflect their times, using contemporary styles which often, thanks to the excellence of their execution, still appear modern. Indeed, those who ran the Underground helped to design London.

Then, of course, there is the impact of the Underground system in wartime (see Chapter 14). Of course everyone thinks of the Second World War, but, as this book shows, the Underground was even used briefly for shelter in the First. Another little-told story is how in the 1950s London Transport changed the demography of the capital by recruiting directly in the Caribbean and Africa for cheap labour to run the Underground and the buses at a time of full employment among the British population (see Chapter 15). Taking this all together, it is no exaggeration to say that the Underground helped build the London we know today.

This book is an attempt to do justice to the achievement of the Underground pioneers not only for having produced a transport system which, for a time, was unparalleled anywhere in the world, but also for having helped create and transform the city. It tells both their story and that of the system they made, and shows that their achievements go far beyond their effect on transport.

Christian Wolmar, July 2004

O N E

MIDWIFE TO THE

UNDERGROUND

Underground railways were invented by a man born in the eighteenth century. Charles Pearson, who first set out the idea of running railways under cities, took his first breath in October 1793, at the height of the worst excesses of the French Revolution and more than two decades before Napoleon met his Waterloo.

As ever with history, there are various theories about who really was the first to conceive of an underground railway with the aim of alleviating the growing problems of congestion on London's streets. But Pearson has by far the best claim. It was Pearson, the City of London solicitor, who first set out his notion in a pamphlet in 1845, suggesting a railway running down the Fleet valley to Farringdon that would be protected by a glass envelope making it 'as lofty, light and dry... as the West End arcades'.[1] The trains were to be drawn by atmospheric power so that smoke from steam engines would not cloud the glass. This, of course, was not the scheme that was eventually built, but Pearson's concept was certainly the kernel of the idea that was to become the Metropolitan Railway two decades later along broadly the same route.

And it was Pearson who masterminded the financing of the Metropolitan which saved the scheme at the eleventh hour. Indeed,

Pearson was a serial promoter of such undertakings, supporting several similar projects in the 1850s, and thanks to his perseverance eventually got his way. While the importance of Pearson's role is open to debate, it is difficult to argue against the proposition that without him, London might not have pioneered a transport system that transformed urban living. One could go further. Without Pearson metro systems might never have been developed, because the advent of the motor car in the late nineteenth century, followed quickly by electric tramways and the motor bus, could have resulted in the bypassing of the underground railways as a solution to city traffic problems given the expense and disruption of their construction as happened in most cities in the US. Paris, after all, was not to get its first Métro line until 1900 and the New York system did not open until 1904. Both learned much from the mistakes and tribulations of London's pioneers.

In the early decades of the nineteenth century, London metamorphosed from a busy commercial centre into the world's first megalopolis. It was not surprising, therefore, that it would be the first to have underground railways, but it is, perhaps, remarkable that it beat its French counterpart by thirty-seven years.[2] Whereas previously London's rural surroundings had never seemed very far away, now the sprawling slums were interspersed with elegant Georgian squares and swathes of little factories and warehouses which had sprung up in the capital as the Industrial Revolution gathered pace. Greater London's population in 1850 had grown to 2.5 million from just under 1 million in 1800. The Georgian enclaves which had sprouted in the late eighteenth and early nineteenth centuries on fields, snapped up cheaply by eager speculative developers, had enabled the relatively well-off to enjoy a new type of suburban living, away from the throng of the city. These areas, such as Camberwell, Kennington, Islington and Mile End – all fashionable again now as they were built by what Simon Jenkins calls 'men of taste and discrimination'[3] to high standards – were within a mere hour's walk of the City in those days before traffic lights, congestion and pedestrian barriers.

Picture, for a moment, the London when Pearson's idea for underground railways first emerged. As one historian, Hugh Douglas, eloquently put it, 'towards the middle of the [nineteenth] century, London was dying – slowly, painfully and with a great deal of protest. No physician had to be called in to diagnose the trouble; it was all too apparent to those who lived there, for, wherever they went, they encountered the great thrombosis of traffic which clogged the highways that were the veins and arteries carrying the city's blood.'[4] The cause of the clogging of the arteries was too much affluence and good living. London – indeed, the whole country – was prospering mightily. Britain was becoming the hub of an empire and her capital was emerging as the richest city in the world. With the huge increase in population, nearly a quarter of a million people were daily coming into the City to work.

The turmoil on the roads was, however, more like a Third World than a Western city today. There were wagons whose drivers walked beside the horses, blocking a large part of the roadway; and large advertising vans pulled by horses whose very purpose – to be seen by as many passers-by as possible – meant their progress was bound to be slow. Costermongers with carts and animals being driven to market ensured that speeds in the central area rarely rose above walking pace. The bridges were particular bottlenecks and rain would add to the chaos by turning the roads into muddy quagmires.

More and more housing was needed as increasing numbers of jobs were created in the burgeoning factories and workshops, and, most important, in the offices of the City where the demand for clerks, before the days of typewriters, was almost unlimited. Demand for transport soared. No longer did people work within the district where they lived. The first commuters[5] were hardy souls who had walked from areas of low rent to commercial districts, but as London spread, this was no longer possible. Successive new transport methods were introduced throughout the Victorian era in attempts to cope with the demand, starting in 1829 with the omnibus. George Shillibeer opened the first service using twenty-seater carriages from Paddington to the Bank of England, anticipating the same route that the first Underground railway would take thirty-four years later. Although Shillibeer's pioneering status can be questioned, as his omnibus service was little more than a stagecoach which made a shorter journey with more stops, the introduction of his service was a momentous event in the history of London's transport. However, it was not for the masses. The fare of one shilling to travel from Paddington to Bank was expensive and would have deterred all but the wealthiest of potential commuters – in contrast the workmen's trains of the Metropolitan Railway would, three and a half decades later, offer a whole week's travel for just one shilling.

Horses, which from 1870 also pulled trams along iron rails, remained the mainstay of much of the transport system until the turn of the century; oats and hay were as important a source of energy as coal. The rich had their own horses and carriages, a phenomenon which, rather like the growth of the private car a century later, was a major contributor to the congestion problem, but it was damned expensive as the horses required looking after, feeding and grooming. And what came out of the rear end of horses remained a major problem: 'The best estimate is that by the 1830s, English towns had to cope with something like three million tons of droppings every year'[6] and three times that by the end of the Victorian era. And, contrary to those nostalgic pictures of old crones rushing after carriages to pick up fresh manure, the stuff was virtually worthless, barely five shillings a ton to the farmer. Therefore it was dumped in vast dung heaps in the poorer areas of town, contributing greatly to the squalor, stench and unhealthiness of Victorian London.

With the arrival of the omnibus, London grew at an even greater rate. The censuses of 1841 and 1851 show that during this decade alone an extra 330,000 migrants had flooded into the capital, making up more than one sixth of the population. These incomers were partly attracted to London by the prospect of golden streets, but mostly they were fleeing from rural areas where the crisis in agriculture had reduced employment, or from Ireland where the appalling potato famines had led to emigration on an unprecedented scale. London's rate of growth was to continue and the capital, boosted by the burgeoning wealth of the empire and, particularly in the second half of the nineteenth century, an economy that was almost continually expanding, became a vortex, sucking in an ever greater proportion of the nation's population. It was the most exciting city in the world and everyone wanted or needed to live there. While it was inevitable that the transport system had to grow to accommodate this multitude it was no means certain that underground railways would become the chosen solution.

However, in the middle years of the nineteenth century, none of the alternative forms of transport were particularly enticing. Apart from walking and the new omnibuses, there were the hackney cabs, which were expensive, at eight pence per mile, and uncomfortable, and the drivers would often go by circuitous routes to boost their income. So as more and more omnibuses, carriages and hackney cabs piled onto London's roads in the early decades of the 1800s, it is easy to see how the idea of digging big holes under the city to transport the masses gradually began to be put forward and grudgingly accepted. Nevertheless, it took a massive leap of imagination to adopt such a radical solution and it is impossible to exaggerate the extent to which the notion of building railways under cities was radical and far-sighted.

In the mid 1840s, when the concept of an underground railway was first being elaborated, the railway age was a mere fifteen years old. It helped, of course, that the railways were also a British invention. The first locomotive-hauled railway linking two major cities, the Liverpool & Manchester, had only begun operating in 1830. As freight was the initial *raison d'être* for the construction of railways, London came rather late to the new technology, several years after the industrial heartlands of the north of England, where the need to move coal and other primary material more quickly than by canal led to a rapid burgeoning of the railway system. The iron road was, however, still unproven and evolving.

When in 1837 the first major line out of London to the north was completed, with Euston as its terminus, the developers of the railway did not bother to build many stations on the southern sections of the line around the capital. Other lines were also completed without serving the capital's hinterland. This was partly because the railways reached open countryside within a mile or two of what was then a compact city, but it also represented a failure of imagination by the railway companies. They saw their role as straddling the country and carrying people long distances, rather than linking the capital with outlying villages, and failed to recognize that such short journeys were a potentially lucrative market. So the Great Northern, for example, had just four stations in the eighteen miles between its grand terminus at King's Cross and Hatfield – Hornsey, Southgate, Barnet and Potters Bar – the middle two of which, incidentally, are now Underground stations. On the Euston line, the first stop was Harrow and on the Great Western it was initially West Drayton. Despite the railways' dramatic effect on the country, as one historian puts it, 'until the 1860s, and arguably until the end of the century, their least important impact was in providing transport within London itself'.[7]

With few trains, and omnibuses slow and expensive, walking continued to be the preferred method of travel for the majority of Londoners. And even when the first suburban London railway was built, the London & Greenwich, the developers, insufficiently confident about their own project, provided a walkway alongside, charging users a small toll. The London & Greenwich opened in 1836 and was a remarkable engineering achievement as, to save on land, it was built on 878 arches, which remains to this day the longest set in the country. The grandly named 'pedestrian boulevard' next to the line soon disappeared as more tracks were added to the railway, which became the main artery linking the centre of London with its south-eastern suburbs.

As an urban railway for people making short journeys, the London & Greenwich was a precursor to the Underground. The experiment of running short-distance trains in an urban context proved successful despite doubts as to both the viability of the technology and the extent of the potential market. The line was soon carrying 1,500 people per day at fares of one shilling for 'imperial carriages' and half that for 'open cars' on trains that ran every quarter of an hour throughout the day. Initially the line struggled to make a profit, given the high cost of constructing all those arches, and it was not until a system of local railways centred around London Bridge emerged over the next couple of decades that shareholders began to get an adequate reward. By the middle of the 1840s, with other companies running tracks on the line, 5,500 people were being carried daily and holiday times proved highly lucrative as people used the line for day trips out of London. Had north London developed such an extensive system so early, today's Underground map would look very different and much less dense. But it was no geographical accident. Property was cheaper in the southern suburbs, which meant that they grew more quickly, thus creating a larger potential market for local rail services. The terminus at London Bridge, too, was on land that was much less expensive than property on the City side of the Thames, where it would have been unthinkable to carve out huge swathes of the estates owned by powerful aristocrats antipathetic to the new iron roads. In South London the land was the property of the Church, and the bishops who managed it – mostly the dioceses of Winchester, Rochester, London and Canterbury – were relatively welcoming to rail schemes. The bishops had also allowed cheap houses to be built on their land whose occupants were too poor to resist demolition, unlike the more affluent landlords north of the river.

So a pattern familiar to today's Londoners was set, providing the answer to that oft-asked question as to why only the northern half of the capital is well served by the underground network: more suburban lines were built on the surface in south London than in the north, obviating the need for underground railways. It was not until the invention at the end of the nineteenth century of tube railways, which ran deep into the London clay, that the underground system was to reach across the Thames. And even then, as we shall see, the geological conditions favoured underground railways north of the river.

The first railway through north London was something of an oddity, as it followed an orbital rather than a radial route. Originally intended primarily for goods, the North London Railway opened in 1850 between Fenchurch Street and Islington and was extended, in the following year, to Hampstead Road (Chalk Farm), via Bow, from where a spur went deep into London's Docklands. Within a few months, 7,500 people were using the quarter-hourly service every day, even though the line pootled aimlessly around north and east London before diving into the City. By linking lots of other railways, it demonstrated the enormous latent demand for rail services which was to be the spur for the creation of the Underground.

Of course there were also other social forces helping to create the conditions that enabled Pearson's concept to come to fruition. The phenomenon of travelling long distances to work, mostly on foot, had begun: as early as 1836, 175,000 people crossed London and Blackfriars bridges daily, most paying tolls. While there were also poor districts in growing industrial areas such as Spitalfields and Shoreditch in the East End, the slums of central London remained the worst in the capital until the second half of the century. Censuses reveal that a modest-sized house in areas such as Seven Dials or the southern end of Baker Street might be crammed with thirty or forty people.

There was a growing clamour among the political classes to clear the slums and improve transport communications. The railways fulfilled, at least in part, both roles. Although railways would be banned by a Parliamentary commission from reaching the centre of London, they were driven through the poorest parts of the capital outside the central area with little regard for the local inhabitants, while the richer estate owners were able to ensure that their property was not breached. In the middle years of the century the development of the railways transformed London. As Simon Jenkins puts it,

> the coming of the railways to London from the mid-1830s onwards dealt the metropolis a bigger, and certainly more lasting, blow than anything since the Great Fire. Like the Great Fire, the railways shattered both the living and working arrangements of hundreds of thousands of Londoners. Like the Fire, they ate up vast quantities of labour, material and capital, and destroyed acres of the metropolis in the process. Most important of all, like the Fire, they spun the population of London ever further from the core, speeding the decay of the central districts, yet at the same time enabling Londoners to enjoy higher standards of space and cleanliness in their housing than in any other city in the world.[8]

While this process was initiated by the suburban railways, of which the London & Greenwich was the pioneer, the Underground was to play a major part, with whole sections of London owing their existence to its arrival. Gradually the elements which made a London underground railway feasible were coming together. The relative popularity of the London & Greenwich showed that railways could successfully be used for short journeys and it stimulated a host of other such projects; employment was increasingly rapidly, creating, as we have seen, the notion of commuting; the continued growth of the City was leading to more and more congestion; and it was apparent that the horse was both an inefficient and an expensive source of power. Soaring land values and the vested interests of the major estate owners made surface developments in the centre of London prohibitively expensive and prompted a plethora of schemes for creating railways underneath and through London.

Pearson, therefore, was promoting an idea whose time had come. He was a visionary and an idealist, who recognized that the railways were the key to transforming the city and improving the lot of the masses. Pearson had two, somewhat conflicting, ideas: a huge central London station and an underground railway connecting the main line stations which were then emerging on the periphery of the capital. Pearson's station would have been on the edge of the City, at Farringdon, and as well as serving the four corners of Britain, its aim – in line with his zeal for social reform – were to allow working people to live in decent conditions outside town. This would have been achieved by linking it with a new town at Hornsey or Tottenham where 10,000 cottages, each with its own garden, were to be built cheaply enough for artisans and clerks to rent. Train fares, too, would have been low enough to ensure that they could travel daily up to town for work. Pearson's visions, therefore, were never simply about transport but had at their heart the aim of creating a better life for his fellow citizens.

Pearson had a long line of social campaigns behind him. He was born in the City, and came from comfortable middle-class stock – his father, Thomas, was an upholsterer and feather merchant – but throughout his career he took on radical causes. He became a solicitor in 1816 and was soon elected a councilman of the City of London, possibly helped by the fact that his wife Mary was the daughter of another member of the Corporation. He came to prominence by exposing the system of packing juries in trials for political offences, and his progressive views led him to take on an eclectic range of issues, from prison reform to the ban on Jews becoming brokers in the City and the removal from a monument of an inscription attributing the Great Fire to Catholics. Until his long campaign for the Underground, Pearson's most celebrated battle on behalf of the common people had been when he tried to break the monopoly of the capital's gas companies, each of which had carved itself out an area where it was the sole supplier. Pearson had wanted the mains and pipes to be owned by co-operatives of consumers, a remarkably far-sighted concept for the 1840s; but, after a pitched battle over the installation of a gas main between workmen employed by the Commercial Gas Company and a rival group enlisted by Pearson for the Commissioner of Sewers, he was forced to withdraw, leaving the monopoly unchallenged. It was as City Solicitor, a position he held from 1839 until his death in 1862, that he was able to smooth the way for the creation of the world's first underground railway. Pearson had first set out the idea of 'trains in drains' when standing unsuccessfully in a by-election in Lambeth, but the idea survived his failure, although it was shelved while the excesses of the railway mania of the mid 1840s ran their course.

In many respects, poor Pearson can be seen as a serial but heroic British failure. He stood in several other by-elections for Parliament apart from Lambeth, always being roundly defeated, and many of his schemes and ideas never caught on, but his tenacity, perhaps prompted by these setbacks, was essential for bringing the scheme for an underground railway to fruition.

Given this patchy record it is not surprising that Pearson's contemporaries were sceptical about his early dreams of a rail line under the streets and that it took two decades for the railway to be built. Vague ideas for underground railways had been mooted as early as the 1830s, but, in truth, they were fanciful because the tunnelling technology was not really yet available. Of course, tunnels had been dug under hills and cuttings had been hewn through the countryside to create large embankments for railways, but these were in open country, not underneath the most expensive properties in Britain where the slightest subsidence would lead to exorbitant compensation claims. Victorian entrepreneurs were notably more prepared to take risks than today's engineering companies, but not so gung-ho that they would consider such a foolhardy enterprise. Moreover, as we shall see, the method of powering the underground trains was to be a troublesome issue as electricity was the only effective means and the technology to harness it would not be available for another three decades.

Nor in these early days of the railway age were the political climate and administrative infrastructure conducive to building underground lines, which were fraught with risk while seeming to offer little potential for making money. The motivation of the railway developers was always dominated by the need to make a profit. There was little consideration of the public good in these schemes, even if they happened to be of great benefit to society. As one historian puts it, 'the paramount consideration therefore in the minds of the projectors and managers of Britain's nineteenth century railway system when making decisions was a simple one: what balance could be expected between the direct private costs and private benefits of the investment? . . . The Victorian railway entrepreneur was guided by experience and commonsense, raised to a very high order, not by systems analysis.'[9] Considerations other than short-term profit occasionally came into play, such as building a line to stop a rival company establishing a route or to cream off business from an existing railway, but developers, unlike Pearson, were not inclined to consider the social benefits.

Inevitably therefore many railway companies got it wrong (although today's major project developers are not much better at getting their sums right, despite the panoply of analytical tools at their disposal). After the early railways, which tended to be profitable, they built many which never made an adequate return for investors – but most of them, particularly in urban areas like London, were of great social benefit. To the entrepreneurs and their shareholders, this was no use as they had no mechanism of capturing and profiting from that benefit. So the railways were not popular, and were often portrayed in the press as rapacious and irresponsible monsters wrecking the bucolic bliss of the countryside and forcing themselves on the unwilling inhabitants of towns and cities. As one historian puts it, the railways were cast 'in the role of a mindless juggernaut, grinding private rights into the ground in the blind quest for profit'.[10] They had to be controlled, and in London, without a city-wide government, it was Parliament's job to take a strategic view, despite the politicians' *laissez-faire* instincts. From 1846 onwards, there was a series of inquiries, roughly one every decade, by Royal Commissions and select committees of Parliament into the various plans of the railway entrepreneurs. Their decisions largely shaped the rail map of the capital as it exists today and, indeed, the findings of the first one, the Royal Commission on Metropolis Railway Termini of 1846, led directly to the development of the Metropolitan line. The establishment was a response to the fact that at the height of the railway mania of the mid 1840s, no fewer than nineteen urban lines and termini were projected and it was clear that this potential wholesale demolition, and the chaotic traffic conditions it would engender, could not be countenanced, even by the Victorians obsessed with keeping government out of business.

The Commission took evidence from a diverse range of people and interests – valuers, parish bodies, the Corporation of London, even Her Majesty's Woods and Forests, and, of course, railway developers with their retinue of traffic managers, solicitors, engineers and land agents. The key issue for the Commission was the location of the London stations. Should they be on the edge of the current conurbation or should they be allowed to make incursions right into the centre, creating a much more convenient service? The commissioners had to balance two clearly conflicting needs: on the one hand, 'if they allowed the wholesale invasion of central London presently intended, they would fill in an area already crowded beyond endurance'; on the other, if they left the termini too far out they would block up the thoroughfares with 'leviathan waggons and vans sometimes creeping about the streets, having a few articles at the bottoms of the waggons [while] at other times with loads overhanging on each side the foot-pavement of the narrow streets and lanes through which they pass'.[11]

In the event, the commissioners found that the advantage of 'bringing the railway stations further into the city appear to us exaggerated'.[12] They were, of course, wrong: think how wonderful it would be to have a series of city centre railways, bringing people right into the heart of London without the need to transfer onto buses or the Underground. It was, though, an impossible dream. Even if the railway companies had been given permission to build deep into the City, the economics would have proved an insuperable barrier. The nearer the railways ventured into town, the more they had to pay for the land and the more likely they were to come up against the powerful interests of the great landowners of London. As John Moxon, chairman of the London & Croydon Railway, said: 'Every railway we apprehend in its first mile costs more than in any other part of the line'.[13] The early London termini were, therefore, crude sheds, one-storey brick houses containing little more than a ticket office. It was only when the railway companies wanted to demonstrate their power that they began building palaces like St Pancras and Euston, or elegant sheds like King's Cross.

So the railway developers were defeated – the commissioners rejected seventeen of the nineteen proposed schemes before them, and gave only conditional assent to the other two, both extensions south of the river. Moreover, the Commission recommended a no-go area for the railways, extending from Park Lane in the west to Bishopsgate in the east and from the New Road (now Marylebone and Euston roads) in the north to the Borough in the south. The ban held, with the small exception of the incursion of the London, Chatham & Dover Railway over the Thames (see Chapter 3), until the building of Victoria station in 1858, and the line of terminals stretching today from Marylebone to King's Cross shows how the Commission's findings determined the future shape of railways in London.

The side effect of the Commission's decision was to ensure that London would need an underground railway, because any link between the various stations could not possibly be built on the surface: even viaducts would have affected too much highly expensive land. The Commissioners had heard evidence from Pearson on his idea for an 'Arcade Railway', but the concept elicited little interest and no finance.

Although Pearson continued, in vain, to battle for his scheme for a central station long after the Commission had rejected the idea, he began to focus on his other project, an underground line joining the termini. For the next inquiry, in 1854–5, Pearson was better prepared and had dug up hard evidence for the need for his railway by taking the first ever traffic count of people coming into London. He had appointed traffic takers, checking those entering and leaving between 8 a.m. and 8 p.m. on all the principal roads to the City of London. The results revealed that omnibuses were the main method of coming into town with 44,000 passengers, on 3,700 vehicles. On the railways, 27,000 people came into Fenchurch Street and London Bridge combined, but barely any – a mere 4,200 – to the three stations to the west, King's Cross, Euston and Paddington, a fact that did not seem to help his case for an underground railway. A further 26,000 people entered on private carriages or hackney cabs but all these numbers were dwarfed by the 200,000 who walked into the City. Pearson drew the rather obvious conclusion that

> the overcrowding of the city is caused, first by the natural increase of the population and area of the surrounding district; secondly, by the influx of provincial passengers by the great railways North of London, and the obstruction experienced in the streets by omnibuses and cabs coming from their distant stations, to bring the provincial travellers to and from the heart of the city. I point next to the vast increase of what I may term the migratory population, the population of the city who now oscillate between the country and the city, who leave the City of London every afternoon and return to it every morning.[14]

The committee again threw out the vast majority of the railway schemes, but did recommend that there should be a railway connecting the various termini as well as the Post Office and the docks. In this it had clearly been strongly influenced by Pearson's scheme for a railway from Farringdon to King's Cross. It was, as one historian puts it, a seminal report: 'The direct results of the select committee of 1854/5 have tended to be underestimated. The Metropolitan railway and the Thames embankment were both foreshadowed in the report and both were based upon recognition of the principle that railways in towns should make a contribution to public amenity and not merely intrude at will.'[15] In other words the social benefit of railways had begun to be recognized, but nevertheless the committee argued that the underground railway should be developed by the private sector alone. However, as we shall see, it did eventually receive some support from the state.

Given the range of improbable schemes put forward by Victorian inventors and entrepreneurs, there was understandable scepticism about the notion of 'underground railways'. Viewed from the twenty-first century, it appears easy to distinguish between the ill-thought-out schemes that were inevitably heading down a technological cul-de-sac, such as atmospheric or cable railways, and those that are the roots of today's transport systems. But that is to abuse the benefit of hindsight: for the Victorians, backing the winning systems was a veritable gamble by brave shareholders, many of whom lost their money. Indeed, Pearson's idea of an underground railway was just as far-fetched as many of the other ideas which were circulating at the time and came before the committee. Digging a huge hole in an urban area for a railway tunnel was no more or less mad than, say, the two separate schemes for a 'crystal' railway, developments of Pearson's original idea of an arcade railway. The first, put forward by an architect, William Moseley, was for a railway twelve feet below street level between St Paul's and Oxford Circus, a route which nearly half a century later would become the core of the Central line. The 'crystal' was a bit of Victorian hype to describe a railway enclosed in glass with a walkway above, and shops, houses and even hotels on either side, a sort of nineteenth-century shopping mall complete with atrium.

The second scheme for a 'Grand Girdle Railway and Boulevard under Glass', suggested by Sir Joseph Paxton, the designer of the Great Exhibition's Crystal Palace four years earlier, was even grander, a twelve-mile railway built above ground but within a glass arcade and, like Moseley's scheme, also containing houses and shops. It too broadly followed the route of what would eventually become an Underground line, since the aim was to link London's railway termini, as forty years later the Circle (which fortunately escaped the fate of being called the Girdle) was to do. Paxton's scheme, for which he sought public funding and which he cannily called the Great Victoria Way to curry royal favour, was quite liked by the committee but was ultimately rejected on the grounds of cost.

Eccentricity and technical innovation were not always an insuperable barrier for the promoters of what today would be considered as crackpot schemes, only fit to be laughed at in museums. After all, Eiffel got his tower and the Crystal Palace was built. Both the schemes for crystal railways were to be powered by atmospheric pressure, a system by which a cylinder under the train was sucked through a sealed pipe between the tracks by creating a vacuum at one end using huge pumping engines. Several atmospheric railways were, in fact, completed, including a line between Forest Hill (later extended to New Cross) and Croydon in south London. The great advantage was that the coaches did not need smelly and noisy locomotives to haul them as all the power came from a static engine house. While the theory was sound, in practice there was constant difficulty in keeping the seal tight, especially as the continuous valve between the rails had to be kept closed with a leather flap on top of the pipe but had to be opened to let the connection to the cylinder under the train through. Although the leather was kept oiled with lime soap, this would dry quickly and all the pressure would be lost. Far from being cheaper, the power for the trains cost three times more than conventional engines and all the various schemes soon changed over to locomotives. The demise of Croydon's railway killed off another scheme, the idea of a tube railway, also operated by atmospheric pressure, which was intended to be cut through London's clay from Hyde Park to the Bank and was the brainchild of Frederick Bramwell, the president of the Institute of Mechanical Engineers.

There was, too, the concept of cable railways. The London & Blackwall, which stretched from the Minories on the eastern fringe of the City (extended in 1841 to Fenchurch Street) to Blackwall, on the river three and a half miles away, operated on this principle. It was the first London railway to cross an area which was already fully built over with streets and houses and, like the Greenwich, it was constructed on viaducts. There were stationary engines at the Minories and Blackwall and the method of operation was bizarre. Carriages were attached to a rope at the end station (Blackwall) and at each of the five intermediate stations. After telegraph messages – an early use of this technology – had been dispatched to ensure that all the carriages were attached, the rope holding the carriages would be hauled in by the stationary engine. From the Minories to Fenchurch Street, the carriages coasted down a slight incline.[16] Despite frequent breakages of the rope (not entirely solved when hemp was replaced by wire after a couple of years) and the fact that it was impossible to travel between intermediate stations without going to one of the termini, the railway proved highly successful, carrying 10,000 travellers per day by 1846. Cable operation, which enabled speeds of up to thirty mph to be reached, was finally replaced after nearly a decade with conventional steam locomotives. Interestingly, part of the Blackwall route survives on the line of the highly successful Docklands Light Railway.

So, in the context of a world in which atmospheric and cable railways were being built and used by passengers, and a plethora of other outlandish schemes dreamed up by developers were being considered, Pearson's plan for an underground railway does not appear too far-fetched. Nevertheless, it took a lot of bloody-minded persistence and effort to persuade investors to stump up the money, even though the scheme had been endorsed and supported by Parliament. Even Pearson aficionados did not always have faith that the idea was truly viable. Henry Mayhew, the writer and campaigner, discussed 'our joint schemes' and 'often smiled at the earnestness with which he advocated his project for girding London round with one long, drain-like tunnel and sending the people like so many parcels in a pneumatic tube'.[17]

Mayhew pointed to the difficulties Pearson faced in trying to persuade his contemporaries of the viability of the idea. Writing after the opening of the first section of the Metropolitan, Mayhew recalled how Pearson had to overcome all kinds of superstition and pseudo-scientific mumbo-jumbo:

> Such a scheme, though it has proved one of the most successful
> of modern times, met with the same difficulties and oppositions
> that every new project has to encounter. Hosts of objections were
> raised – all manner of imaginary evils prophesied – and Charles
> Pearson, like George Stephenson before him, had to stand in that
> pillory to which all public men are condemned and to be pelted
> with the dirty missiles which ignorance and prejudice can always
> find readily to their hands. The proposal was regarded with the
> same contempt as the first proposal to light the streets with
> gas . . . so learned engineers were not wanting to foretell how the
> projected tunnel must necessarily fall in from the mere weight of
> the traffic in the streets above, and how the adjacent houses
> would not only be shaken to their foundations by the vibrations
> of the engines, but the families residing in them would be one
> and all poisoned by the sulphurous exhalations from the fuel
> with which the boilers were heated.[18]

For his doggedness and stubbornness alone, in overcoming such prejudice Pearson deserves to be remembered as the man who gave us the underground railway. His original concept would go through manifold versions, often forced upon him by financial and practical constraints, and incorporate many ideas from fellow visionaries and developers, but essentially he was the midwife of the Underground.

T W O

THE UNDERGROUND
ARRIVES

To build a railway in Victorian times, developers needed three things in addition to luck and gumption: Parliamentary permission, capital and labour. Railway companies were fortunate in having a privileged position which allowed them to adopt a corporate form that meant they were able to raise capital from more than six people. Other companies operated under a restriction which limited the number of investors to five or fewer, a result of legislation introduced in response to the scandal of the South Sea Bubble in the eighteenth century; which remained in force for manufacturing companies until the 1860s. Moreover, the railways could compulsorily purchase property, but to obtain planning permission they had to introduce a private Bill and successfully negotiate it through both houses of Parliament. This was not a straightforward process since Parliament was chock-full of people with vested interests, which might incline them to be in favour or against a particular Bill, irrespective of its merits or obvious failings. This explains how all sorts of absurd schemes for railways that had no chance of making any money or which did not serve any real purpose managed to slip through the process while other, much worthier, projects never materialized. In practice, the Lords rarely rejected a project that had been accepted by the Commons and it was the lower house which became the scene of major battles on railway bills.

The first step, therefore, towards the building of the Underground was a Bill for a line between Edgware Road in West London and Holborn Hill on the edge of the City, which was successfully taken through Parliament in 1853 by a group that had no connection with Pearson. However, as the developers had foolishly cut the line short of Paddington in a late concession to opponents, their Bill was superseded the following year by an Act for a line between Praed Street, opposite Paddington station, and the Post Office near St Paul's, later shortened to reach only Farringdon Street.[1]

As with all such legislation, the successful passage of the Bill gave the developers permission to obtain the land and anything that stood on it. Therefore, the landowners had to be satisfied by the Parliamentary process that they were to receive compensation for their loss – otherwise their objections could kill it. Generally, during the promotion of their bills, railway developers reached accommodations with the large landlords, the aristocratic estate owners, but rode roughshod over the smaller ones who did not have the clout – or the lawyers – to fight their corner during the Parliamentary process. As for tenants, trifling compensation was paid to some of the occupants of the squalid housing demolished to make way for the railways but those who rented on a weekly basis got nothing.[2] The first part of the Metropolitan line from the west was to be built under what is now Marylebone and Euston roads.[3] Since that section was under a road, it required no demolition of buildings, but the second part, when the line turned southwards towards Farringdon down the Fleet valley, necessitated the demolition of many homes.

The blithe manner in which the builders of railways were allowed to cut a swathe through slum areas was one of the ongoing scandals of Victorian life and was the subject of several attempts at legislation promoted by reformers. The Underground was responsible for less damage than most railways because it was largely built underneath the streets, using what became known as the 'cut and cover' method – simply digging a hole, installing the railway and covering it up again;

nevertheless the poor in the way of the route suffered. There is some dispute about the precise number. While an 1853 law required railway companies to set out 'demolition statements' listing the numbers displaced, no one checked the accuracy of these figures. The companies indulged in dirty tricks, such as paying landlords to evict their tenants a few weeks before their houses were needed.[4] The official figure for the number of people displaced by the building of the Metropolitan from Paddington to Farringdon Street was just 307; but a contemporary source[5] claimed that merely in driving the line through the Fleet valley from King's Cross to Farringdon, 1,000 houses containing 12,000 people were swept away.

There were suspicions, too, that the Metropolitan had deliberately drawn up its route to go through poorer areas where the residents were easier to displace. An outraged local vicar, William Denton of St Bartholomew's near Smithfield, wrote: 'The special lure of the capitalist is that the line will pass only through inferior property, that is through a densely peopled district, and will destroy the abode of the powerless and the poor, whilst it will avoid the properties of those whose opposition is to be dreaded, the great employers of labour.'[6]

The developers were also required to pay compensation to owners of houses under which the tunnel passed, but since for the most part the line was designed to go beneath roadways, the Metropolitan also largely escaped that requirement. To show its benevolent intent the company bought and converted a court in St Bartholomew's to rehouse some of those displaced. This was a cynical exercise designed to appease public concern in the short term: within two years the company had evicted the tenants and converted the houses into profitable warehouses. Pearson's lofty motives proved, therefore, not always easy to reconcile with the practicalities of a commercially minded company beholden to its shareholders.

After the second Bill received the Royal Assent in August 1854, there were several alterations and changes to the route over the ensuing four years but the basic concept remained the same. Construction was delayed while the company tried to overcome the second big obstacle, raising the required capital. The process for obtaining money for railway projects was remarkably haphazard. The sums required were vast, especially given that the total amount of available capital was relatively small as the banking system was still in its early stages of development. It is no exaggeration to say that railways were the principal catalyst for the creation of capitalism. As Nicholas Faith has observed, 'railways were by far the biggest projects undertaken since the time of the Romans. Before the railways, the world's financial markets were, at best, primitive affairs, incapable of providing the unprecedented amount of capital railways absorbed . . . The railways did more than create markets: miraculously they conjured up whole new breeds of men: the promoters and financiers [who] found the money.'[7] Investing in railways was a risky business. A few people, particularly early on, made good returns; many received barely any dividends for years but did, at least, retain their capital; and an unfortunate minority lost everything. The investors in Underground lines during the ensuing fifty years, in which the core of today's system was built, largely belonged to the middle of those three categories.

The project for the Metropolitan Railway nearly foundered several times on the difficulties of the search for capital, made all the harder by the fact that the scheme involved underground travel, a revolutionary concept which understandably scared off investors. It was only through a Victorian version of a public–private partnership that the money eventually came through. The Great Western had always been willing to invest a part of the cost – £175,000 out of a total estimate of just under £1m – but the Great Northern, the other railway which was to benefit through a connection at King's Cross, was reluctant to put up any money. The other railways were obvious sources of investment because the Metropolitan was to have connections through to the main line at both Paddington and King's Cross, so that the Great Northern and the Great Western could run trains, including freight, on the new railway. However, the railway companies were not prepared to stump up sufficient finance and by 1857 the Metropolitan's directors were so dispirited that they almost wound up the business.

Instead, in early 1858 they decided to spend £1,000 in a last-ditch effort to attract investors. And this is when Pearson became the saviour of the project. Although he was not a director of the company, he used his role as the City of London's solicitor to persuade the Corporation to invest in the project. Basically it was the nightmare of congestion on the city streets which won over the case for the railway. The political head of the Corporation, the Lord Mayor, David Wire, accepted the case for the railway by admitting that business in the City was being damaged by the crowded streets, and that rising land prices were driving low-paid workers out of the centre. Since it was impossible for these people to travel long distances to work each day, they were crowding into unfit dwellings with forty or fifty jammed into a small six-roomed house on the outskirts. The line was seen as a way of enabling people to live further away from their place of work, relieving both the congested roads and the cramped and insalubrious housing conditions.

However, public corporations like the City were not in the habit of investing in commercial ventures and the opponents of the railway even argued that it was illegal. The laissez-faire Victorian ethos did not normally allow for government involvement in commercial enterprises. But Pearson found a precedent in the Corporation's contribution to the construction of the West India Dock at the turn of the century and used this to convince the city fathers that they could invest in the railway. The City's involvement was a bit convoluted. The Metropolitan Railway was allowed to purchase the land it required in the Fleet valley, much of which had recently been cleared to make way for what is now the Farringdon Road, for the bargain price of £179,000; in return the City subscribed £200,000 in shares which were later sold at a profit. To clinch the deal, Pearson persuaded the directors of the Metropolitan Railway to threaten to withdraw from the project if the City did not invest, a rather dubious piece of lobbying given his position.

It was not only Pearson's direct intervention with the City which gained him his reputation as the saviour of the railway. For the previous couple of years, he had lobbied tirelessly to persuade other investors to fund the scheme. He spoke at meetings, wrote letters and pamphlets, used his City contacts to press potential investors to stump up the cash and wooed the reluctant Great Northern to invest. Pearson sent out a *Twenty minutes letter to the citizens of London*, which gave a history of attempts to raise capital, stressing that he did not stand to gain personally as he only owned fifty shares and was not a director.[8]

The changes in the route to reduce the cost and allay opposition were sanctioned by a Parliamentary Bill in August 1859 and, thanks to Pearson's efforts, construction was able to begin in the spring of 1860 with the hope that services could start running within a mere two years. And now, of course, the third element required for building a railway came into play: a team to build it within the budget, led by an engineer with the ability to carry through what was an unprecedented project – a railway carved out of city streets. The cut and cover method was used to build the entire three-and-a-half-mile stretch, apart from a 700-yard tunnel hewn out under the hill of Mount Pleasant in Clerkenwell.

The crucial job of engineer was carried out by John (later Sir John) Fowler who remained with the project from his appointment in 1853 right through to its opening a decade later, a loyalty which, in truth, was guaranteed by the extremely generous remuneration of £137,700 he received. Given that this represented almost 15 per cent of the project's costs, it was much more, relatively, than any of today's fat cats receive, although Fowler would have had to pass on a proportion to his colleagues and assistants. Fowler was one of the great Victorian railway engineers and his skills were undoubtedly responsible for turning an ambitious project into reality. He came from Sheffield and his early work was on railways in Yorkshire and Lincolnshire. He moved to London in 1844 with a burgeoning reputation for innovative engineering and he was either the main or the consulting engineer on most of the London underground railways that were built until his death in 1898.

From an engineering point of view, the new railway involved a myriad of technical problems that had not been previously encountered. Shallow tunnels had never been built under city streets that contained all kinds of sewers, drains and pipes, many of which had to be diverted. Little was known about how the particular stresses and strains of an 'under the streets' railway would affect the brick arches used for the tunnels. And how to avoid undermining the foundations of nearby buildings was another new problem. Carving a railway line under a city was such a pioneering concept that it is impossible to exaggerate the courage of all concerned in pushing through and building the Underground.

Of course, the thousands of 'navvies' who supplied the brawn took the most risk, as construction methods were primitive. With labour incredibly cheap and a seemingly endless pool of men who had left agriculture to try their luck in the cities, there was little problem in finding workers to build railways such as the Metropolitan. The term 'navvy' derived from the word navigator, first used to describe the workers who built the navigation canals in the eighteenth century, and the nickname stuck when they went on to build docks and the railways. They had a fiercesome reputation for drinking and brawling and while they were not quite the wild men so often portrayed, their lives were tough and frequently cut short by accident or disease. Usually most of the navvies came from local agricultural areas through which the railway lines were being laid but, obviously, the Metropolitan was forced to look for labour further afield and men were drawn from across the nation, including Ireland and the Highlands of Scotland.

There were two shifts of navvies on the building of the Metropolitan and men worked through the night by the light of blazing flares. Despite this, the schedule of two years proved optimistic and construction dragged into a third year, much to the consternation of the residents and the traders who were affected by the building work. The building created an awful mess of mud and muck in the streets along the route and this affected tradesmen, who called meetings to fight against the threat to their livelihood. One group even formed the Euston Road Trade Protection Association to try to obtain reparations for the damage caused by the diggings and, as ever, the lawyers did well. The Metropolitan made some efforts to limit the damage it caused, particularly in wealthy areas. The best example occurred when, a little later, the railway expanded westwards: the Metropolitan built a fake façade in Leinster Gardens, near Bayswater, complete with windows and doors to cover the fact that this elegant terrace now had a big gap where numbers 23–24 had once stood. The mock houses, which remain a tourist curiosity today, were, reportedly, frequently used to play practical jokes on rookie messengers and post office boys.

Despite these efforts at mitigation, the disruption created by the building of the line must have been unbearable, as little consideration seems to have been paid to the needs of the local residents and businesses affected by the construction. A Victorian observer was rather understated in his perception:

> The work of constructing this remarkable railway eventually became . . . somewhat wearisome to the inhabitants of the New Road [now Euston Road]. A few wooden houses on wheels first made their appearance, and planted themselves by the gutter; then came some wagons loaded with timber, and accompanied by sundry gravel-coloured men with picks and shovels. A day or two afterwards, a few hundred yards of roadway were enclosed, the ordinary traffic being, of course, driven into the side streets; then followed troops of navvies, horses and engines arrived, who soon disappeared within the enclosure and down the shafts. The exact operations could be but dimly seen or heard from the street . . . but paterfamilias, from his house hard by, could look down on an infinite chaos of timber, shaft holes, ascending and descending chains and iron buckets which brought rubbish from below to be carted away; or perhaps one

morning he found workmen had been kindly shoring up his family abode with huge timbers to make it safer. A wet week comes, and the gravel in his front garden turns to clay; the tradespeople tread it backwards and forwards to and from the street door; he can hardly get out to business or home to supper without slipping, and he strongly objects to a temporary way of wet planks, erected for his use and the use of the passers-by, over a yawning cavern underneath the pavement.[9]

Although – through both legitimate and illegitimate means – the Metropolitan did not have to pay much in compensation to landowners whose property was affected by its construction, the railway company faced all kinds of other legal claims for loss of business or disruption. There is no doubt that there was considerable hardship caused to businesses along the New Road when the railway works made the street impassable, and many went broke. There was a series of claims from publicans whose buildings, and trade, were affected. The first to try his luck was a man called Hart, publican of 1 Chapel Street just off the Marylebone Road, who complained that railway workmen had torn down part of an outer wall and nearly caused the house to collapse, forcing his lodgers out. He was given £120. The owner of another pub, the Pickled Egg in Clerkenwell, was granted £100 because the railway had put up a hoarding outside the house which had apparently shaken the foundations of the hostelry. The courts, though, tended to view claims, particularly large ones, with suspicion. The landlord of the Rising Sun in the New Road claimed £1,100, arguing that cracks had appeared in his wall, but the jury only awarded him £20. Others got nothing for their pains. Numerous households obtained small sums while Clerkenwell Vestry sought unsuccessfully to stop the company making excavations, arguing that they would endanger its workhouse.

The work was speeded up by a remarkable wooden contraption, some forty feet high, an early version of a conveyor belt, which hoisted excavated earth from the vast holes being dug by the teams of navigators. The spoil went to a site off the Fulham Road in West London called Stamford Bridge, which forty years later became home to Chelsea football club, whose fans unknowingly stood on embankments carved out of the extra soil dumped there by the Metropolitan. Not surprisingly, given the novel nature of the undertaking, there were several mishaps during construction which contributed to the delay in completion beyond the very ambitious target of mid 1862.

The first occurred quite soon after the start of work, in May 1860, when an excursion train on the main line with a guard who was too drunk to apply the brake overshot the platform at King's Cross and ended up in the Metropolitan workings. There was much damage but remarkably no one was killed. A few months later, the boiler of an engine pulling wagons exploded, a regular hazard of the primitive steam locomotives of the time, killing the driver and his lineman. Most seriously, in May 1861 there was a collapse of the earthworks in the Euston Road which destroyed the pavement, gardens, telegraph wires and gas and water mains. Fortunately, creaking in the wood supports had alerted the workers, who fled, and no one was injured; but the damage to the frontages of the houses gave further succour to the compensation-hungry lawyers.

The worst accident during construction was the bursting, following a torrential storm, of the Fleet sewer, which crossed the line between King's Cross and Farringdon three times. The foul 'black river' of London was largely enclosed in a brick sewer the top of which, in June 1862, had been weakened by construction of the railway and eventually broke. After an unsuccessful two-day battle to prevent flooding, water poured out, breaking up the network of scaffolding and beams which was being used to build the tunnel walls, and flooded the works to a depth of ten feet. Amazingly, the railway, together with the Metropolitan Board of Works,[10] managed to set up a diversion for the water into the Thames and the old sewer was quickly rebuilt, causing a delay of only a few months to the scheme. Inevitably, the difficulties encountered by the builders meant that costs overran, as ever with large projects, and a further £300,000 had to be raised through the offer of shares, this time with a guaranteed 5 per cent dividend to ensure that the subscription was taken up.

But within a couple of months of this disaster, which fortunately claimed no lives, the railway's directors ran a special train for shareholders and other grandees. The Metropolitan, ever conscious that it had to overcome basic fears of going underground in order to attract sufficient custom to make a profit, was very adept at public relations. It had first run trial trips in November 1861 when it still expected the line to be open on time the following year. The inaugural trial over the whole line, with a distinguished group of guests including William Gladstone, then the Chancellor of the Exchequer, was made in May 1862. This was part of the company's policy of regularly inviting journalists and illustrators onto the worksites in order to help allay fears about travelling on the railway. Its efforts were well rewarded with favourable coverage like this report from an optimistic and presumably well-lunched scribe on the *Illustrated London News*:

> Although this curious and unique Metropolitan Railway has been termed underground, or subterranean, for nearly half its length it is open to the light and air of heaven, and where it does pass for various lengths beneath the surface, it is so well lighted and ventilated that the tunnels, instead of being close, dark, damp and offensive, are wide, spacious, clean and luminous, and more like a well-kept street at night, than a subterranean passage through the very heart of the metropolis.[11]

This would not be the experience of many travellers when the line opened a year later.

Another VIPs' ride was organized for August 1862 after the repairs had been completed following the Fleet sewer collapse. These trials are immortalized in a series of well-known engravings of men travelling in top hats in open wagons, which are often wrongly taken to show the service on the day of the opening of the line. In fact, such open freight wagons were never used in service and the well-dressed guests were generally only taken for a short run along an outdoor section of track. Another well-used image, of Baker Street station looking extremely spacious and wide, with a few relaxed and well-dressed passengers, is also inaccurate in that the perspective taken by the artist is illusory, suggesting far more room than there is in reality – as visitors to the station today can testify. These examples of the Victorians' tendency to present their world in the best possible light demonstrate the difficulty of trying to convey what it was really like on the Underground for these early pioneers. While it is hard to imagine the smoky and damp atmosphere caused by the steam engines, there are some contemporary descriptions, more of which later, to help us. Certainly the experience of those who went on these carefully stage-managed trips was atypical, not least because they were hauled by 'smokeless' engines that were eventually found to be too unreliable and consequently were never used in service.

While the technical problems of tunnelling in towns seemed like a sufficient obstacle to progress, probably the most intractable problem in those pre-electricity days was for the Underground's engineers to devise a way of operating trains that did not choke their passengers. As one account puts it, 'Pearson's main problem was finding an engine suitable for use underground. The users' problem was managing to breathe'.[12] In fact it was more Fowler's problem than Pearson's and, canny engineer though he was, not all his ideas were sensible. He had originally envisaged that trains should be blown through an airtight container using giant compressors at each terminal but, as we saw in Chapter 1, the problem with such 'atmospheric railways' was the difficulty of keeping a tight seal.[13]

The search for alternatives to conventional steam engines was prompted by the pollution caused by their smoke and, to a lesser extent, steam emissions. An engine developed by Robert Stephenson at

Fowler's behest – known as Fowler's Ghost – which used bricks as heat storage when in tunnels and operated normally outside, proved to be too unreliable, and was rejected after trials.[14] Instead, the Great Western's engineer, Daniel Gooch, was asked to design a conventional engine which prevented steam escaping by diverting it into a cold water tank and used coke rather than coal. However, while coke emitted less smoke than coal, it was even more toxic and the Metropolitan later reverted to coal.

Despite the flood, the problems with locomotives and smoke, and the innovatory engineering techniques used to build the line, the railway was ready for testing by the end of 1862 – late, of course, as the Metropolitan's directors had hoped it would be open in time for the International Exhibition of that year, but in hindsight commendably fast for such a groundbreaking project. The commissioning of the railway was achieved with impressive speed by today's standards. After the test runs of August, there was an official Board of Trade inspection on 22 December, which found that some modifications needed to be made to the signalling. These glitches were resolved remarkably quickly and, following official inspections on 30 December 1862 and 3 January 1863, there were further trials for just five days until the official opening ceremony on 9 January.

In keeping with the Metropolitan's sophisticated campaign to win over the public to its novel railway, it was a grand occasion attended by around 600 shareholders and VIPs. The timing was a bit odd, though, as the directors and the guests set off at 1 p.m. to travel down the line from Bishop's Road, Paddington, the initial terminus, to Farringdon Street, taking time off to view the intermediate stations which while pleasant were not, with the possible exception of the one at King's Cross, of great architectural merit. By the time they got to a specially created temporary hall at the other end of the line, well after 3 p.m., they must have been ravenous and it is to be hoped that they did not have to suffer the interminable speeches until after the food was served.

There were two absentees. Lord Palmerston, the prime minister, then seventy-nine, had excused himself, stating that at his age he wanted to remain above ground for as long as possible; in fact he died two years later. More importantly, poor old Charles Pearson, to whom a toast was drunk at the banquet, had died in September 1862: late enough, at least, to know that the line would become a reality. Dominated by his sense of duty to the end, when Pearson was offered a reward by the Metropolitan he refused it, saying: 'I am the servant of the Corporation; they are my masters and are entitled to all my time and service. If you have any return to make, you must make it to them.'[15]

But thanks to Pearson and his fellow pioneers, London had the world's first underground railway and gave English, and many other languages, a new word: the metro.

THREE

LONDON GOES
UNDERGROUND

London had its new railway, but would anyone use it? *The Times* had been certain that Londoners would take the same view as Lord Palmerston and seek to stay on the surface. A year before the opening, the paper had concluded that the railway would never pay because of people's reluctance to venture underground:

> A subterranean railway under London was awfully suggestive of dark, noisome tunnels, buried many fathoms deep beyond the reach of light or life; passages inhabited by rats, soaked with sewer drippings, and poisoned by the escape of gas mains. It seemed an insult to common sense to suppose that people who could travel as cheaply to the city on the outside of a Paddington 'bus would ever prefer, as a merely quicker medium, to be driven amid palpable darkness through the foul subsoil of London . . .[1]

But they did. Londoners had few concerns about trying out their new invention, the world's first subterranean railway. Right from its opening, the Metropolitan was extremely popular. On the first day, Saturday 10 January 1863, 30,000 people journeyed on the line, many travelling out of sheer curiosity and clearly oblivious to the horrors of the London subsoil described in *The Times*. They travelled in three different classes, paying threepence, fourpence and sixpence for a single journey and fivepence, sixpence and ninepence return, bringing in impressive receipts of £850. The fares were high compared with those charged by subsequent lines – notably the Twopenny Tube, the Central Railway which, when it opened at the turn of the century, demanded just twopence for any journey on its five and three-quarter-mile length.

The 120 trains in both directions that day suffered no serious breakdowns and the only major delays were caused by the crush of people trying to get on the trains, each of which only had four carriages in addition to the locomotives. The scheduled fifteen-minute interval service, therefore, proved wholly inadequate to meet the demand and, according to the *Illustrated London News*,[2] the Great Western quickly had to lend some of its locomotives and carriages to cope with the numbers.[3] The *Daily Telegraph* described how people at King's Cross seeking to go east to Farringdon Street bought tickets to travel in the opposite direction towards Paddington so that they could pick up a train further down the track,[4] a ploy with which many of today's Londoners living on the busier lines will be familiar.

It might not have been luxury, but the *Daily Telegraph* commented that of 'the general comfort in travelling on the line, there can be no question, and the novel introduction of gas into the carriages is calculated to dispel any unpleasant feeling which passengers, especially ladies, might entertain against riding for so long a distance through a tunnel.' The paper was particularly enthusiastic about the gas lighting, a radical innovation: 'On Saturday, throughout every journey the gas burnt brightly and in some instances was turned on so strong in the first class carriages, in each of which there are two burners, that newspapers might be read with ease. The second class carriages are nicely fitted with leathered seats, and are very commodious, and the compartments and arms in the first class render overcrowding impossible.' The mode of lighting was, indeed, innovative and was an essential part of winning over the public to this new form of transport by making them feel safe when they went down into the cellar-like tunnels. The gas was carried in long India rubber bags within wooden boxes on top of the carriages and was piped through to the lights. There were gauges on each carriage to ensure that the gas was replenished as soon as the reservoir was low. 'Gas will supply the place of the sun' was the proud boast of the company.

There are conflicting reports about the atmosphere in the tunnels during those early days, though most are negative. Right from the beginning there were accounts of 'singular occurrences' on the railway. The *Morning Advertiser*[5] described how, on the opening day, a train appeared to get stuck at Portland Road (now Great Portland Street) station and 'the station began to get full of steam, the passengers became alarmed and got on to the platform'. The train could not proceed as the signal was not clear and 'passengers began to run about in all directions, and many of them left the station and proceeded on their journey by omnibus'. The reporter was told by a local publican that 'he had to assist some of the porters over to his own house and bathe their heads and temples with vinegar, as they were exhausted and suffering from the effects of bad air'. After the train finally got under way, there was a noise like 'an explosion or the letting off of a small cannon' which caused 'great alarm amongst the females and children' and the gas went out in the carriage in which the reporter was travelling. The paper said that a porter had to be admitted to hospital, but gave no details of the incident. Another account, in a letter to the *Daily Telegraph*[6] four days later, describes a similar incident when a train broke down in a tunnel between Farringdon and King's Cross, causing 'great alarm' to passengers as the carriages filled with smoke and steam.

A history of Clerkenwell written a couple of years after the opening of the Metropolitan summed up these complaints, suggesting that the public had been deceived in being 'promised to be carried in handsome and well-lighted carriages through a tunnel free from smell; but very shortly after the line was opened, old dingy carriages, lighted with oil, were no rarity, and, worse than all, the tunnel was far from being free of sulphuric fumes, and of blended smells from coke and steam'.[7]

Obviously it cannot have been as bad as that the whole time, since so many people were prepared to use the system. Indeed, as drivers became more skilled at managing their engines, the atmosphere may well have improved. A couple of weeks after the opening Sir John Hardman, describing his trip along the line – which he called the Drain[8] – was impressed that he and his wife 'experienced no disagreeable odour, beyond the smell common to tunnels'.[9] He was taken by the fact that the compartments were so spacious that a six-foot man could stand upright with a hat on. His principal problem was that all the stations looked the same and he reported that it was so difficult to know where to get off that many people were carried past their destination. This may have been because the drivers were always in a hurry to get out of the steamy tunnels and tended not to stop for the full minute specified in the timetable. A passenger, Irving Courtenay, wrote to *The Times* complaining that he had not been able to board a train at Portland Road because it had not stopped long enough. He took the next train and timed its stay at the following three stations, finding they were a mere twenty, fifteen and twenty-five seconds respectively.

Within weeks of the opening, the Metropolitan Railway's PR machine was in full flow on the issue of the smoky atmosphere, a problem that was to dog the railway for years to come. When the shareholders gathered, in April 1863, for their first half-yearly meeting after the opening, apart from granting an annuity of £250 per year to Charles Pearson's widow (a notable act of generosity given that he had not even been a director of the company), they heard from the company's engineer that 'the experience of working for some months has quite dispelled all fears as to the noise and vibration to either streets or houses. I have heard no complaints of any kind and the feeling generally appears to be that a vast convenience is accomplished without interference with streets or otherwise and that the appearance of London is not prejudicially affected by anything we have done'. The company claimed to be using the coke 'made from the best and finest Durham coal' that was pre-burnt in the ovens for long enough to 'deprive it of every trace of sulphur and other objectionable exhalations', and that consequently 'the fuel is much better than that used on any other railway through the country'.[10]

The noise and vibration may well have been less than expected, but there was no getting away from the fact that, despite Sir John's account, the sulphurous fumes emitted by the engines – 'choke damp' as it was called – did not make for a pleasant atmosphere, especially for staff who worked long hours. The Metropolitan found itself in real difficulties over the problem when, in 1867, three people died in separate incidents in circumstances where choke damp seemed to have been a contributory factor. The company's damage limitation strategy was just as sophisticated as those presented by today's government spin doctors. Despite the fact that in one of the cases the coroner specifically mentioned that the death be attributed to the fumes in the tunnel, the Metropolitan's board argued there was no connection. The company rousted up three tame medical experts who found that the sickness rate among staff in 1866 had been less than half that among Great Western rail workers. Indeed, the company went further, suggesting that the atmosphere underground in the steam days 'provided a sort of health resort for people who suffered from asthma, for which the sulphurous and other fumes were supposed to be beneficial, and there were several regular asthmatical customers who daily took one or two turns round the circle to enjoy the – to them – invigorating atmosphere'.[11] Such accounts should be taken with more than a pinch of salt, although one must remember that the Victorians were great hypochondriacs and therefore eager enthusiasts for patent medicines and bizarre remedies of the most obscure kind.

The drivers, in fact, were conscious of the problem and took care not to stoke up the fires in their engines while they were in tunnels, intent on saving their own lungs as well as those of the passengers. When the smoke nuisance persisted, the guards, policemen and porters petitioned the company for leave to grow beards in the misguided notion that they would provide protection against the sulphur. The matter was solemnly discussed at a Great Western board before permission was granted. *The Times*, siding with the Metropolitan's board, argued that the unpleasantness was greatly exaggerated and, on rather thin evidence, attributed the illness among station staff to exhaustion from long hours of work in circumstances where the constant throng of passengers and running of trains meant that they had no time off for meals, a sad commentary on the conditions faced by the staff.

As complaints persisted, ventilation shafts were installed between King's Cross and Edgware Road, in the early 1870s, creating blowholes whose sudden emission of smoke and steam frequently startled passing horses. Glass was removed from some of the roofs of the stations in order to allow the smoke to escape but this did not seem to help much. A letter to *The Times*[12] several years later describes how a passenger, a mining engineer, reported that he was 'almost suffocated and was obliged to be assisted from the train at an intermediate station'. He was taken to a nearby chemist who said, 'Oh, I see, Metropolitan Railway,' and gave the poor fellow a wineglass full of what he concluded was 'designated Metropolitan Mixture'. The chemist reported that he did a roaring trade in this potion, often dealing with twenty cases a day. In truth, despite the attempts at better ventilation, the problem of foul air was never really overcome until electric trains replaced steam in the first decade of the twentieth century.

Finding locomotives which created the least pollution was the main technical problem facing the Metropolitan. At first the Metropolitan had used the Great Western ones designed by Gooch but a dispute with the company led to the withdrawal of all of its trains, locomotives and staff at the end of September 1863. With superhuman effort, the Metropolitan had obtained stock from the Great Northern which fortuitously was building locomotives to use on their own services on the Metropolitan's line, but they were far too crude to be a long-term solution. Therefore, the Metropolitan was anxious to commission its own locomotives specifically designed to operate on the Underground[13] and ordered eighteen tank locomotives from a well-established company, Beyer, Peacock, which had earlier supplied similar engines for a Spanish railway. The key feature was the condensing equipment which prevented most of the steam from escaping in the tunnels although partly this depended on the diligence of the driver who needed to refill the water as often as possible in order to keep it cool. Oddly, though cabs had become standard on the main line railways, these locomotives had none, just a weatherboard to protect the driver and his fireman. Perhaps this design was aimed at ensuring that drivers would make every effort possible not to allow steam to escape – or perhaps it was an economy measure since the drivers on the Underground would not have to face the elements as the main-line drivers did. They were beautiful little engines, painted green and distinguished particularly by their enormous external cylinders. The design proved so successful that eventually 120 were built, providing the basis of traction on the Metropolitan and all the other early 'cut and cover' Underground lines until the advent of electrification in the 1900s.

Despite the improvement provided by the new Beyer locomotives, running steam engines in long tunnels was a fundamentally bad idea, necessitated by the available technology. Indeed, the situation was so bad that a Board of Trade inquiry was set up in 1898 to examine ventilation in the tunnels, which were then being used by a staggering 550 passenger and goods trains daily. The Metropolitan again mounted a campaign to allay concerns. The General Manager, Colonel John Bell, repeated the line of his predecessors that the company's employees were the healthiest railwaymen in the country and that Great Portland Street was 'actually used as a sanatorium for men who had been afflicted with asthma and bronchial complaints'.

The staff would have taken issue with Colonel Bell. According to a Mr Smethurst, President of the Short Hours League, 'hours of men on the Metropolitan, although not so long as others, are yet in my opinion dangerous, excessive and injurious. The effect of a daily journey on the underground railway is too well known to need description. What must the men feel who spend their lives in whirling round the sulphurous tunnel?'[14] He reported that drivers and firemen worked up to thirteen hours per day. Signalmen normally worked eight or nine hours per day but they also did thirteen on Sundays. Most Met staff worked three out of five Sundays, too.

These hardworking men were largely newcomers to London. Henry Mayhew, the journalist and social reform campaigner, visited the line in May 1865 and was most impressed with the railway officials who 'struck us as being so smart a body of men'[15] that he wondered how they had been gathered together in such a short space of time. Mayhew was accompanied by Myles Fenton, the general manager of the Metropolitan, who told him that most of them, particularly the inspectors, guards and signalmen, came from the West Country, with Somerset and Wiltshire contributing the greatest number. 'It is surprising,' noted Mayhew patronizingly, 'how soon a raw rustic is converted by a severe course of discipline into a smart civil and skilful officer.' The drivers, however, were mostly local people who had been poached from main line companies, especially the Great Northern.

Another objection was that there were no waiting rooms at any of the stations. These had not been deemed necessary by the Metropolitan since trains were so frequent, but one small shareholder, a civil servant commuter, suggested that this was mistaken: 'I can assure you that the draughts during the winter months are enough to kill a bronze rhinoceros.'[16] There were buffets, but he argued that he should not have to lay out sixpence merely to seek shelter. Another option was the penny-in-the-slot weighing machine. Every station had one and they were a popular feature of platform life in the Victorian tunnels. They were large balances fitted with red velvet cushions which, in effect, provided a free comfortable seat for old gentlemen waiting for a train.

Yet, despite the awful conditions for the staff and the various complaints from passengers (vitiated, perhaps, by other reports like those of Sir John Hardman and by the Metropolitan's effective PR), most Londoners seemed to have been prepared to venture down to use the line. Indeed, the bad publicity before the opening may even have contributed towards the Metropolitan's success by lowering expectations so that travellers were then surprised to find it was not quite as bad as they had been led to expect. By the standards of Victorian railway building the Metropolitan was highly successful, even in financial terms. In the first full year of operation, 11.8 million people used the line, more than four times the population of the capital – a daily average, including Sundays, of 32,300, which was a remarkable achievement given the limited route it served. There was, incidentally, only a partial timetable on Sundays, since the trains were suspended during the morning church service hours, a practice which survived on the Metropolitan until October 1909. The peak day in the first year for the Metropolitan was Saturday, 7 March, when Princess Alexandra of Denmark arrived in London for her marriage to the Prince of Wales: 60,000 people, double the usual number, travelled on the line. The Princess did not venture onto the Metropolitan herself, but thousands used the line to travel to Paddington to see her off on her journey to Windsor.

The Metropolitan's receipts were so healthy, with profits of £102,000 in its first year, that initially generous dividends could be paid to the shareholders: 6.25 per cent in 1864, a much better return than most railway companies received. In May 1864, the Metropolitan made a staggering £720 per mile per week, compared with the £80 for the London, Chatham & Dover, the next best performing railway, and just £22 for the Great Eastern & Midland. Yet there were still attempts to do down the Metropolitan. William Pinks, the Clerkenwell historian who wrote that analysis of the early traffic, suggested there were only half the expected number of passengers, providing a weekly income of £1,885 rather than the £4,000 or so needed to make a profit.[17] But this seems at odds with the Metropolitan's figures and it was apparent that the line was well used and profitable. It was only when the railway started expanding that it hit financial difficulties as the cost of the work was normally too high to earn shareholders a decent return on the capital invested. As the authors of the definitive history of London's transport put it:

> Shareholders were not to reap the full reward of this important pioneer venture, for the board had already become involved in much less remunerative expenditure. The initial successes had played into the hands of those who have a vested interest in extending the line: the contractors who built the railway, the engineers who supplied the technical advice, and the solicitors who looked after the parliamentary proceedings and the subsequent conveyancing.[18]

While this is a somewhat harsh judgement, which ignores the enormous social benefit for London of the Underground, it is one that has resonance today given that the infamous public–private partnership introduced by the Labour government in 2003 cost a staggering £500m in fees for lawyers, consultants and engineers before a single improvement had been made.

The speed with which the Metropolitan was accepted as a vital part of London is shown by the fact that a music hall ditty about the railway soon became widely sung. To the air of 'Yankee Doodle Dandy', it went:

The underground railway's a fact
It's made cab-owners groaners
Sent drivers and conductors crack'd
And riled the great 'bus owners.
LGOC monopolists weep,
That railway each one curses;
It's sure to do, because it's cheap,
And runs under the 'buses.

The 'monopolist' of the London General Omnibus Company no doubt preferred the comic song 'The Underground Railway' by Watkin Williams. Although its publisher claimed it was widely sung, that seems unlikely and it is too tedious to set out here in full. It laboriously relates how a man and his sweetheart, Mary Jane, decided to journey to Paddington from Farringdon Street. In the crush on the platform Mary Jane collapsed, as young Victorian women were wont to do, and was helped by another traveller. In the meantime her fiancé had to rescue another woman who had fainted in his compartment. The net result was that when reunited at the end of the journey, the couple found they had been the victims of clever pickpockets:

And of our little stock, they eas'd the whole lot,
We'd sav'd to get wed when we'd a little more got,
Now till more is earn'd that bliss is adjourned,
Through going on the underground railway.

So what was the explanation for the immediate phenomenal success of the Metropolitan? Underpinning the heavy usage was the fact that the system was remarkably safe and, more importantly, was perceived as such, allaying the natural fear of walking down those steps to go beneath the streets. Had there been a big accident early on, the whole concept might never have taken off. Indeed, in France during August 1903 the number of passengers slumped by more than half, just three years after the opening of the first Métro line. A fire was allowed to spread as a result of staff incompetence and panic, and eighty-four people were killed. Despite the predictions and, at times, rather haphazard safety practices, there was no such disaster on the Metropolitan.

The signalling, for example, was simple but effective. Clearly, it was necessary to have a proper signalling system rather than just leaving a time gap between departures, a method still prevalent on the main line railways.[19] Mayhew cited an article in *Railway News* which described how signalmen at each station had to press keys to communicate with the next one, making a dial show either 'line clear' or 'train on line'. With this simple but clever system, trains could run at intervals of two minutes while without them Mayhew reckoned it would have been a quarter of an hour. Moreover, there was also a system of interlocking which meant that the points and the signals worked together and could not be set in a conflicting way – a safety device that was becoming standard in the railways at that time.

While there were no serious accidents, there was, of course, the odd mishap. Within weeks of opening, in February 1863, there were two minor crashes at the same spot at Farringdon Street station. On 17 February, a train leaving the station was switched onto the wrong track and collided head-on with one arriving, but as it was at low speed only a few passengers were injured. The interlocking had been temporarily disconnected. Ten days later much the same thing happened again at the same location, this time causing thirty injuries and providing another proof that the 'compensation culture', generally considered a modern scourge, was already flourishing in Victorian times. Most of the passengers accepted under £20 in compensation, but one victim, a Mrs Mee, was more persistent, turning down £150 and eventually receiving £220 for her pains in an out of court settlement.

Bearing in mind the novelty of the whole concept of underground railways, it is impressive that eighteen months passed before there was a fatality on the line, and even then it was caused, as many since have been, by drunkenness. A couple rushed for the last service from Portland Road (now Great Portland Street) to Edgware Road and the woman, Kate Gollop, somehow got onto the tracks underneath the train, where the porter on duty found her dying. The man, Thomas Powell, disappeared, having caught the train. In the subsequent court case, when her husband John sued the Metropolitan Railway – yet another example of Victorian litigiousness – it emerged that both had drunk large quantities of alcohol. Powell remembered taking her to the station and seeing her fall, but he then went home without realizing she had been hit by a train. Other evidence was conflicting and the precise circumstances never emerged. Although Gollop won his case, the jury only awarded him one shilling, despite the fact that he was disabled and had relied on his wife as the breadwinner.

Despite isolated incidents such as these, the Metropolitan had a remarkably unblemished safety record and in its first forty-four years did not experience a single railway accident resulting in the death of a passenger, which is excellent given the intensity of service, the use of steam engines and high passenger numbers. Indeed, according to the definitive history of London's transport, 'during the whole period of steam operation, there was no fatal accident to any passenger in these cuttings and tunnels'[20] caused by a train collision or derailment. The first serious accident on the underground system involved a head-on collision near Earls Court in August 1885 between a District train and a Great Western service, which killed the two crew of the Great Western train. Safety was the cornerstone of the rapid success of the railway but its excellent economic performance was based on the fact that the line fulfilled a hitherto unmet need offering the convenience of reaching Farringdon from Paddington far more quickly and for the same fare (sixpence) as the lumbering omnibus. What a joy it must have been to escape the hurly-burly of the streets for the relative, if smoky, peace below. With 650 services per day, each train of four coaches carried, on average, only fifty people on its whole journey. Of course there were peak hours when the trains were crowded, just as there are today, but for the most part the experience – especially in those early days when passenger numbers were building up – must have been relatively pleasant.

The Metropolitan's attitude to smoking provides a comic counterpoint to the constant complaints about the foul air in the Underground. Uniquely for the time, the Metropolitan – of all railways – banned smoking in its carriages, presumably not wishing to add to the already smoky atmosphere. Yet, five years after the opening of the line, the provision of smoking carriages was made compulsory when the MP for Dudley, H.B. Sheridan, successfully moved an amendment to the Railway Regulation Bill requiring all railways to provide a smoking carriage, unless excused by the Board of Trade. The amendment attracted the endorsement of none other than the political philosopher, John Stuart Mill, who devoted the last speech he would ever make in the House of Commons to supporting the clause, and it was largely thanks to his advocacy that the amendment was passed by a majority of twenty-two. Although the Metropolitan was initially excluded from the requirement and endeavoured to continue to prevent people lighting up, other railway companies using its lines all had smoking carriages and there was a public clamour for the Metropolitan to follow suit. In fact, when the smoking coaches were officially introduced in 1874, the company was probably merely meeting the demands of its passengers since contemporary reports suggest that the ban was being widely flouted.

The people who flocked to the new subterranean railway were a disparate bunch. Top-hatted bankers travelled on the same trains as the artisans, albeit, of course, in different classes. While the fares represented a substantial amount of money for some low-income earners, most Londoners in work could afford to use the service. The Metropolitan realized that there was a whole new market to exploit, using spare capacity in the early mornings when their more affluent customers were still tucked up in bed. In line with Pearson's aspirations, it became the first railway to provide cheap workmen's trains when in 1864 the Metropolitan started running two trains in each direction before 6 a.m. at a return fare of just threepence (later reduced to twopence return), with the right to go back by any train, which greatly increased their attractiveness. The workmen's service immediately attracted 300 daily users, a number which soon doubled. In fact, overall, the working classes provided by far the greatest proportion of the Metropolitan's passengers since 70 per cent of tickets sold in those early years were for third-class travel, with 20 per cent and 10 per cent respectively for second and first. Only a minority of travellers, around a sixth according to figures given to Mayhew by Fenton, travelled between the two termini, with the rest joining or alighting at one of the intermediate stations. Fenton told him: 'Each additional station produces a large accession of traffic creating as it does an interchange with each previous station; whilst great numbers of passengers now travel between the terminal stations, yet the numbers conveyed between the several intermediate stations are much greater.' In other words, Londoners were learning to use the Underground for short hops around town and railway managers were beginning to understand the real benefits of an urban rail network.

The Metropolitan had been the first railway to be required to run such cheap workmen's trains, as this was a condition of being granted powers, in 1861,[21] to extend the line through to Moorgate and double the tracks to four between King's Cross and Farringdon. The condition had been suggested by the Metropolitan to allay criticism that the railway was destroying large swathes of housing and therefore turning working men out of their homes. However, the Metropolitan began running these trains even before the extension was completed, exploiting what was a very useful source of extra revenue. The London, Chatham & Dover Railway, which, as we see below, connected over the Thames with the Metropolitan in 1866, was also required to provide similar cheap trains but those using them had to go through huge bureaucratic hoops. The trains were to be for the exclusive use of 'artisans mechanics and daily labourers, both male and female' going to their work or returning from their jobs to their homes. They were required to buy a weekly ticket for a shilling, and, to prevent abuse, the ticket holder was required to give not only their name and address but those of their employer and not vary the journey or carry any luggage except for a workman's basket of tools 'not exceeding 28lbs in weight'.

The Metropolitan imposed no such conditions on its trains. Mayhew, travelling on a 5.15 train one Saturday morning in 1865, complained of having to get up at such a 'ghostly and burglarious' hour in order to catch the workers' train. He was most impressed with the whole set-up, though one slightly suspects that he was in a frame of mind to be positive about the new invention from the outset. His book of reportage about Britain's industry, which took him around the country, starts with a typically florid and upbeat description:

> It was so novel a means of transit, so peculiar and distinctive a feature of the great English capital, that to omit this underground mode of intercommunication from a publication professing to be descriptive of the foremost institutions and establishments of the British metropolis would be the same as playing the tragedy of Hamlet with the principal character left out. Indeed this subterranean method of locomotion had always struck us as being the most thoroughly Cockney element of all within the wide region of Cockaigne.[22]

Mayhew's positive feelings about the railway may well have been encouraged by the fact that his book had an advertisement for 'J Willing, Advertising Contractors, 366 Grays Inn Road, WC', who were sole contractors for advertising on the Metropolitan, the North London, Hammersmith & City and several other railways and had paid £1,150 for the right to sell books and post advertisements at the stations for a period of three years. The deal must have been a real money-spinner since Willing paid more than £34,000 to renew the contract for a further seven years in 1866. Despite what may appear to readers as a potential conflict of interest, Mayhew's account is invaluable as it is one of the most detailed contemporary reports of early Underground travel and has the added advantage of being written by someone with an acute eye and a reporter's instinct.

Mayhew found the carriages to be 'extremely handsome and roomy vehicles', forty feet long, and in first class, luxuriously fitted up 'with six compartments arranged to hold as many as sixty passengers in all'. But even the second and third class, which had eight compartments, he described as 'fine spacious vehicles; indeed there are no third class carriages on any other line which are the least comparable to them'.

When Mayhew reached the platform at Bishop's Road, there was, despite the early hour, 'a bustle with men, a large number of whom had bass baskets in their hand or tin flagons or basins done up in red handkerchiefs. Some few carried large saws under their arms, and beneath the overcoat of others one could just see a little bit of the flannel jacket worn by carpenters, whilst some were habited in the grey and clay stained fustian suit peculiar to ground labourers.'

His compartment was full of plasterers, joiners and labourers: 'All present agreed that the cheap and early trains were a great benefit to the operative classes. The labourer assured us that he saved, at least, two shillings a week by them in the matter of rent only. He lived at Notting Hill and would have to walk six miles to and from his work every day, if it were not for the convenience of the railway.' Moreover, the labourer had benefited from better housing conditions in the way that Pearson had hoped. Thanks to the railway, he was able to live in greater comfort further out of town than he would otherwise. He had two rooms, almost in the open country, for the same price as he would have had to pay for one in a much less salubrious court in the heart of London, and thereby, Mayhew noted, avoided needing 'medicine for his wife and family'. A plasterer, on his way to Dockhead, joined the conversation and said 'it was impossible to reckon up how much workmen gained by the workmen's trains, especially if you took into account the saving in shoe leather, the gain in health and strength and the advantage for men to go to their work fresh and unfatigued by a long walk at the commencement of the day'. The plasterer added that there was a moral benefit, too, 'since it enabled operatives to have different sleeping rooms for themselves and their young children'.

Mayhew later met another man who also benefited from improved accommodation out of town. He had rented 'a six roomed house, with a kitchen and for this he paid £28 the year, rent and taxes. He let off four rooms for 8s the week so that he stood at about 3s a week rent for himself and for the same accommodation as he had now, he would have to pay from 6s to 6s 6d, the week in some wretched dog hole in town.' The only problem was that the local food was more expensive than in the centre of town, but he bought most of his provisions after work and took them home.

At Gower Street (now Euston Square) Mayhew moved to the next compartment where he found a butcher on the way to the meat market, a newsvendor going to fetch his morning papers, and others connected with the building trade. Most of those he met were extremely supportive of the railway but inevitably he found the odd grouch, a carpenter who 'was one of those growling and grumbling characters so often met among the working class' and who failed to perceive the benefit of paying a shilling a week for the service. The carpenter was interrupted by another passenger who extolled the virtues of commuting: 'If a man gets home tired after his day's labour, he is inclined to be quarrelsome with his missus and the children, and this leads to all kinds of noises, and ends in him going off to the pub for a little bit of quiet; while if he gets a ride home, and has a good rest after he has knocked off for the day, I can tell you he is as pleasant a fellow again over his supper.' This might not quite chime with the experience of today's commuters, crammed by the hundreds into tiny Underground trains.

Mayhew also noted the excellent refreshment bars provided by Messrs Spiers and Pond and here his report seems so like advertising copy that one wonders how many free cakes he was offered: 'So moderate are the prices and excellent the fare that 300–400 people come daily to dine at the Farringdon Street terminus.' The company, which also had the concession for the London, Chatham & Dover Railway and the station at Birmingham New Exchange, were 'manufacturers of all the biscuits, cakes, ices and even soda water which they dispense to their customers and are able to supply better articles at cheaper prices than usually prevail at the wretchedly served refreshment bars of other railways'.

Although Mayhew may have been slightly too ready to accentuate the positives and ignore the negatives about the railway, there is no doubt that the Metropolitan's immediate impact on London was enormous. It had the same kind of regenerative effect as modern urban railway systems in London such as the Docklands Light Railway and the Jubilee Line Extension. Landlords and businesses were quick to exploit the potential of the new railway. Its convenience was unrivalled – a mere eighteen minutes from Paddington to Farringdon was the normal schedule (fast non-stopping trains which did the journey in fourteen minutes were briefly introduced but soon dropped because such a schedule was impossible to maintain). Newspaper advertisements for shops began to stress their proximity to the line. Messrs Samuels Brothers of 29 Ludgate Hill, for example, explained how 'Underground railway passengers have the great advantage of a speedy transit to within four minutes walk of the warehouses' where they would find that 'every description of plain and fashionable clothing is supplied to gentlemen and their sons, ready made or made to measure'. Thus, part of the success of the railway was that it not only provided a new mode of transport for existing travellers but generated its own business, a lesson that is still not sufficiently taken account of when ideas for new lines for the twenty-first century are conceived. Even this short section of line was having a major impact on London's economy.

But the railway was not only for Londoners. The Metropolitan had been forward-looking right from the start by encouraging other rail companies onto its tracks as a way of contributing revenue. They carried people from stations on their own lines, before connecting with the Metropolitan at Paddington or King's Cross. This, however, caused the row between the Great Western and the Metropolitan as, very soon after its opening, the latter wanted to increase the frequency of its trains from four to six per hour throughout the day. The Great Western, whose rolling stock was being used, was only willing to provide that intensity of service during the peak hours, because it wanted to retain sufficient train paths for its through trains coming off its network into the Underground at Paddington.

Although, as we have seen, the Great Western rather childishly withdrew its stock, the company continued to run its through trains along the subterranean railway track to Farringdon Street. Indeed, to understand the role of the Metropolitan in these early days, it is best to visualize the railway as a part of the main line network which happened to go underground when it reached London. Through trains for the Great Western via Paddington and for the Great Northern via King's Cross, which started to operate in October 1863, gave Underground users a host of destinations in the suburbs and beyond. The Great Western, for example, ran trains between Farringdon Street and Windsor, initially using its commodious broad gauge trains. The Great Northern ran trains out to Hatfield and Hitchin and their popularity was clear from the beginning, when the passengers on the first through train to Farringdon Street were reported as expressing their delight by swooping down in force on the newly opened station refreshment buffet and consuming all it contained.

And while the Metropolitan was conceived as primarily a passenger railway, there was also, surprisingly, freight. Mayhew suggests that the 'the original idea was that [the Metropolitan railway] would receive its chief income from the conveyance of goods from the west to the eastern district of London' but concedes that 'this proved so complete a fallacy that, whilst millions of passengers have been carried by it annually, the goods traffic has been comparatively inconsiderable'. However, he predicted this would change when the Circle was complete. In fact, there is little evidence for Mayhew's assertion. The railway was principally seen by Pearson and its other promoters as a people mover, with goods playing only a small role towards helping the finances of the project. An early example was the carriage of carcasses from the cattle market, which previously had been at Smithfield but had moved a couple of miles north to Islington. After the connection at King's Cross was opened, the underground line was used to take the dead animals through to Smithfield where there was a special underground spur for deliveries of meat. There were, too, various new warehouses on the section between King's Cross and Farringdon which had been built near the line specifically to make use of it and freight was carried until well after World War Two.

The principal use of the Metropolitan was to service the needs of the City of London, which was rapidly growing towards its zenith as the centre of an empire. The City was a magnet for employment throughout the region, ensuring that the Metropolitan's lines were well used but also putting immediate pressure on the railway company to expand. Indeed, the little stub of a line between Paddington and Farringdon was never intended to be anything but the basis for a much larger network, and even before its completion plans were being drawn up for extensions and branches, with the ultimate aim of a circle around the centre of London. But that aspiration was to take a quarter of a century to become a reality. In the meantime various connections and new lines were added to the system to allow London's burgeoning major railway companies to make use of the Metropolitan, which had realized that allowing other services onto its tracks for a fee was the quickest and easiest way to achieve profitability.

The success of the Metropolitan also brought forward a spate of proposals for new railways in the capital. There were a staggering 259 different projects for creating around 300 miles of railway – many, of course, duplicating each other and several being little more than lines drawn vaguely on a map – in and around London. If all the lines had been built, four new bridges would have been needed across the Thames and only a quarter of the existing city would have been left standing. That is not as fanciful as may be imagined. In Paris, at around the same time, nearly half the housing was razed to construct the great boulevards, the centrepiece of the grandiose and revolutionary schemes devised by Napoleon III and Baron Haussmann. As one historian put it: 'The splendid new Paris had many admirers in this country, and a similar havoc could easily have been wrought in London.'[23] Britain, even at the height of Victorian entrepreneurship, was always more conservative in planning matters than its European neighbour and more fearful of riding roughshod over the populace, eschewing the *grands projets* so beloved of the French. Muddling through has always been the chosen method of progress and the untidy structure of today's Underground could be seen as a result of that failure of imagination. In effect, the British state was much more willing than some of its European counterparts to defend the property interests of the landowners, particularly the big ones, against the demands of the railway developers (and the passengers they served). Parliament, therefore, could not stand back idly while the City and Westminster were torn to pieces by competing companies and so, as in the 1840s, fresh parameters for future urban railways had to be established. The score or so of serious schemes were referred to a joint committee of both Houses of Parliament which, reporting in 1864, rejected all but four of the additional lines affecting the Metropolitan – three for various sections of what was to become the inner Circle and one allowing the company to expand out of Baker Street into the north-west suburbs which, as we shall see later, was to be a far-reaching decision both for the Metropolitan and London.

The Metropolitan had prepared itself for growth from the start. It had obtained powers for two extra tracks between King's Cross and Farringdon, called, oddly, 'the City Widened Lines', and the completion of the Midland's awesome station at St Pancras, together with a connection to the Metropolitan, necessitated their rapid construction to meet the demand. They were brought fully into use in 1868 and it is a testimony to the success of the Metropolitan's original concept that the busiest part of the track had to be doubled within five years of the line opening.

Even before the completion of the City Widened Lines, the Metropolitan had begun its extension into the City, reaching Moorgate (with an intermediate station at Aldersgate Street, now Barbican) in 1865. There was, too, a connection from the south which added to what had become one of the world's busiest railways. The London, Chatham & Dover railway had crossed the River Thames at Blackfriars – where its coat of arms still adorns the bridge – in 1864, reaching Ludgate Hill and then connecting with the Metropolitan at the rebuilt and extended station of Farringdon Street two years later to form what remains today the only main line railway link through the heart of the capital. It was not a popular development since it wrecked one of London's most famous views, the sight of St Paul's sitting ever larger astride the rest of the City as one descends Fleet Street. An ugly bridge cut the sight of the cathedral in half, but surprisingly there were few objectors during the scheme's long gestation period. It was only when the bridge was completed that the Victorian environmentalists suddenly woke up to what had been done. As one contemporary observer put it, 'That viaduct has utterly spoiled one of the finest street views in the metropolis, and is one of the most unsightly objects ever constructed, in any such situation, anywhere in the world.'[24]

With half a dozen main line railways – both the South Eastern and the London & South Western also sent in trains – now connected to the Metropolitan, the journey possibilities were almost endless. They were further increased in 1871 when a connection was built from Snow Hill Junction to Smithfield to provide a triangular junction which enabled the Chatham's trains to reach Moorgate Street. Had there been trainspotters in the 1860s, the Metropolitan would have been their paradise. All kinds of services, pulled by a variety of locomotives, many with hastily conceived adaptations to try to reduce their emissions during their journey through the tunnels, were to be found using the railway. The Great Northern, for example, began working freight trains from King's Cross to Herne Hill while the Chatham ran a circuitous passenger service starting at Victoria and running out to Brixton, back into town via Ludgate Hill, on to the Metropolitan through King's Cross, and out to terminate at Wood Green – a wonderful tour of much of south and north Victorian London all in one train journey.[25]

There was fierce competition over this cross-London route. The Chatham's chairman for the last thirty years of the nineteenth century was James Staats Forbes, an emollient fellow who specialized in rescuing railways in financial trouble. His much more vituperative rival on the South Eastern, Edward Watkin, was another formidable railway entrepreneur and when, as we see in the next chapter, they controlled respectively the District and the Metropolitan, their refusal to cooperate with each other hampered the development of the Underground and delayed the completion of the Circle line.

The South Eastern had built a spur above the rooftops of Southwark to connect with the Chatham line over the Blackfriars railway bridge and in 1878 the railway ran its own series of strange services, linking Woolwich and Greenwich with Muswell Hill and Enfield, via Ludgate Hill and King's Cross. Shared lines, however, did not mean shared services. These trains called at all stations but because of the Forbes–Watkin rivalry, South Eastern tickets were not accepted at the Chatham stations of Ludgate Hill and Snow Hill. And as the railway historian O.S. Nock puts it, 'woe betide the passenger with a London, Chatham & Dover Railway ticket for Wood Green (Great Northern Railway) who attempted to make use of a South Eastern train that turned up at Ludgate Hill while he was waiting'.[26] At the height of this crazy competition, the Chatham was running eighty trains per day in each direction between Ludgate Hill and Moorgate Street alone, but these services were legendary for their lateness and, as Nock says, 'one can well imagine that the service extended far into the night before the last ones struggled home'.[27]

This was an old disease of the railways, the tendency to build and operate them for their own sake rather than to meet any real demand. The Metropolitan, which had largely avoided this trap, having fed and created an important market, was happy to make money out of this profligacy, routing the majority of these services on the City Widened Lines and thus reserving its original tracks for itself. Most of these cross-London passenger services were withdrawn in the early years of the twentieth century when the motor bus began to provide a more flexible and less circuitous option for people making occasional journeys across the City. Goods trains continued, however, to be heavy users of the line. The vital link through the Snow Hill tunnel fell into disuse in the 1960s but was reopened, at the prompting of the Greater London Council, in 1988 and is now used by the very heavily loaded Thameslink trains. Indeed, the serious overcrowding on today's Thameslink trains suggests that the opportunities created by the Victorian pioneers in building railways through the centre of London were not sufficiently exploited by their successors. While roundabout journeys from Victoria to Wood Green may not have made much sense commercially, there were plenty of other potential cross-London services which did. The problem was the lack of coordination between the railways and the absence of any state intervention in trying to plan a network of services, a recurring theme throughout the early history of London's railways, including the Underground.

Indeed, the competition and rivalry between the various companies meant that the infrastructure they created was not always used to best effect. Nowhere was this more true than for the Circle line (see next chapter), which was run by two separate and rival companies. The rivalry and lack of coordination explains, too, why London was never traversed by a main line train company. There were minor exceptions, such as the Chatham's incursion across the river to Farringdon, and, on the edges of central London, the East and West London lines, both principally used for freight but with a few sporadic passenger services.

For its part, the Metropolitan saw itself partly as a main line railway and had designs on extending far out of London into the relatively uncharted north-western suburbs and their hinterland, which would see the company reach as far as Amersham, Aylesbury, and the strange outpost of Verney Junction in the middle of the Buckinghamshire countryside some fifty miles from the capital. In a way this was more a story of the Underground extending overground, since all the lines emanating outwards were built on land that was cheap enough not to require tunnels, once they had left the confines of central London. The key was Baker Street, from where its first extension, a line to Swiss Cottage, was completed in April 1868.[28] It was London's second underground line, not the section of today's Jubilee, which is a deep tube line, but the sub-surface tunnels which are now used by Metropolitan line trains. The original idea had been to run through to Finchley Road, but as usual money was short, and eventually a single-track railway was built to Swiss Cottage with intermediate stops at Marlborough Road and St John's Wood. The latter was very near Lord's cricket ground, perceived already as such a vital market that it had its own temporary ticket office within the ground on match days. At first this seemed an insignificant little branch line, especially as the junction at Baker Street proved difficult to operate and through services from Moorgate were replaced the following year by a shuttle along the extension line. Financially, the line was hopeless because it did not reach Finchley Road, which would have offered a bigger catchment area, and nor had a projected branch to Hampstead been built. Nevertheless, this little branch, owned initially by a seperate company, was to be the start of a major extension of the Metropolitan that would stimulate the growth of a whole quadrant of London.

Another significant, but ultimately less important incursion had been made westwards by the Hammersmith & City line. This, too, was a separate railway created with backing from both the Metropolitan and the Great Western Railway, a surprising liaison given their disputes during the early days of the Metropolitan. In fact, the Hammersmith & City opened in June 1864, less than a year after the damaging argument between the two railways that had led to the Great Western withdrawing its rolling stock. The line was a rather tortuous one: starting from the Great Western line at Green Lane (now Westbourne Park), a mile out of Paddington, it took in the fields of Porto Bello (as they were then called) and Notting Barn farms, via Latimer Road and Shepherds Bush, to reach its terminus near Hammersmith Broadway.

The line was designed to serve the newly growing residential areas of Shepherd's Bush which, according to Roy Porter, 'became plastered with two and three storey houses and small shops, bought by traders and clerks with building society mortgages'[29] and Hammersmith, a village which had long been known for its spinach and strawberries, but now had begun to assume its present-day reputation as a transport interchange, a place to pass through. The railway also served Ladbroke Grove, where the once elegant terraces had deteriorated quite quickly through multiple occupation by less well-off people and were now quickly being infilled by smaller dwellings aimed at the burgeoning middle classes, and as Porter points out, the 'planting of stations in the open fields (Latimer Road, Goldhawk Road) encourag[ed] speculators to buy up smallholdings'. This was the first example of a pattern that was to be repeated throughout the development of the Underground: its arrival would prompt a rapid change in the character of an area and make many developers their fortune. Indeed, there was a bit of judicious profiteering by a couple of the Hammersmith & City directors, Charles Blake and John Parson, who had bought land on the path of the line and made a fortune by reselling it back to the company, a not infrequent type of scam during the development of the railways.

The Hammersmith & City had the added advantage of connecting with the West London railway, a sad little line which was testimony to the lesson that enterprise was not a sufficient precondition for commercial success. It had been built in 1844 as the only section of the grand-sounding Birmingham, Bristol & Thames Junction railway ever to be built and was spectacularly unsuccessful. It ran along the main Great Western line at Willesden, down to the Kensington canal basin, by the site of the Olympia exhibition hall, where its terminus survives as a station. It only carried passengers for six months and then became the butt of jokes in the satirical magazine *Punch*, to such an extent that it was called *Punch*'s railway. The magazine cruelly wrote: 'Omnibuses have been put on to meet the trains but the meetings have been so strictly private, no one having been present [save] the driver of the 'bus and the guard of the train.'[30] The line, however, which had fallen into disuse, was revived by its connection with the Metropolitan and some trains ran directly from Farringdon through to Kensington (Addison Road, as it was often known) station. However, the station was a mile from the centre of Kensington, which meant few passengers used it and therefore most trains remained on the Hammersmith branch.

Present-day users of the Underground would find some of the early service patterns on the Metropolitan reassuringly familiar and others totally improbable. Mayhew describes the schedule of ten trains that left Farringdon in the hour after noon on the Saturday in May 1865 when he visited: four to Hammersmith, three Metropolitan (to Bishop's Road, Paddington), two to Kensington and one Great Northern train. Three of them depart in the first five minutes, showing how closely together the services could operate. In fact, Mayhew had chosen a relatively quiet period as the average hourly total was around twenty per hour. By the time of Mayhew's trip along the line, a staggering 352 trains were scheduled to depart from Farringdon every weekday and 200 on Sundays, demonstrating that leisure was already a strong market. The weekday services, which departed between 5.15 a.m. and midnight, consisted of 116 Metropolitan trains to Bishop's Road, 110 to Hammersmith, sixty-two Great Western trains to Kensington, ten to Windsor and thirty Great Northern services while the rest were empty stock and locomotives.

Such a cascade of trains may have been a bit excessive but it did not matter. Spurred by the requirements of capitalism to make a return for their shareholders, these Victorian railway pioneers did not hesitate in sweating the assets they had so painstakingly built up by persuading investors to stump up the risk capital. Labour costs were low and coal was cheap, so running a few extra little-used trains to create a full timetable was not an expensive business.

Twenty years after the Metropolitan opened, a system of lines had built up using the underground section as the key link through London. Some might say this account is a bit selective because the early history of the Underground is so difficult to separate out from that of London's suburban railways, as witnessed by the bizarre array of services offered by the various rail companies south of the river. But over the following twenty years, the whole pattern of the Underground map would change with two major developments which led to its current shape: the completion of the Circle and the development of the deep tunnel network, the real Tube, the greatest part of which was constructed within an astonishing seventeen-year period.

The Metropolitan was spreading its tentacles, but first London was to get its Circle line, a tribute to long-term planning as it had first been set out in a Parliamentary committee as far back as 1846, but also a demonstration of the haphazard nature of the development of the Underground and the politicians' obsession with competition; the line would be controlled by two rival companies, led by railway pioneers who hated each other: James Staats Forbes and Edward Watkin.

FOUR

THE LINE TO
NOWHERE

Until the completion of the Circle line, the Underground carried more through services than trains that simply shuttled between the two Metropolitan termini. It was little more than an underground tunnel below London which happened to serve several local stations. The Circle changed all that. London would, thereafter, have a genuine underground railway with many journeys both starting and ending beneath the streets.

The decisions of the Commissions in 1846 and 1855 had made it almost inevitable that there would have to be an underground line connecting the various railway stations springing up on the edge of the metropolis. However, both planning and construction were to prove a lengthy process, hampered by the lack of an overall coordinating body and the unresolved tension of whether to encourage cooperation between various companies or stimulating competition. The whole process was made more difficult because the Circle was built as a result of government diktat, yet it was the private sector which had to fund and construct the line. The Metropolitan, as we have seen, had begun its crawl around London with the extension to Moorgate but then progress in the east halted for a decade while various extensions proceeded in the west. A House of Lords committee, in 1863, investigating, yet again, London's communications, had concluded that a connection between the main line termini would best be achieved by extending the Metropolitan eastwards from Moorgate and westwards from Paddington, eventually meeting along the Thames. Various promoters came forward with schemes, including the ubiquitous John Fowler, whose idea was that the Metropolitan would extend its line from Paddington to South Kensington in the west and to Tower Hill in the east, while a new railway, the rather confusingly named Metropolitan District, was to complete the rest of the circle.

The following year, yet another committee, this time a joint select committee of the Lords and Commons, examined all these proposals and found in favour of the one put forward by Fowler. As all the preliminary work had already been done, three Bills were quickly drawn up and were on the statute books by July. Two of these covered the extensions for the Metropolitan and the third was for the Metropolitan District (referred to below as the District to avoid confusion) route from Tower Hill, along the Thames through to South Kensington.

Work on the extension from Paddington to South Kensington began soon after the passage of the Bill. It proved to be a more difficult railway to build than the original section of the Metropolitan because it went across the street pattern, and consequently under houses, rather than being dug under a road as with the Paddington to King's Cross. Landowners thus affected had to be bought off, requiring large compensation payments to property owners on the way. The effect of the Underground in this section of west London must, indeed, have been much more noticeable to local residents than on the initial part of the Metropolitan. At times, as mentioned in the introduction, this line runs in short open-air sections, hidden between the backs of houses, and several property owners must have felt much as the benighted residents of Richmond do today about the aircraft flying over their heads. The 'cut and cover' method used for most of the line was enormously disruptive and while there was only one sizeable tunnel, under Campden Hill between Kensington and Notting Hill, there were several short sections left uncovered, where noise and smoke affected the local neighbourhood. Resistance was strong: 'Once the disruption along the route of the original Metropolitan railway had been seen, owners of properties all over London fought vigorously against the introduction of the underground railway in their area. The "not in my back yard" brigade were just as forceful in Victorian times as they are today.'[1] Quick to resort to the law, they feared that there would be severe damage to their property from the relatively crude digging methods then employed.

By the end of 1868, the Metropolitan was operating to South Kensington, the site of the planned connection with the District which had also began to make slow progress. Unlike the huge fanfare that had accompanied the start of work on the Metropolitan, there was no ceremony in 1865 when the first sod was turned, nor, in fact, when the line opened on Christmas Eve 1868, a date chosen because revenue on Christmas Day was expected to be high – rather different from today when the whole Underground system is closed for the holiday.

Like the Metropolitan, the District was building on expensive land, through Kensington to Sloane Square, Victoria and Westminster; and by the middle of 1866, according to *The Times*,[2] 2,000 navvies were carving out the tunnels assisted by 200 horses and fifty-eight engines. At Earls Court, huge kilns were at work producing the 140 million bricks needed for the tunnels and embankments. The stretch from South Kensington to Westminster was completed in three years but the effort had brought the company to its knees because it had cost £3m – three times as much as the Metropolitan had paid five years earlier for its longer line from Paddington to Farringdon. The progress of the District line had been obstructed at every turn, especially by the big landowners who disliked the idea of underground railways traversing their land and, where possible, extracted large compensation payments out of the railway. Lord Harrington banned ventilation shafts from his South Kensington estate; a pipe containing the River Westbourne had to be channelled over the platform at Sloane Square;[3] and the company had to pay for the widening of Tothill Street and avoid the precincts of Westminster altogether. Several new sections of streets had to be provided and many others improved. There were many petty restrictions too: to avoid disturbing the barristers, the steam whistle of any locomotive engine could not be sounded near the Temple except in an emergency.[4]

The Westbourne was not the only problem with water for the new railway. Pumps had to work all day extracting it at the rate of 4,000 gallons per minute and, moreover, a large sewer near Victoria had to be reconstructed, putting the effluent into a cast-iron cylinder eleven feet high and fourteen feet in width. The complexity of the task of digging under London, even in those days, before the advent of electricity and telecommunications, was nevertheless daunting: 'Water pipes, gas mains, sewers and monster beams of timber presented themselves in all directions overhead while workmen, as numerous as bees in a hive, were excavating, getting bricks and fixing arches with as much dexterity as if they had served their apprenticeship in underground railways.'[5]

Construction of the Underground lines was used as the catalyst for reshaping large swathes of London. A *Times* journalist, who went on a site visit with directors of both the Metropolitan and the District during construction of the latter in Victoria and Westminster, wrote: 'The "slums" of Westminster will be very much improved by the construction of the line. In Broadway[6] a number of dilapidated houses have been pulled down and many more are "ticketed" [scheduled for demolition].'[7] Further towards Victoria, a brewery owned by Eliot, Watney and Co. (Watney was to survive as the name of an awful beer until the end of the twentieth century) was being rebuilt using the roofing of the tunnel as the foundations. The company had been forced out of its old premises by the building of the line and, to ensure its cooperation, the District offered the brewery a new site. At Victoria itself, there was to be what *The Times* called a large 'exchange station' with the new terminus being built by the London, Chatham & Dover. All the scepticism about the viability of underground railways had disappeared. The reporter was enthusiastic, and was aware of the fact that the Metropolitan was only the start of a much bigger system: 'Judging from the results already shown by the working of the Metropolitan line, even in its imperfect state as only a partial system, a traffic such as never has been known on any line is expected to be secured by this circular scheme.'[8] Indeed, that was to be true – but not until the circle was complete which meant that in the meantime the District struggled financially, as it would for most of its forty-year independent existence.

Moreover, there was a problem in beginning work on the District's section along the Thames as ideally it should have been combined with the construction of the Embankment, to which the Metropolitan Board of Works was now, after years of prevarication, finally committed. The works had, in effect, to be integrated but the District's shortage of cash precluded further major expenditure, especially as the climate for investment in such projects had worsened as investors saw that the substantial early dividends paid by the Metropolitan had been too generous and such rates of return could not be expected in the long term. The District wanted a period of running its trains between South Kensington and Westminster to ensure that some revenue was coming in, but the Board of Works was pushing hard to get the railway to press on with the building of the line rather than opening sections of it. Eventually, work on the Embankment started in 1869 but it was not until the following year that the District obtained powers to raise a further £1.5m to continue its progress eastwards. The line reached Blackfriars at the end of May 1870 but there were few early users. A historian of the District postulates: 'Although it was expected that traffic levels would match those of the Metropolitan on the north side of the city, they were comparatively light, perhaps due to the variety of main line termini, any of which could be reached easily from south London and which removed the need to travel between them once reaching London.'[9] Indeed, the various termini north of the Thames had comparatively small suburban networks and each area tended to be connected with a single station, whereas in south London the rivalry between the London, Chatham & Dover and the South Eastern had resulted in much duplication with many outlying towns and suburbs being connected to two major termini, thereby giving local travellers a choice of their destination in London, reducing the need to take an onward journey by the Underground.

Six weeks after the District's extension to Blackfriars had started operating, the Embankment along the Thames opened and according to contemporary reports, following the departure of the royal guests who had performed the ceremony, 'a great mob of roughs tried to push westwards along the Embankment but their progress was arrested "in a masterly manner" by the police'.[10] The East and West Ends were very different worlds and it would be another fifteen years before the underground line linked them as well.

Once the District had reached Mansion House, effectively three quarters of the way around the circle, it started running trains all the way round to the Metropolitan's new terminus at Moorgate, providing half the services on the line. This sort of joint service pointed the way to the solution to the operational difficulties – a merger with the Metropolitan. However, that obvious move was made more difficult by the appointment of two men who were intense rivals to lead the respective underground railway companies. Both companies were ailing financially and turned to major figures in the railway industry to help them out of their difficulties. Unfortunately, the two men chosen, James Staats Forbes and Edward Watkin, had a history that meant they would never be able to cooperate.

Forbes and Watkin were very different characters who had headed rival railways. James Staats Forbes had worked for Brunel on the construction of the Great Western and had gone on to save the London, Chatham & Dover Railway – which had been on a path of almost suicidal expansion and cut-throat competition with the South Eastern – from bankruptcy. He started there as general manager in 1862, taking the railway out of receivership and then going on to stay nearly four decades, the last twenty-five years as chairman and managing director. He was an early exponent of spin doctoring, being described as 'a past master in the art of bunkum',[11] and was, on the surface, an easygoing and cultured character who built up an extensive art collection on the money he made from the railways. He also had a steely backbone that was to help fuel the thirty-year feud with Watkin, who had an even more aggressive and domineering personality. The District's directors were so desperate to obtain Forbes's services that they reduced their own allowance by £1,250 in order to pay him a salary of £2,500 without imposing a further financial burden on the shareholders. Forbes became managing director of the District in 1870 and chairman when he ousted the Earl of Devon a couple of years later, a position he held until 1904.

While Forbes was in the mould of a company doctor, trying to sort out a legacy of unrealistic expansion, Watkin, who took over as chairman of the Metropolitan in August 1872, within a month of Forbes assuming the same post at the District, was a great visionary, ever espousing grand plans. He came from a more affluent background than Forbes. As the son of a prominent cotton merchant, he was not only born into wealth but had immediate access to the rich who could help promote his considerable railway ambitions. Like that other underground pioneer, Charles Pearson, he was also something of a campaigner, having written a book pleading for public parks and helped start the half-day Saturday movement, campaigning to allow workers to have Saturday afternoons off. He was, as many prominent people of the time were, an MP for a while; but it was the railways which were to become Watkin's lifelong obsession, inspired, perhaps, by the fact that his father took him to the opening of the Liverpool & Manchester in 1830.[12] At one time or another during his long career he was a director of most of the major main line railway companies in England, and he was involved in many railway projects abroad, notably in Greece, and in Canada where his efforts to save the Grand Trunk Railway ensured that the country eventually obtained a cross-continental line.

He had, as one historian puts it, 'business acumen, superb negotiating skills with tremendous flexibility to manipulate several options to achieve a personal objective'.[13] Other descriptions are even less kind: 'He could be fairly described as a nervous and aggressive workaholic who from his twenties onwards suffered from anxiety, depression and nervous breakdown.'[14] There is no doubt he was a difficult man to work with. Although he was, at times, extremely affable, he was ruthless and enjoyed nothing more than a good fight, including public disputes with the directors of companies he chaired. His belligerence resulted in a battle with Forbes that lasted for over three decades, but fortunately for Londoners, most of the conflict between the pair was fought out in the Kent countryside. Even today, the pattern of the railway network and the existence of two stations in many modest-sized towns such as Maidstone, Sevenoaks and Margate, serving different London termini, is a reflection of the long battle between the two railways at the time when they were led, respectively, by Forbes and Watkin. Watkin was secretive and abrasive in negotiations, while Forbes, possibly disingenuously, presented himself as more amenable. Forbes refused to bow to pressure from his rival and set out to expand to survive.[15] The ruinous competition, which was to the detriment of both passengers and shareholders of both railways, only ended when Watkin retired in 1894; within five years, the two companies had effectively merged.

In London, the battle was less wasteful but still damaging to the long-term interests of the capital. After the District reached Mansion House, at last the Metropolitan started its journey east, with an extension opened in February 1875 into Great Eastern's huge new Liverpool Street terminus. Later that year trains were rerouted to a nearby station at Bishopsgate. A further extension to Aldgate was completed in 1876, largely because of pressure from the Corporation of London, but by then the Metropolitan realized that building cut and cover lines through expensive City property was not viable and stopped its expansion.

Even before the arrival of Forbes and Watkin, relations between the District and the Metropolitan railways had been fraught. The idea of having two railways was already creating conflicts which made life harder for passengers. At Kensington, for example, the ownership pattern was confusing. While the track from Moorgate round to South Kensington via Paddington belonged to the Metropolitan, the two companies jointly owned the stations at Gloucester Road and Kensington High Street where the eastern platform belonged to the Metropolitan and the western was in the hands of the District. At South Kensington there was another silly situation: the entire station was owned by the Metropolitan, and the District, unwilling to share it, started building an entirely new one which required the demolition of thirty recently built houses in Pelham Street.[16]

Usage increased when the District reached Mansion House in July 1871 but the money problems continued. Indeed, it was rather ironic that the District had been created as a separate company from the Metropolitan in order to raise money and yet throughout its history it struggled to do so. At first the District trains were run by the Metropolitan, but inevitably squabbles arose over the precise level of payments. The two companies had signed an operating agreement in 1866 by which the Metropolitan was supposed to get 55 per cent of the receipts for providing the trains, but it actually got 62 per cent since it ran additional services beyond those in the contract. This forced the District to provide its own trains and it bought the same Beyer, Peacock locomotives which had proved so effective for the Metropolitan. That did not stop the constant bickering over the amounts each should receive from the fare box and it was only in 1878, several years after the completion of the initial stages of the District, that the money was shared equally.

There were all kinds of other disputes. For example, the District had rather cheekily built two extra tracks parallel to the Metropolitan's between Gloucester Road and High Street Kensington, the Cromwell curve (named after Cromwell Road under which it runs), without either Parliamentary authority or an agreement with the Metropolitan. This allowed the District to avoid running over part of the Metropolitan's tracks, for which it had to pay a usage charge, but did much to sour relations between the two companies, and arguments over the use of the curve carried on into the next century until, in a court case in 1903, the Metropolitan prevented the District from using the curve.

Even before the completion of the circle, the public were beginning to get a genuine underground service that covered much of London north of the Thames. The District's rapidly built extension to Mansion House was opened by the Prime Minister, William Gladstone, and brought the line tantalizingly near to Tower Hill, just three quarters of a mile away, where eventually it was to meet the Met. By July 1871, when the District started running its own trains, there was a ten-minute frequency, half operated by each company, from Mansion House to Moorgate and a five-minute frequency between Mansion House and Gloucester Road. The trains were not luxurious but were relatively comfortable. They were painted green on the District and consisted of eight carriages: two first, two second (later a third second-class carriage was added) and four third. The first class only had four compartments per carriage, upholstered and roomy, while the others had five, and whereas the second class had a modicum of comfort the third's furnishings were confined to a strip of carpet on the wooden seats and a padded back strip at shoulder height. Once the ninth carriage was added, there was space for 430 people on each train, impressive given the frequency of service. As with the Metropolitan, the District started out as non-smoking but was forced to allow it from 1874, adding to what was already an unpleasant atmosphere.

Like the Metropolitan, the District realized that there was money to be made by feeding trains from suburban lines onto the underground section. It first started operating services from West Brompton, on the West London line, through to Kensington High Street; but there was no station at Earls Court, between the two termini.

Earls Court is an early example of how quickly the arrival of the underground railway could transform an area. At the time, Earls Court was fertile market garden land with few houses. The residents petitioned for a station and this was eventually completed in October 1871. The early building, a modest affair with a wooden booking office, lasted only four years before being burnt down, an event which enabled the company to provide a much grander station to meet the demands of the population, as the surrounding area had developed rapidly in the intervening period.[17]

The Earls Court and West Brompton connection was to be the start of the District's drive westwards, just as the little spur from Baker Street to St John's Wood would be the basis of the Metropolitan's great expansion, both described in the next chapter. Meanwhile, though, the Circle needed to be completed and work was stalled. The antagonism between Watkin and Forbes delayed the completion of the Circle line, both being more concerned with doing each other down than ensuring the completion of the project.

There was, as ever in this story, a shortage of capital; and the state of the Metropolitan's finances, which had been the main reason for employing Watkin, was, he discovered, worse than originally thought. The handsome returns paid by the Metropolitan in the mid 1860s were partly coming out of capital raised for future projects,[18] forcing the company to cut dividends, which in turn prompted a shareholders' revolt and a boardroom coup. The new board discovered that the books had not been properly kept and, according to one account, there was the suggestion of widespread corruption: 'there was a considerable amount of slackness and waste in the stores and engineering departments'.[19]

Indeed, Watkin was incensed at what he found when he took over the chairmanship of the Metropolitan. He was scathing about John Fowler, the engineer, who had been paid the enormous sum of £152,000[20] and who also received a further £157,000 from the District. While obviously part of that had to be passed on to his own employees and contractors, it represented a staggering amount given that the whole of the original section of the Metropolitan had been built for £1m. As Watkin pointed out in an indignant letter to the engineer at a shareholders' meeting, it was a poor example to other professionals involved in the construction: 'No engineer in the world was so highly paid. Taking it any way you like – time, speciality, risk, quantity, value or all combined, you have set an example of charges which seems to me to have largely aided in demoralization of professional men of all sorts who have lived upon the suffering shareholders for the past ten years.'[21] Watkin went on to lambast contractors generally: 'At the opera, if we look at the lady occupants of the best boxes, who are glittering with the best diamonds, and ask who they are, we are told that they are the wife and daughters of Clodd, the great railway contractor. In the park whose carriages, horses and equipages are the most fashionable? Why, those belonging to Plausible, the great railway engineer. And if we hear of some poor nobleman's estate being in the market, who buys it? Why, Vampire, the great railway lawyer.'[22] It is interesting that Watkin, the son of a merchant, felt impelled to side with the landed gentry, rather than the ranks of the new entrepreneurs to which he belonged, in the great class battle which had been raging since the start of the Industrial Revolution nearly a century before.

The need for the completion of the Circle was apparent from the high usage of the sections that were already built. By 1875 the Metropolitan was carrying 48 million passengers per year, and the District, though continuing to struggle, managed to carry around half that number, still a substantial achievement. Three quarters of these passengers used third class, suggesting they were manual workers and low-paid clerks attracted by the low fares, but interestingly, as it expanded, the Underground managed to attract a substantial body of first-class passengers who were vociferous in their complaints about travelling on the slow and uncomfortable services. But where had these new travellers come from? Without the railway would they simply not have undertaken their journey, or were they transferring from other modes?

The steamboats, which were first introduced in 1815, had once been the mainstay of travel from south-east London but were in decline, hastened by a disaster in 1878 when the overcrowded *Princess Alice* capsized, drowning over 600 people, mostly day-trippers. New forms of transport undoubtedly generate journeys, as witnessed by the rapid filling of any new motorway, and it was the same here: rather than the Underground eating into the traffic of its main rival the horse-drawn omnibus, usage of both modes of travel increased after the creation of the Metropolitan. The number of omnibus users rose from 40 million in the year of the Metropolitan's opening to nearly 50 million in 1875. Partly this was the result of clever strategies by the omnibus owners: they reduced fares to cope with the competition, which, along with the fact that the average journey was now shorter, resulted in a fall in revenue in this period, despite the upsurge in passenger numbers; and they also provided, with encouragement from both the District and the Metropolitan, feeder services to the Underground, an early recognition of the importance of integrated transport. In some cases, the Underground companies had to subsidize these feeder services in order to boost passenger numbers on their trains. When the District first opened, there was no public transport between Regent Street and Church Lane (now High Street) Kensington, or anything along Park Lane or Palace Road. The reason was that in this affluent area of Central and West London people could afford their own carriages and therefore the District had to guarantee the revenue for the first omnibuses between Victoria and Paddington along Park Lane. Similarly, the Metropolitan paid for services from Piccadilly along Regent Street to what is now Great Portland Street station.

With suburban railways springing up – especially in south London – as well as the growing Underground in central London, it was the end of the half-century-long dominance of horse-drawn public transport and one estimate suggests that by 1875 there were three times more train passengers than omnibus riders.[23] The omnibus still had a niche market for shorter journeys and those for which there was no rail alternative, but the train services, both underground and suburban, were becoming the main way for Londoners to get about, not least because they were so much faster for any journey of more than a mile, despite the problems of access up and down often quite difficult stairs. And interestingly, the London General Omnibus Company managed to pay much more handsome dividends to its shareholders during this period than did the train companies, because of external changes such as the reduction in the cost of horse feed and various savings in tolls and taxes. The Underground companies, moreover, were burdened with a huge capital base, together with continual pressure to raise more in order to expand.

With both the Metropolitan and the District ailing, others tried to fill the gap in getting the Underground circle completed. In June 1873, a group of City financiers, who later called themselves the Metropolitan Inner Circle Completion Company, published a plan to build a link between Mansion House and Bow, not only completing the circle but linking with the North London, Great Eastern and East London railways. This scheme, which obtained Parliamentary powers in 1874, prompted a couple of years of wheeling and dealing with Watkin, as ever, behaving badly. He tried to block the completion company's scheme by starting work on the Metropolitan's extension and introducing another bill for the completion of the inner Circle by a shorter line from Aldgate to Cannon Street, but that was rejected by Parliament. Watkin kept on trying delaying tactics against the Completion Company as well as pushing the Metropolitan on as far as he could, but when the line reached Aldgate in November 1876 there was neither money nor permission to go any further. As with its westward extensions, constructing the line was a much more difficult task than the original section because not only did its path take it under buildings, but as the line was now heading for the heart of the old City, the property was increasingly expensive. For example, the Roman Catholic chapel at Moorfields needed thirty feet of costly underpinning and even then part of the building collapsed.

One example of Watkin's skulduggery was that he opposed the 1878 extension of time bill for the Completion Company, claiming it contained a clause about the underpinning of buildings that was 'unusual and onerous'. Yet, according to one historian, 'the same clause appeared in the Metropolitan and Regent Circus Bill he was promoting in the same Parliament'.[24] The District, on the other hand, realizing it could never raise the money to complete the circle, supported the Completion Company's efforts.

But to no avail. Despite being offered £370,000 from the Metropolitan Board of Works (MBW) to support the building of a new street linking Fenchurch Street and another £130,000 by the Commission of Sewers, the Completion Company could not raise the cash to build the link. So at last, after several wasted years, the only realistic outcome emerged – the Metropolitan and the District decided to cooperate. After the failure of the Completion Company scheme, a contractor, Charles Lucas, persuaded the two enemies, Forbes and Watkin, to meet and agree a short-term peace agreement in order at last to complete the Circle. They managed to persuade the Commissioners of Sewers to raise their offer to £250,000 and the MBW's to £500,000. Even then, it took an outsider to knock the heads of the two companies together. With several other schemes being put forward by promoters, there was an inquiry chaired by Sir John Hawkshaw who, arbitrating, recommended that the joint scheme by the two existing railways should be selected, presumably on the basis that the involvement of a third party would have led to chaos. As we see below, it was bad enough trying to run an integrated service like the inner Circle line with two players, let alone three.

At last, in August 1879 a joint act was passed granting powers to the two railways to complete not only the Circle but also a spur to Whitechapel and a connection with the East London which ran between Whitechapel and New Cross. For its part, the Metropolitan, which was more affluent than the District, started work on the Aldgate–Trinity Square (now Tower Hill) extension which opened in September 1882. At this stage, the line ended abruptly at Tower of London station, then a rickety wooden construction which had been jerry-built in just three days but which lasted until it was bombed in 1940.

After yet more bickering between the District and the Metropolitan, the two started working together almost immediately on the last section of the circle, between Tower Hill and Mansion House. The Metropolitan initially financed the work, with the proviso that the District would become a financial partner at a later date. The cost was a severe burden for the Metropolitan. As the engineer and railway writer O.S. Nock put it, 'all constructional difficulties experienced in earlier underground lines in London were accentuated on this extraordinary 2¼ miles of railway and the ultimate cost worked out at a million pounds a mile'. The main cost was labour: to build the circle extension, 850 men were employed by day and 500 at night for two years. Of course, even if translated to today's money, making, say, £70m per mile, that is very cheap compared with the estimates of the Crossrail link under London which it is reckoned could cost at least £10bn for a tunnel of less than four miles (£2,500m per mile) under central London between Paddington and Liverpool Street. An estimate soon after construction[25] reckoned that the thirteen-mile-long circular railway cost about £11m, including almost another five miles of spurs and early extensions. London had got a bargain but the expected financial bonanza for the two underground companies never materialized.

Any hopes that operating a line together would finally make the two companies, and, in particular, their bosses, behave in a grown-up way were quickly dashed. But first there was the opening ceremony, on 17 September 1884, to be got over with. Forbes and Watkin reportedly sat in the same train as it ran round the Circle, but unfortunately there is no photograph to record their discomfiture. At the inevitable banquet, Forbes rose at the end of the meal to tell the assembled VIPs that differences between himself and Watkin were slight and only on the surface. It was pure cant. There was an immediate series of disputes which continued until the end of the century. Far from peace breaking out, it was the lawyers who enjoyed a field day as innumerable suits and countersuits were filed by the two rivals.

Public services started on October 6 and there was turmoil, caused partly by the two companies' mistrust of one another. They had agreed that the Metropolitan trains should run clockwise around the outer track, while the District operated in the opposite direction on the inside line.[26] Of the fifteen route miles (which included a few spurs and sections of four-track which counted double) of the Circle, seven were owned by the Metropolitan, just under six miles by the District, and just over two were jointly owned. While this could, with goodwill and sensible management, have been an effective way of operating the seventy- to eighty-minute round trip covering twenty-seven stations, the hostility and antipathy between the two ensured that it was a recipe for chaos.

According to the initial timetable, the companies attempted to run eight trains per hour in each direction but underestimated the difference between operating on a horseshoe, with a terminus at each end, and a continuous circle. The locomotives had to be watered which took place during a two-minute stop at Aldgate where a special drain had to be fitted to run the hot water, a colossal 218,000 gallons daily, into the Thames. The longer servicing and inspection involved taking the locomotive off the train and replacing it at one of the Kensington stations – High Street for the District, South for the Metropolitan. Spare engines were left wherever there was space in odd corners of the railway, of which there was little, putting extra pressure on running a punctual service.

In addition to the 140 trains scheduled on the inner Circle in each direction, a further 684 were timetabled to use part of the line, entering at Cromwell Road from the west, Praed Street (near Paddington) from the north-west and Whitechapel from the east. That meant a total of 964, around a hundred more than the line could cope with. The financial arrangements between the Metropolitan and the

District were at the root of this attempt to run too many trains as the District essentially paid a fixed fee irrespective of the number of trains it operated.[27]

Oddly, the very first day seems to have passed off without trouble, at least according to the man from *The Times*. The reporter describes[28] how the first morning service which left New Cross for Mansion House was a workmen's train soon after 5 a.m. and that the first westward Circle service was at 5.35 a.m., revealing a service pattern which is not much different from that of the early twenty-first century: 'The trains run at frequent intervals from before 6 o'clock in the morning until about midnight'. He also offers a possible explanation for some of the higher costs of the new section, as he mentions that 'the new tunnel and the new stations are great improvements upon the tunnels and stations of the older underground railways. The platforms are wide and the stations are airy.' But the rolling stock and its lighting was no better than when the Metropolitan first opened two decades previously. The reporter, too, was a bit grumpy about the prospect of the cost of fares: 'The joint companies promise a reduction of fares, but these have not been issued.' Nevertheless, he concluded that 'the traffic worked smoothly yesterday, and many of the public made a trial trip of a run around London'.

But the service soon deteriorated. According to one 'young man', writing to the paper ten days after the start of the service,[29] his job was at risk because he could 'never feel safe as to what time we shall arrive at our destination. As a daily traveller between Turnham Green and Sloane Square, I can assure you that the best time our morning train has kept since the opening of the Inner Circle completion has been 9 min late and the general time 15 min and 20 min late, and before this our train used to keep admirable time.' His problem was that his train was often held at Earls Court to allow the Circle line trains from Kensington High Street to pass. No wonder that control over this section of line, the Cromwell curve, was to be the subject of a legal dispute between the two companies until 1903.

The disruption was so bad that several trains came to a standstill for many hours and on at least one occasion, near Kensington High Street on 16 October, the passengers abandoned the carriages to walk along the track to escape by the nearest station.[30] Even without such outright failures – which were eventually rectified by cutting services back to six per hour on the inner Circle – passengers were much put upon, largely because of the silly rivalry. For instance, they were supposed to be encouraged to travel by the shortest route, their tickets bearing either the letter I for the inner, largely District, services, or O for the outer Metropolitan-run trains. Each company had its own booking office at joint stations and inevitably there were disputes about what route should be recommended between two stations that were broadly opposite each other on the Circle. Worse, however, was that when relations between the two companies went through one of the regular bad patches in 1886, both companies began issuing tickets for their own trains to hapless passengers irrespective of the fact that it might involve a journey of, say, twenty-two stops instead of five. Tickets bearing the wrong letter were not accepted for travel by the rival company and they ran fierce advertising campaigns against each other. 'Metropolitan railway, the best cheapest most convenient and expeditious route' boasted one, listing fares to various stations, 'note the fares and time occupied . . . save your time'.

The rivalry was undoubtedly exacerbated by the financial pressures of the two railway companies. Both had promised to pay dividends of 4 per cent on their respective shares of the £2.5m capital raised to build the line and therefore there was great pressure to maximize revenue through intense usage and, when that proved impossible, by trying to screw as much as possible out of the other company. The Metropolitan was always the senior partner, able to run more through trains and generally being able to call the shots over the District. There were disputes over sharing the cost of construction, over the amounts of interest that should be paid, about an agreement over the Cromwell curve and, inevitably, about fares.

The most ridiculous row led to the chaining of a locomotive to a disputed siding at South Kensington. As the *West London Advertiser* reported, 'The right to a siding is disputed by the respective companies . . . The District, in order to enforce their right, have run an engine and train into a siding and have actually chained it to the spot, notwithstanding the fact that the engine fires are kept alight, steam kept up and night and day, a driver and stoker are in charge. A day or two ago, the Metropolitan sent three engines to pull away the train and a tug of war ensued in which the chained train came off the victor . . .'[31] In between these arguments, there were attempts to do the obvious and amalgamate the two railways, something both Watkin and Forbes supported, but they could never agree on the terms.

The financial problems were mostly a result of the high cost of construction but were exacerbated by the fact that the route, as we have seen, was largely chosen at the instigation of a Parliamentary commission rather than by entrepreneurs assessing the needs of the market. Though the line was fairly well patronized, it was not very useful until a broader network of Underground lines was connected with it. Whereas two decades previously, when there was only a small section of the Metropolitan line, just under 9.5 million people had travelled on the Underground, bringing in receipts of £101,000, in the first year of full operation of the Circle there were 114.5 million passengers who paid receipts of £1,012,000. However, that was still not enough to pay adequate dividends given the expenditure on the Circle's construction and the cost of operating the line.

Compounding these problems was an unexpected revival in the fortunes of the horse omnibus. Intuitively, one would have expected the omnibus to have been on a declining curve since the start of suburban train services fifty years previously. However, several factors combined to make omnibuses cheaper and, while still slower than the train, at least faster and more reliable than hitherto. Their finances had been helped by the scrapping of turnpike tolls and mileage duties. Moreover, they paid low rates for their stables and depots while the railways had to pay the full amount on their stations and yards. Ironically, the underground railways even paid more towards the upkeep of the roads than their omnibus rivals as they frequently had to pay a ransom towards improvements in the thoroughfares under which they built their lines. Interviewed just before the end of the nineteenth century, the general manager of the District, Albert Powell, complained: 'The omnibuses are practically free from taxation; do absolutely nothing to maintain the roads over which they run; and while their expenses . . . are thereby kept down to the lowest figure, enabling them to charge fares out of all proportion to the service rendered, the District Railway is not only compelled to construct, at its own expense, the railways over which it runs . . . but is forced to contribute £32,000 per annum in rates and taxes towards the roads over which its competitors – the omnibuses – run.'[32] While railway operators the world over are in the habit of making similar complaints, Powell had a point. The railways even had to pay a passenger tax (on fares above a penny a mile) for which there was no equivalent for the omnibuses.

Secondly, these road improvements were part of a London-wide project to create wider and better streets. There were several new highways such as Northumberland Avenue, Shaftesbury Avenue and Charing Cross Road built in the 1870s and 1880s that did much to unblock the constant congestion on the London streets and make it easier for the clumsy omnibuses to thread their way through them.

Thirdly, the horse tram, highly successful in the suburbs, was excluded from central London, leaving the omnibus the lucrative pickings in the City and West End for journeys not covered by the Circle. Finally, the price of maize, a major factor affecting the profitability of the omnibus companies, dropped considerably in the 1880s. With all these advantages, the bus operators were able to offer much lower fares, attractive to the poorer passengers. For example, it was possible to travel from Putney to South Kensington, a distance of three and a half miles, for just a penny and from Putney to Charing

Cross for twopence. While many people would have been put off by the slower journey times of the omnibuses, they nevertheless represented damaging competition to the new underground services and certainly dented the profits of the rail companies, especially as their costs were virtually fixed and they provided enormous amounts of capacity through the frequency of service.

The completion of the Circle had done little to improve the situation of the District. Nothing could change the inherent problem for the District that many passengers from south of the river could choose their London terminus precisely to avoid having to change onto the Underground. For example, the advantages of the through services (mentioned above by *The Times* reporter) from New Cross to Mansion House were not that great compared with taking a train directly on the South Eastern Railway to, say, Cannon Street or Charing Cross. Passengers from Brighton had the choice of going into either London Bridge with easy access over the Thames to the City, or to Victoria.

Moreover, the geography of the line was not helpful to the District. The Circle is really an ellipse when viewed on a conventional map, a couple of parallel lines joined at the eastern and western extremities. At the eastern end, the lines are barely a mile apart and given that progress on the trains was held up at Aldgate for watering and the various junctions for traffic heading east, it was often quicker to take a brisk walk through the City rather than brave the Underground – especially as the true heart of the City, the Bank of England, was about half a mile away from several stations but not directly served by any of them. While the northern section of the line was profitable from the start as it benefited from greater usage and lower construction costs, the southern one probably never could be. Without a joint operation, there was no hope of paying adequate dividends. In 1886 Forbes had to admit to the District's shareholders that the venture of completing the Circle had been 'almost disastrous' and two years later he claimed that it was costing the company nearly £60,000 per year without any return.[33]

There had, indeed, been scepticism right from the beginning as to whether the Circle line was a viable railway. The *Railway Times*,[34] far from celebrating the completion of the line, ran a highly critical editorial under the heading 'The Inner Circle Delusion', which questioned whether there would ever be an adequate rate of return on the cost and suggested that the whole enterprise was an example of 'aerial castles, pleasing to the imaginative mind' but of little practical use.

The *Railway Times* was, of course, guilty of a lack of imagination and failed to realize that the fundamental problem was the one that was to dog all the Underground entrepreneurs – the fact that they were building a fantastic resource for Londoners whose value could never be adequately reflected through the fare box which was their only source of income.

The line may have been a financial failure, but at least the Circle, a strange concept for a railway line as it goes nowhere in particular, was complete. And while the short-term economics may have been disastrous, along with the continued development of the suburban railway network, it was to prove a boon to London's economy. It was to be used by both commuters and, importantly, leisure travellers and it quickly became an essential part of the capital's infrastructure. Yet, oddly, it was to take another sixty-five years and the creation of Harry Beck's famous diagram before the name 'Circle Line' appeared on the London Underground map.

FIVE

SPREADING OUT

Neither the Metropolitan nor the District wasted the years of waiting to complete the inner circle. Both were pursuing markets further afield – in the south and west in the case of the District and to the north and west for the Met. While strictly these were not underground lines as they largely ran on the surface or on elevated viaducts, they were to become an essential part of London's underground network. It was not until the concept of deep tube lines was developed that any new lines crossed the central area of the capital. In the meantime, suburban expansion was essential to satiate the appetite of the entrepreneurs and the various professionals – lawyers, financiers, brokers – who fed off them.

The beginnings of what was to become the extensive network of lines on the western side of the capital had started almost as soon as the first section of the Metropolitan had been completed. As noted earlier, through associated companies, the Metropolitan had already developed two extensions: the Hammersmith & City line whose trains ran into the underground tunnel at Paddington, and the initially unsuccessful branch to St John's Wood and Swiss Cottage. However, it was to be the latter, called for a long time the 'extension railway', that was to prove far more significant in the history of the Underground and of London, ultimately creating a whole new area of the capital which, through its unofficial name, Metroland, encapsulated the importance of the railway in bringing about this growth.

As early as 1874, Sir Edward Watkin already had far-reaching visions for extending the Metropolitan, expressing to shareholders his desire to 'break through the iron barriers which . . . larger railways have constructed around you . . . and connect your great terminus with Northampton and Birmingham and many other important towns'.[1] There was one slight lacuna in this grandiose scheme: he had not yet worked out from which terminus these trains would operate. At first, Baker Street, with its little branch line that was gradually being extended out into north-west London, became the focus of the Metropolitan's network but later this would shift to a new terminus at Marylebone because of the physical difficulties of expanding the older station.

Watkin's ambitions were both grand and inconsistent. He wanted, simultaneously it seems, to create out of the Metropolitan an extensive suburban railway; a main line service – a plan to extend the line to Worcester was rejected in the early 1880s; and ultimately, even more extravagantly, a through railway from the north-west of the country via London to Kent where it would connect with a putative Channel Tunnel. Watkin, who had interests in a French railway company that could create a connection with Paris, even built a test bore for the tunnel, stretching more than a mile under the sea. He reckoned he could have the whole scheme, which included huge lifts on the shore to carry trains down to the level of the tunnel, completed within five years. It was not only the understandably sceptical shareholders of his wonderfully named Submarine Railway Company who were wary of the project, but the War Office which had fanciful visions of crack foreign troops being whisked through the tunnel to invade Britain. The fears of the military can be summed up by the views of Lieutenant General Sir Garnet Wolseley, the Adjutant General, who told a committee enquiring into the scheme that 'the proposal to make a tunnel under the Channel . . . will be to place her under the unfortunate condition of having neighbours possessing great standing armies'.[2] Given the disadvantage any invading troops would face in trying to overcome the entrenched positions of the defenders, such considerations were obviously nonsense in military terms and were motivated by xenophobia. Nevertheless, Watkin tried to allay these fears by saying the whole construction could be blown up at the touch of a button from London or, somewhat ridiculously, that he would build a spiral railway, rather than a lift, out of the tunnel to give the British a better chance of shelling any foreign troops attempting to invade. To no avail. The military's objections prevailed, though lack of cash also ensured that the project never really had a chance.

Despite his failure on the Channel scheme, Watkin pressed ahead with a host of other ideas in which the Metropolitan was intended to play a central part. Given the lack of diaries or correspondence to explain Watkin's thinking and his innate secretiveness about his long-term intentions, even to shareholders, it is unclear exactly how he reconciled all these various visions and how the growing Metropolitan was to fit into them. While some historians suggest that Watkin had a grand master plan but was keeping his cards close to his chest, others suggest that he was merely muddling through, intent on expansion and growth wherever possible. The Metropolitan, though, was key to his grand ambitions because he realized that if the through trunk line were built through London, it would be the central part of 'a sort of backbone for the commerce and industry of the country'. Watkin's initial power base had been the Manchester, Sheffield and Lincolnshire Railway but as he also gained control of the South Eastern based in Kent, the obvious role for the Metropolitan was to link the two. And as a history of the Metropolitan puts it, 'Watkin perceived that it would be politically easier for the Metropolitan to break out of London than for the Manchester, Sheffield and Lincolnshire Railway to break in'.[3] Moreover, having the direct connection into the Underground and into the heart of the City gave Watkin's plan a leading edge in order to compete with the existing north–south railways where people had to get off at the terminus to change trains. In the event Watkin managed to complete the Grand Central Railway just before his death in 1901, but this ran on Metropolitan tracks into

Marylebone rather than creating a through route to the south, and his national aspirations for the Metropolitan were never achieved.

Watkin's ambitions therefore ensured that the line to Swiss Cottage, which at first was a single track railway,[4] was quickly extended even though it was poorly patronized. The extension was made easier by the fact that once out of the immediate vicinity of central London, the railway was built on the surface, which of course was much cheaper. Powers were quickly obtained for the tunnel to be continued from Swiss Cottage to Finchley Road and then for the railway to run in the open air through to West Hampstead, Kilburn and Willesden Green, which were reached in 1879.

Already, the Metropolitan was aware of the potential role of the railway in opening up a whole new area of London. It is difficult nowadays to believe that one contemporary account could cite that 'amongst the charms of Kilburn is its proximity to the country. Within half an hour's walk, the pedestrian is among trees and fields and pleasant places'.[5] An extension to Harrow[6] was completed in 1880 where, although there was already some housing around the railway stations built by the London & North Western at Wealdstone and Harrow Weald, it was essentially still a natural and undeveloped environment: 'The whole neighbourhood is more rural than any part of the country within the same distance from the interminable brick and mortar wilderness of London. The district about Kingsbury and Neasden is intersected by flowering hawthorn hedges, while the River Brent meanders through them.'[7]

And so it went on. Within another five years the Harrow line reached Pinner, and Rickmansworth and Chesham were added before the end of the 1880s. The Metropolitan waxed lyrical about the way these extensions created the possibility of rural trips, saying that they 'opened up a new and delightful countryside to the advantage of picturesque seekers; ancient houses and old-world ways. Within 50 minutes from Baker Street and for the cost of less than a florin [two shillings], if the visitor can be economically disposed, he can enjoy a feast of good things, fresh air, noble parks, stately houses, magnificent trees and sylvan streams.'[8] But, of course, the only way that the railway could become profitable was to ensure that developers, stimulated by the arrival of the railway, destroyed much of that bucolic splendour (as described in Chapter 12).

The extension to Rickmansworth reveals that Watkin was certainly aware of the fact that the only way the railway could make money was through attracting the developers. There was little immediate railway traffic to be had from a town of just 1,000 people and it was hardly surprising that only 561 passengers were carried to the capital in the first month, though income was boosted by a bit of freight, principally coal and gravel, and by leisure traffic on Sundays attracted by the Metropolitan's flowery publicity. For example, the *Watford Observer* reported that 450 people had used the line to go to Harrow and 250 to Northwood on a hot day in September 1887.

There were, however, sceptics about the line, a letter writer to the *Financial News* complaining that 'so boring was the country passed through and so few people on the train' that he considered the extension 'a waste of money and doomed to failure'.[9]

Chesham, a larger town of 6,500 people, was connected to the Metropolitan in 1889, becoming the terminal of the railway for the next three years. Hitherto it had been an isolated self-contained community but the arrival of the Metropolitan transformed it into a focal point for excursions. Soon after the opening, the Metropolitan had one of its own, taking 3,000 employees by special trains for one shilling apiece to march behind the Harrow Town Band to the cricket ground where they saw their staff cricket team play the local Chesham side.

The station at Aylesbury, which had been on a minor railway, was rebuilt by Metropolitan and in 1892, proved to be a fantastic boon to the local traditional duck egg trade, whose 'egglers' were now able to collect large numbers for the London trade. While the line attracted reasonable patronage from the town of Aylesbury, the intermediate stops were pretty deserted and financially the service did not appear to make immediate sense. An early contemporary account[10] in the local paper records that '71 people booked on the first journey which left Aylesbury at 7.15 a.m. and the great majority got out at Stoke [Mandeville] and Wendover'. The reporter reckoned that 'for a village Stoke may be said to have one of the largest and most comfortable stations to be found anywhere. In the event of their houses being destroyed by fire or flood, the whole of the inhabitants can be found shelter in the station building.'

The Metropolitan now extended nearly 50 miles from central London, making it an odd combination of a suburban – rural, really – railway stretching far out of the capital linked to an underground system that ran under much of the City and the West End. With the benefit of hindsight, it is obvious that this expansion was more a product of Watkin's main line aims than of any coherent strategy to use the railway as a tool to develop a large area of the countryside outside London. Aylesbury had long been Watkin's principal target, because it was at a junction just outside this town that the Metropolitan would eventually, in 1899, meet the Manchester, Sheffield & Lincolnshire, creating the through connection to London he had sought for so long. It had become clear, though, that the idea of running trains through the Underground section out to the south coast, creating a direct link between Manchester and seaside towns such as Brighton and Dover, could never be realized. The overused stretch of line which had formed the original section of the Underground between Paddington and Farringdon, now encumbered with hundreds of Circle Line trains and used, in 1897, by 528 passenger trains and fourteen goods trains – with a train every three minutes in each direction at peak time – did not have the capacity despite the doubling of the track[11] between Kings Cross and Farringdon.

Baker Street, which was both a terminus for the Metropolitan and the connection into the Underground, was clearly inadequate for the task of handling main line trains too. Watkin was forced to run his trains into a new terminus, prompting the building of London's last new main line station, Marylebone, which has throughout its history been something of a white elephant – especially as it is rather poorly served by the Underground. Indeed, when the station opened, it had no connection whatsoever, forcing passengers to walk to Edgware Road or Baker Street. Watkin had some difficulty pushing through his plan for a new station, not least because the tunnels would have to run under the sacred turf of Lord's Cricket Ground, whose membership were, quite simply, the Establishment. The routing of the main line trains to Marylebone left the suburban services of the Metropolitan to run into Baker Street, either stopping there, or continuing into the Underground as they still do today. Watkin, weakened by a stroke a few years earlier, died in 1901 without seeing the far-reaching effect of the twenty-year-long series of extensions into the countryside, which were to prove an astonishing success when the company realized that its future was in stimulating the creation of Metroland.

As part of his expansion plans, Watkin had also managed to gain control of another semi-underground line, the East London, the third connection across the Thames – along with the West London line and the Chatham's Blackfriars bridge. The East London line was a strange railway and remains an anomaly on today's underground map as it connects two rather unfashionable districts of the capital, New Cross and Shoreditch, with a desultory shuttle that has half a dozen intermediate stops.[12] The East London was built primarily because the tunnel was already there, rather than to fulfil any immediate railway purpose. The line uses a tunnel constructed by the father and son team of Marc and Isambard Brunel and its importance lies not so much in the resulting construction, amazing though that was, as in the techniques used to build it. Brunel's tunnel was conceived as a pedestrian – and possibly carriage – thoroughfare between the two banks of the Thames, a mile and a half downriver from the then lowest crossing point, London Bridge. Several unsuccessful attempts to burrow under the Thames had been made in the early nineteenth century but it was not until Brunel *père* developed a new building technique that the idea became feasible. His innovation was to create a shield, a huge frame on three levels, each with twelve little compartments with just sufficient room for a man to dig out the earth in front of him with a pick and shovel. The spoil was taken out by a series of buckets and when the thirty-six men had dug out all in front of them, the shield was moved forward by a series of jacks. As the shield advanced, a team of bricklayers working behind would create the lining of the tunnel, ensuring that there was no collapse.

Not surprisingly, with the combination of the pioneering method and the difficult geological conditions – the solid London clay often giving way to gravel and sand – there were frequent floodings and, as with so many of these great Victorian enterprises, the money put up by the investors – who were never to receive any return on their investment – soon ran out. Work had started in 1825 but was halted several times due to flooding – which at one point nearly drowned Isambard and killed six other men – and lack of funds. The government bailed out the project, originally costed at £179,000 (the best estimate is that in today's money this represents around a thousand times more, £179m), with a loan of a quarter of a million pounds and the tunnel eventually opened in March 1843, nearly two decades after the start of construction and at over twice the projected cost.

While the tunnel was an engineering triumph, the first in the world to be built under water, financially it proved to be a disaster. Although 2 million people, many of them sightseers rather than those needing to get across the Thames for business or commercial purposes, paid the penny toll in the first year, the receipts of just under £9,000 were nothing like sufficient to service the debt, let alone repay the loan. The biggest mistake had been the decision not to incur the extra cost of building a road access to the tunnel, which meant that the carriages, which were to have been charged sixpence, could not use it. For a time, thanks to a series of 'Fancy Fair' promotions and the encouragement of stallholders to sell food and souvenirs, the owners managed to turn the tunnel into an major attraction for both tourists and leisure-seeking Londoners and briefly it became London's most successful gift shop. One plucky trader, who hailed from Leipzig, even advertised that he was German-speaking (Britain was on friendly terms with Prussia at the time) by putting up a sign saying *Hier spricht man Deutsch*. Ultimately, though, there was a limit to how attractive the stallholders could make a narrow, though elegantly built, tunnel. By the 1860s, Brunel's wonderful construction had degenerated into a low-life den, inhabited by drunks, the homeless and prostitutes. The solution, for the poor shareholders, was to sell the tunnel for use as a railway line to the East London Railway at a loss. The East London paid £200,000, not enough to cover the debt which had, by then, risen to nearly double the original sum.

This was another hapless enterprise. Having installed the railway, the company started operating services in 1869 between New Cross and Wapping. North of the river, this was extended first to Shoreditch and then, in 1876, to Liverpool Street via Whitechapel and Bishopsgate junction; but the enterprise was doomed financially since the connections with the rest of the railway network were poor and (just like today) few people wanted to travel to the obscure parts of town it served, especially on a route that was effectively a slow dog-leg. Moreover, the one useful destination, Liverpool Street, could only be used by a very limited number of East London trains because the Great Eastern jealously guarded its grand fiefdom.

Inevitably, the East London fell into financial difficulties and Watkin was ready to pounce. The line was taken over by a consortium of six railways, with Watkin becoming first the receiver, in 1878, and then chairman. While there was some modest improvement in the line's fortunes, particularly as a useful route for freight to avoid the already overcrowded route through London on the Metropolitan, none of the grand plans for the East London was ever realized. There had been suggestions that New Cross could become the 'Willesden of the South', a major junction linking several routes, but that was never a realistic concept. Watkin had hoped the East London would be part of his scheme to connect the north-west of England with the south coast and Paris through the Channel Tunnel; but instead, from 1884, Brunel's beautiful tunnel ended up being used only by a few underground trains connecting into the Circle. In yet another illustration of the petty rivalry between the Metropolitan and the District, those trains belonging to the latter went into New Cross Gate while the Metropolitan's stock used New Cross, a few hundred yards down the road, because it was owned by the South Eastern, another company chaired by Watkin.

Forbes had ambitions for the District to make other incursions into east London, but these had to wait until 1902, two years before his death, when the long-mooted Whitechapel and Bow section finally opened. It was the last shallow underground railway built in London, as the first two miles out of Whitechapel ran under the Mile End and Bow roads, after which the line continued on the surface, joining existing railways to go all the way to Upminster, thereby opening up large swathes of the Essex countryside.

In the west, however, the District had advanced much earlier in the same way that the Metropolitan did in the north-west: stage by stage helped by occasional takeovers of existing or proposed railways. But unlike the Metropolitan, the District was not encumbered by aspirations to be a main line railway. There was, however, one almost equally ambitious scheme that was briefly put forward by the District: a huge outer circle whose route was set out by John Fowler. Starting at Clapham Junction, it would have described a fantastic ellipse around what were then the limits of the Metropolis, taking in such diverse places as Battersea, Chelsea, Kensington, Kilburn, Camden, Finsbury Park, Stamford Hill, Bethnal Green, Limehouse and New Cross where it would have used existing lines to regain Clapham. This was not merely a fanciful idea, as the concept of an outer Circle had even found favour with the 1863 Parliamentary Select Committee which had recommended the completion of the (inner) Circle line, but in truth the plan was always unrealistic. Despite the success of the North London railway, which happened to link many places that had little alternative transport, people did not want to travel in huge circular routes around the capital and the number seeking to make trips between outlying districts and suburbs will always be much fewer than those seeking to go in and out of the centre.[13] Moreover, the scheme trod on too many toes of the existing railway owners, who feared, probably wrongly, that it would take much of their business away.

This ambitious but doomed plan should not be confused with the services that were called the outer Circle, which started running in 1872. This started at Broad Street, the North London terminus sited, until its demolition in 1986, next to Liverpool Street station (completed in 1874), and ran along the North London to Willesden Junction, down the West London and through on the District to Mansion House. There was, too, a middle Circle service which ran from Moorgate to Mansion House, but taking the long way round by using the Hammersmith & City branch, the West London and the District. In effect, these types of service were designed to get people from one side of town to the other by train, a kind of journey which was only made easy once the tube railways started to be built from 1890 onwards.

Stymied in such grandiose ambitions, the District was intent on spreading westwards as fast as possible. Most of the area west of Kensington was open land, scattered with a few villages which then, as now, were prosperous and, mostly, eager to be connected with through trains to London. The scarcity of passengers on the District's central London section between Mansion House and South Kensington meant that rapid extensions were vital for the company's finances – but only possible if the company could raise the capital to build them. Forbes looked towards Hammersmith, Kew and Richmond as potentially lucrative markets.

The District's first western extension, opened in 1874, took the railway to Hammersmith. This was a controversial destination for a company laden with debt, given that it seemed to be deliberately trying to take passengers away from the Metropolitan's branch which had opened in 1864. Watkin, of course, was furious. As Hugh Douglas neatly put it, 'this tapping of the Metropolitan market was a further thorn to scratch the sensitive skin of Sir Edward Watkin and his shareholders'.[14] But Hammersmith was rightly seen by the District as a better prospect than the intermediate parts of west London, especially as it was a good interchange point for places further afield such as Richmond and Ealing. What infuriated Watkin even more was that not only did the District's services offer a more direct connection with central London, but the new station was exploiting patronage which had been stimulated by the arrival of the Metropolitan a decade earlier. In that time, Hammersmith had changed from providing strawberries and spinach to Londoners into an expanding suburb that was rapidly attracting development and, therefore, was becoming a more mature market for the railways. Certainly, Hammersmith became the area west of London best served by the Underground, a position it still enjoys now, but local passengers had to suffer the inconvenience of the two stations being separated by the busy Hammersmith Broadway, a situation that pertains today, with passengers transferring between the two still having to brave a perilous road crossing.

Indeed, the way developers and the railway went hand in hand was well demonstrated three years later when the District reached Richmond partly using London & South Western tracks. This extension stimulated the development next to Turnham Green, one of the intermediate stations, of the first garden suburb, Bedford Park. The inspiration for Bedford Park, which pre-dated the more famous garden city at Letchworth in Hertfordshire by a quarter of a century, came from the Arts and Craft Movement, the group of artists who argued that attractive objects, and indeed surroundings, should be the right of everyone, rather than simply the affluent, and who thus encouraged the appreciation of beauty in revolt against the dominant materialist and, as they perceived them, vulgar Victorian values. However, Bedford

Park was developed by a rather dubious and financially stretched builder, Jonathan Carr, a cloth merchant, whose aims were an amalgam of materialism and idealism, and while initially some small houses were built, the latter ones were large and intended for the better-off City gentlemen who could afford the high rental of £40 per year for the advantage of being able to reach their offices within half an hour of getting on the train. In defence of Carr, the design of the estate by its first architect, Norman Shaw, was notable, mostly in Queen Anne style with the long rows of houses being individualized through the use of gables, tall prominent chimneys and large windows. There was a church and a mock-Tudor pub, surrounded by carefully preserved mature trees, to add to the attractiveness and the village feel which was so strong that for a time the estate had its own newspaper. Nor was it Carr's fault that Bedford Park was to prove the precursor for countless far less attractive suburban developments both in Britain and abroad.

The opening of the District to Hammersmith had also led to numerous housing developments near all the intermediate stations between there and Gloucester Road, which spurred the District to build yet more extensions. The District's need to extend deep into rural areas was the result of the massive debts incurred by the construction of its first, very expensive, section of line. Indeed, the District was so focused on growing westwards that it was hardly surprising that progress with the Circle was so slow. The extensions, after all, were likely to be lucrative and Mansion House was a useful terminus with access to the City. So why bother with the troublesome project of completing the loop?

The District duly reached Ealing, a long-term target, in 1879, with intermediate stops at Chiswick Park, Acton Town and Ealing Common.[15] Trains were scheduled to take forty-eight minutes to reach Mansion House from the new terminus at Ealing, little different from the timetable of their electric successors today. From 1883, there was also a service right out to Windsor from Mansion House, using the

Great Western Railway's line. This service, though, was little used, perhaps because the District's four-wheel rolling stock was too crude to give a good ride on the long non-stop stretch from Ealing to Slough; or perhaps, simply, because Windsor was just too far out and too affluent to encourage regular commuting.

The effect on land prices of the arrival of the railway began to be noticed and now landowners in Isleworth and Hounslow sought to see their areas connected in with the District. A new company, the Hounslow & Metropolitan, was formed to build a line from Hounslow Barracks (near the present Hounslow West station) to a junction with the District's Ealing branch; the line opened in stages until its completion in 1886 and was operated by the District. Here, though, more than ten miles from the centre of London, the development pickings were not as easy and the line attracted little new housing along its path until after the First World War.

In the South, by extending the stub of a line to West Brompton towards the Thames and Putney, the target of the District seems to have been leisure traffic. This was extended to the station now called Putney Bridge where people could take steamboat trips and watch the Oxford and Cambridge University boat race, then a huge national event. Indeed, the opening in March 1880 was chosen deliberately to be in time for that year's race. This extension did not attract as much development as the Ealing line and consequently there was less first-class traffic, a key determinant of profitability for the railway, because the areas served were not as fashionable and rents tended to be lower.

The District's management had ambitions to head further south over the river to Wimbledon, taking the line across the Common; but, although Parliamentary powers for this had been obtained in 1881, the railway was prevented from building the line – which was a joint effort with the London & South Western – by its usual financial difficulties. This saved the Common as, following complaints from the residents, a less damaging route was eventually agreed upon and opened in 1889. Visions of reaching Kingston had to be shelved and eventually abandoned due to lack of money. Coincidentally, the running time of the District trains to Mansion House from Wimbledon was exactly the same as from Ealing, forty-eight minutes. Apart from an extension to South Harrow and then Uxbridge (the latter actually eventually passed to the Metropolitan), and a loop to South Acton, all completed in the first decade of the new century, this was the end of the District's expansion westwards.

SIX

THE SEWER RATS

Although the District did not have the vision to create Metroland, the line stimulated considerable development and change in what is now west London. Despite the perpetual cold war with the Metropolitan and its equally permanent impecunious state, the District's achievements in carving out such a large railway in the last quarter of the nineteenth century were remarkable. In fact, by developing a dense network of lines, in contrast to the Metropolitan's single line adventure into the depths of the countryside, the District arguably did more than its rival to accelerate the rapid expansion of London's suburbs. Even before the completion of the Circle, the District's tracks were incredibly busy, not least because of the company's desperate need to reward its shareholders. By 1880 trains were serving Fulham, Richmond and Ealing, as well as running the three circle services described above. This meant that even in quiet periods there were always at least fourteen trains per hour in each direction between South Kensington and Mansion House where, until 1884, they terminated. By 1904, the last year of exclusive steam operation, the District was carrying 51 million passengers per year and it ran, *on average*, nearly twenty trains per hour between South Kensington and Mansion House, with more during the peak. This was achieved despite all the problems of unreliability and slow acceleration of steam locomotion in small and not always well-ventilated tunnels.

The vexed issue of the ventilation had never gone away and remained a source of controversy until the electrification of the lines in 1905, and while the underground companies still argued that the air was beneficial, a more realistic feel for what Underground travel was like in the early days of the Circle Line can be gleaned from one of the rare detailed contemporary accounts of a trip along the line. In the early 1890s, a journalist with the *English Illustrated Magazine*,[1] Fred Jane, concerned about the long hours worked in the sulphurous atmosphere by the railway workers, who were often in the tunnels for sixty hours a week, managed to get a footplate ride on locomotive No. 18 around the Circle one bright June morning, which he recounted in great detail as part of a series entitled 'The Romance of Modern London'. Our hero, travelling anticlockwise, boards at St James's Park and is accommodated on the platform side behind the left-hand tank, from which he gets a supposedly 'uninterrupted' view. The train plunges 'into a black wall ahead with the shrieking of ten thousand demons rising above the thunder of the wheels. The sensation altogether was much like the inhalation of gas preparatory to having a tooth drawn.'

Jane turned out not to be the most intrepid of reporters. He complains of being too hot, hardly a surprise considering the heat emitted by the locomotive and the tank, and fears for his safety: 'Visions of accidents, collisions and crumbling tunnels floated through my mind; a fierce wind took away my breath and innumerable blacks filled my eyes. I crouched low and held on like grim death to a little rail near me. Driver, stoker, inspector and engine – all had vanished. Before and behind and on either side was blackness, heavy, dense and impenetrable.'

Westminster, Charing Cross (now Embankment), and the Temple pass by without the poor chap really noticing, but on approaching Blackfriars there is some relief: 'I looked ahead. Far off in the air, and from it, came four silver threads palpitating like gossamers in the morning breeze. Larger and larger grew the hole, the threads became rails and the hole a station, Blackfriars, with rays of golden sunlight piercing through the gloom.'

Jane's style may be rather overwritten, in the Victorian fashion, but his account manages to convey the drama of the men working with a blazing fire in the Stygian gloom of the tunnels:

> Off again, a fierce light now trailing out behind us from the open furnace door, lighting up the fireman as he shovelled more coal on to the furnace, throwing great shadows into the air, and revealing overhead a low creamy roof with black lines upon it that seemed to chase and follow us. Ever and anon, the guard's face could be dimly seen at his window, more like a ghost than a man; while in the glass of the look-out holes were reflected the forms of the engine-men like spirits of the tunnel mocking us from the black pit into which we were plunging. Then again we would seem to stop, and to fall down, down, down, with always the wild shrieking surge and ceaseless clatter of the iron wheels.

He notes how quickly the water is replenished at Aldgate: 'The fireman at once jumped off the engine and made the necessary arrangements for filling our water tanks. So quickly was this done that probably none of the passengers noticed any difference in the length of stoppage, and in a very short time we were off . . . ' And he gets excited about the train's speed: 'From Farringdon Street to King's Cross is the longest stretch without a station, and the driver here gave us an exhibition of full speed and No. 18 came into King's Cross at the rate of some 40 mph. The average speed of trains between one station and another is from 20 to 25 mph.'

Now he enters the oldest tunnelled section of line, which had, over the past thirty years, elicited the most complaints about the atmosphere. He is no exception:

The road [a railway term for the track] now began to be uphill, and at the same time the air grew more foul. From King's Cross to Edgware Road, the ventilation is defective and the atmosphere more on a par with the 'tween decks, forrud' of a modern ironclad [battleship] in bad weather and that is saying a great deal. By the time we reached Gower Street [now Euston Square] I was coughing and spluttering like a boy with his first cigar. 'It is a little unpleasant when you ain't used to it,' said the driver, with the composure born of long usage, 'but you ought to come on a hot summer day to get the real thing!'

Other than on that notorious section between King's Cross and Edgware Road, the journalist finds the air 'purer than I had expected' and actually blames the travellers for the fetid air: 'The bad air so much complained of by the "sewer-rats" – as those who habitually use this Circle are called in the City – is due in a great measure to their almost universal habit of keeping all the windows and ventilators closed.' He begins to enjoy the journey and notes that 'the finest bit of scenery on the underground is the Baker Street junction, where a second tunnel lead[s] to the St John's Wood branches' which already actually stretched deep into the Buckinghamshire countryside. On the left, he reports, getting a trifle carried away, the station is 'a medley of crimson and gold; on the right, the daylight creeps in and the picture is a harmony of blue and silver. It is a novel and unexpected sight to see the ordinary black coat of respectability look crimson, as it does when seen after the intense blackness of the tunnel. But like all the other scenes, this was brief and momentary; then a dream of the past.'

Now, changing over to the right-hand side of the locomotive, he notes the trains coming the other way: 'Far away in the distance was an ever-increasing speck of light – the headlight of an approaching train. A moment later, it had come and gone – a silent flash of light, so silent that it might have been a phantom.' Not because it was quiet, though, but because 'our own engine made too much noise for any other sound to be audible'. He adds: 'Curiously enough, an approaching train is totally unlike what one would imagine it ought to look like. A strong light bursts from the furnace if it chances to be open, and illuminates the tunnel overhead, the carriage windows and brasswork make lines of light that run off and die in the distance, but the engine itself is lost in the blackness through which it is rushing.'

At High Street Kensington, the engine is changed, No. 7 replacing No. 18. Jane explains how it is necessary to replace the engines because of the strain caused by the numerous stops and that in order to prevent the wheels on one side wearing down faster than the other, 'engines halve their time run "backwards, forwards", as they say in the West Country'.

Off he goes again, rushing past 'men pasting bills on the advertisement hoardings that border on the line below South Kensington' until reaching St James's Park seventy minutes after leaving it, just a few minutes longer than it takes today with electric trains. This rapid progress was made possible, the reporter stresses, by the excellence of the brakes and of the block-system of signalling (which means the system is divided by the signals into blocks in which only one train is allowed at any time). While this timing might appear slow for a mere thirteen miles, he points out that there were twenty-seven stops on the journey and that without the stops it would have taken a mere forty minutes. Rather optimistically, he suggests that if the train were allowed to run full speed around the circle it would take a mere twenty minutes, for what would be a completely pointless trip.

Finally, Jane gives an example of the way that the passengers cause delays: 'The length of the stoppages could not well be reduced; indeed, they are already too short if we are to believe the tale now current of a wandering Jew sort of passenger – a lady of advanced years who can only alight from a train backwards. Every time she begins to get out, a porter rushes up crying, "Hurry up, ma'am, train's going" and pushes her in again.' The apparent paucity of reports of passengers being injured getting on or off the trains seems remarkable, given that each compartment had a door and the station staff must have been under constant pressure to get these all closed and the trains away again to keep to the tight schedule.

Another graphic description, an entirely negative one, was written in 1887 by the journalist and author R.D. Blumenthal. He recorded his impressions of a journey on the Underground in his diary[2] for 23 June 1887:

> I had my first experience of Hades to-day, and if the real thing is to be like that I shall never again do anything wrong. I got into the Underground railway at Baker Street. I wanted to go to Moorgate Street in the City . . . The compartment in which I sat was filled with passengers who were smoking pipes, as is the British habit, and as the smoke and sulphur from the engine filled the tunnel, all the windows have to be closed. The atmosphere was a mixture of sulphur, coal dust and foul fumes from the oil lamp above; so that by the time we reached Moorgate Street I was near dead of asphyxiation and heat. I should think these Underground railways must soon be discontinued, for they are a menace to health.

For all the discomfort described by Jane and Blumenthal, the Underground was becoming a magnet for Londoners making all sorts of journeys, not just commuting to and from work. Economic growth, although spasmodic with periodic strong booms and busts, was transforming the lives of millions of people. This combined with the expansion of the London population, created markets for all sorts of activities, ranging from shopping and visiting fairs and exhibitions to attending sports matches. This was the genesis of the consumer society which only became possible through mass transportation systems. There was more holiday time at Christmas, Easter, Whitsun and August, and, despite the protests of the powerful Sabbatarians, Sundays became days of leisure activity as well as churchgoing. The main line railways catered for the seaside trippers, offering return fares to seaside resorts like Brighton and Margate for between three shillings and sixpence and five shillings while, as we have seen, the Metropolitan extolled the virtues of the countryside for its Sunday strollers.

The District was particularly good at developing markets for its railway aside from peak-hour traffic of people going to and from work. It sponsored many bus services, run by contractors, to feed into its system and it made sure that it laid on extra services for special events. Exhibitions were a major source of traffic and many were held at the then open grounds between the Albert Hall and South Kensington. The District actually built a pedestrian subway under Exhibition Road from South Kensington station, charging users a penny for the pleasure of avoiding the traffic above to reach the exhibitions or South Kensington (later Victoria & Albert) museum. The opening of the passage in May 1885 coincided with the start of an Inventions Exhibition and thereafter the District, rather meanly, only allowed it to be used on special occasions. It was not until December 1908 that it became open permanently and the toll was abolished. Many of the varied set of exhibitions on the grounds in the 1880s attracted huge crowds, including fisheries (attended by 2.75 million people), health, and 'colonial & Indian' (the biggest, which brought in 5.5 million). The District further encouraged this trade by offering 'artisans' a return journey to South Kensington, together with admission for just one shilling. After 1886, when the site was developed for what is now Imperial College, the exhibitions moved to Earls Court.

There, another attraction owed its location, indeed its very existence, to the District: the Big Wheel at Earls Court. The District had already built a covered way to give passengers easy access to the site of the many exhibitions at Earls Court, now the site of the two Exhibition Halls. But it was the Big Wheel, London's response to the Eiffel Tower, which proved the real draw. Built in 1895, the 300-foot-diameter wheel was based on the famous Ferris wheel in Chicago and attracted

2.5 million visitors during its twelve-year life. Ironically, the biggest lure seems to have been the prospect of a breakdown. In May 1896, the company running the tower responded to the one prolonged failure by paying each of the hundreds of people who had spent all night dangling in mid-air the sum of £5, equivalent to several months' wages for many of them. Consequently, a queue of 11,000 people hoping for a similar mishap built up the following day. Just a little north of Earls Court was the Olympia building, opened in 1886 and served by Addison Road station, on the outer Circle route. Olympia was used by circuses, including Barnum's, which attracted massive crowds in the winter of 1889–90, and then was briefly a roller-skating rink when the sport was at the height of its popularity before the Second World War. By the late 1880s, it enjoyed a fantastic train service, with 331 trains daily.

Watkin, incidentally, set about creating an even more direct rival to the Eiffel Tower, a similar but bigger construction at Wembley, also with the aim of attracting passengers on to his railway. But like many of Watkin's schemes, the project was only half completed. Watkin had wanted Gustave Eiffel himself to build a tower higher than his eponymous 900-foot-high steel spire in Paris. When Eiffel turned down the job, the contract was awarded to a rival firm with a similar plan for an eight-legged steel tower with two platforms each containing restaurants, theatres, exhibitions and even Turkish baths. The first stage, 155 feet high, but with only four legs, was opened in 1896 but attracted remarkably little custom. While, in the first six months, 100,000 visited the park where the tower was the centrepiece, fewer than a fifth, barely 100 people per day, paid to climb up it. Most visitors to the site were more interested by the cycle track and the sports ground laid out around the tower or were content simply to view from the ground what soon became known as Watkin's folly. By the time the park opened, Watkin, weakened by his stroke, was too ill to push the project forward and the tower was never completed, but its first stage survived for a decade before being demolished. The site was used after the First World War for the British Empire Exhibition and the internationally famous football stadium, which would have pleased Watkin as they both attracted considerable railway traffic.

Another boost to Underground use was the growing entertainment market. Theatres were booming and, more significantly in terms of numbers, music halls were springing up everywhere in London: by the early 1890s there were thirty-five, with total audiences of 45,000 nightly. Many of these, including the biggest, the Oxford Music Hall at the corner of Tottenham Court Road and Oxford Street, were in central London, within easy reach of a railway or Underground station.

While leisure travellers were an important market, especially in certain key locations and particularly for the District, the financial health of the underground companies was dependent on development around the stations which they served. Although some historians refuse to give credit to the railways or the Underground for creating much of London, arguing that railways tended to follow, rather than stimulate, development, much evidence points the other way. The confusion results from the length of time it took for the whole process of development to unfold. Even once, after a few years, substantial numbers of houses had been built, they would not all be occupied by commuters. The suburbs would soon have a few shops and artisans to service the needs of those with jobs in central London and these roles would not require commuting. Moreover, for every commuter there would also be possibly half a dozen servants and family members whose lives were centred around home. These basic facts, of course, were of no use to the chairmen of the railway companies, who would urge patience on their desperate shareholders by explaining that the passenger numbers would eventually increase.

Nevertheless, there is no doubt that the change brought about by the railways was significant and, most important, long-term. These former villages would never be the same again and over the space of half a century, as they began to merge with one another, their independent origins would be quickly forgotten. Take, for example, West Kensington, a rural area where the arrival of the District line prompted

Traffic chaos on the streets was the stimulus for the creation of the Underground.
This print by Gustave Doré also shows the unsightly bridge, built to connect
the Metropolitan with the railways of south London, which wrecked the view of
St Paul's Cathedral.

The Victorians dreamt up many schemes for urban railways, but most were hopelessly unrealistic, like the 'Great Victorian Way' (above) by Sir Joseph Paxton which was intended to link the main line stations, as the Circle line would eventually do. Some far-fetched schemes, such as the pneumatic railway at Crystal Palace (below left), were actually built.

Charles Pearson (1793–1862), without whose vision the Underground may never have existed.

The 'cut and cover' method of building was incredibly disruptive to anything in its path. Here Parliament Square, with the Houses of Parliament in the background, is being excavated for the building of the District line. Today, the grass of the green in the middle of the square is part of a thin covering over the tunnel.

Early stations, such as Notting Hill Gate, which opened in 1868, were light and airy compared to many of their successors.

Sir Edward Watkin (1819–1901), *left*, and James Staats Forbes (1823–1904), *right*, were bitter rivals when they ran, respectively, the Metropolitan and the District railways.

The London system was the only underground in the world to use steam trains as the principal form of traction. Here a Circle line train approaches Aldgate.

The underground railways made use of every possible space in their stations to advertise their services.

(Left) These first-class passengers on their comfortable, upholstered benches are being advised that their next station is Victoria.

(Right) A gas-lit Earls Court station before electrification. Its appearance is otherwise little different from today, apart from the stairwells that now lead down to the Piccadilly line. Earl's Court was also, later, the site of the system's first escalator.

The designers of the first tube railway thought that windows were not needed on trains because there was nothing to see between stations. They also installed several of these rather perilous island platforms, most of which have now been replaced.

Right from the beginning the system was overloaded at peak times and when there were special events, such as this example of boat race day (probably) at Baker Street.

The Big Wheel at Earls Court, seen in the distance from Barons Court with the recently completed Piccadilly lines in the middle, was built on District Railway land in 1895 and attracted thousands of people onto the Underground system.

C. L. R. Twopenny Tube.
The Train.

The builders of the Central London Railway made the mistake of hauling the trains with extremely heavy locomotives, which caused so much vibration on the surface that they had to be replaced in 1904, just four years after the line opened.

The tube lines were all dug out of the London clay using variations of the Greathead shield. Here, the excavation is larger than normal because the site is to be a station – Museum, now closed.

building that was 'rapidly carried on where speculative builders had money or credit; the tall houses, detached or semi-detached, or in closed lines improperly called "terraces" which ultimately became the sides of streets, rose up in a few months, roofed and windowed, calling for tenants'.[3] It was, to a great extent, happenstance that dictated which markets such developers decided to go for. In West Kensington, the large houses were, according to the local builders Gibbs & Flew, provided with 'hot and cold water . . . while the encaustic tiles, stained glass and marble fenders give them an attractive appearance'. Other areas, such as the squares near Ladbroke Grove station, never managed to attract the kind of people for which they were designed and sank rapidly into multiple occupation, becoming almost as bad as the nearby rookeries in north-west Kensington. It was only with the gentrification process which started a hundred years later, in the 1970s, that these squares started to attract the class for which they had been built. Yet, a few hundred of yards away, at the Holland Park end of Ladbroke Grove, the houses, many perched on the hill, retained their desirability and have always been occupied by the rich.

Paddington, terminus of the first Underground line, even failed to attract the right sort of developer, let alone tenant. Its situation was always precarious because of its proximity to the foul rookeries of North Kensington and to the houses which were run up in the Harrow Road, intended for poor railway workers, smiths and labourers. Indeed, the construction of the Metropolitan Railway made matters worse for Paddington by creating a demand, albeit temporary, for cheap lodgings, prompting the departure of the 'respectable' working class and the decline of the area into a slum.

Crudely, though, the arrival of the Metropolitan or the District stimulated the building of housing aimed at the affluent, even if eventually they could not be attracted there, whereas the horse tram services which simultaneously sprang up catered for poorer folk. The tram network was developed along the major highways of London, making, as Roy Porter put it, 'inner-suburb living easier for those lower on the social ladder'.[4] Trams were banned from the West End and from all but the borders of the City because they were perceived as being only for the lower orders and the local councillors feared they would bring down the tone of the area.

Of course, the railway companies, once they had seen the high usage on the early London suburban railways and of the Underground, also began to provide an extensive network of local services whose stations stimulated massive development. Whole swathes of the Greater London area were filled in as the railways focused on local traffic. In particular, the railways made travel to the outer suburbs such as Croydon, Bromley, Harrow, Wanstead and Walthamstow possible, as no other form of transportation could have brought so many people into the capital fast enough. This was, mostly, a middle-class phenomenon. The working classes could not afford the cost of commuting added to the rents which, in most of the areas reached by the railways, were still relatively high. The exceptions were some of the districts served by the Metropolitan with its workmen's trains and the north-east quadrant of London where places such as Leytonstone, Walthamstow and Tottenham (all now, incidentally, connected to the Underground network on the Central or Victoria lines) saw the rapid construction of large concentrations of low-rent houses in dull, serried ranks, aimed at manual workers who were served by Great Eastern services. That company had been required to provide workmen's trains at the startlingly cheap rate of twopence for journeys as long as twenty-two miles return as a condition for having cleared a vast swathe of working-class housing to build its Liverpool Street terminus, and it continued offering these incredibly low fares until 1920. Slightly more salubrious suburbs, such as Chingford, Enfield and Wood Green, were populated mainly by clerical workers who were able to purchase half-price tickets on trains which ran slightly later than the workmen's services.

This process meant that more affluent residents fled further out to the likes of Epping and Barking, leaving behind houses which were often then pulled down by the rampant developers because they were too large for the rents that the working class could afford and the builders could not be bothered to adapt them. The availability or otherwise of workmen's trains therefore created segregated suburbs, with the appropriate type of developers following the railway. The definition of 'workmen' was sometimes determined more by the time of their regular train than by their true position in society. In 1898, the *Railway Magazine* published a photograph of the arrival of a workmen's train from which, as one historian put it, 'the majority of the passengers passing through the barrier were wearing the silk hats and morning coats that were then *de rigueur* even among junior employees in city offices'.[5]

The Underground played a vital role in stimulating this growth not just because of the suburban incursions made by the District and Metropolitan but also, more importantly, because it took people right into the heart of the City and the West End, whereas rail passengers were left on the fringes. Without the Underground to connect the various termini, the extensive development in the second half of the nineteenth century could never have taken place so quickly. London grew from a population of 2.8 million in 1861 to over 7 million fifty years later. That outward push was further accelerated by the development of a new office economy, centred around the West End which had a burgeoning number of offices and was also establishing itself as London's premier retail centre. Employment in the City was also expanding, with many former residences being turned into offices, and resulting in more commuting. Whitehall, very convenient for Underground travellers, was filling up with civil servants, of whom there were 160,000 by the early 1900s. The ministries dealing with education, the colonies, war and the Navy all grew substantially in the late Victorian and Edwardian periods as the state increasingly adopted a more interventionist role, and the great majority of these civil servants worked in London.

The Underground system was not only used by vast numbers of commuters, both directly and connecting in from the main line railway, but also attracted other sections of the population who travelled on it for business or leisure purposes. For example, there were the innumerable messengers who, before the invention of the telephone, were the principal way of conveying information quickly between offices.

Even more important were the various groups of leisure travellers. The most significant in terms of numbers were the shoppers visiting the large department stores which had begun to spring up following the opening of the Army and Navy store in 1872. Surprisingly, the biggest shops were not initially sited in the centre, but were rather like today's out-of-town developments, attracted to the fringes of the metropolis for the same reason: the cheapness of land. Thus Harrods, which had first been transformed from a small grocery into a general store in 1861, was already flourishing by 1880 and employing 100 people. The biggest success story, though, was at Bayswater where Whiteleys became the most impressive of the early department stores. The Westbourne Grove shop opened in 1863, a few weeks after the first section of the Metropolitan, which terminated a mile away in Paddington. By 1872, the store occupied ten shops and employed over 600 people and was, of course, served by Bayswater station which had opened in 1868. Others were brought in by omnibus, of which 700 per day were serving the area by 1885. The District considered the market to be so important that it even launched a parcels service to relieve shoppers of their goods on the homeward journey.[6] A trip to the shops in Bayswater or Knightsbridge, and later Oxford Street, was little different from a visit today to the huge modern malls such as Bluewater or Lakeside. The popularity of shopping did much to boost the railways' off-peak travel, which was vital for their economic well-being. Catering solely for commuters is never enough to sustain a railway, given that they make two trips per day at peak hours, leaving the expensive rolling stock unused for the rest of the time. There were also, of course, the weekend leisure travellers who came to visit London's parks as well as the museums and exhibitions. The

Underground may not have brought them all in, but it certainly smoothed their passage around the capital.

Even from the perspective of a modern-day viewpoint, it is impossible to disentangle these various phenomena. Certainly the railways, and the Underground in particular, did enable many people to make journeys that would otherwise have been impossible. All these exhibitions, shops and shows would not have sprung up without this new ability to travel around the capital. But the extent to which each mode of travel was responsible is difficult to discern.

Despite the Underground's success in attracting custom, until electrification travelling on it remained an experience which ranged from broadly acceptable to downright awful, depending on the passengers' stoicism. There was growing pressure from the passengers for better conditions. It was noticeable that the numbers using the Underground fell away in the summer because even the vagaries of the slower horse omnibuses were preferable to the unpleasantly stuffy atmosphere in the underground tunnels. While there had been some improvements, such as heaters on trains and station indicators on platforms, during the last few years of the nineteenth century there was a growing clamour for a major improvement of the system. There were suggestions of doubling the District line on its busy section between Earls Court and Mansion House, possibly through a deep tube railway, but this expensive project was never really feasible. Instead, electrification was seen as the only way of making the required modernization.

In spite of this, and the fact that the tube railway, the City & South London (which opened in 1890), was electrically powered, the Metropolitan and District railways were slow to embrace the new technology – known variously as electrolysation and electrization – and it was not until fifteen years later that steam was finally dispensed with. While the rival companies, which were still in a puerile state of permanent dispute with each other, at least concurred over the principle that electrification was essential to their success, they could not agree over what method to use. Understandably, the boards of both companies argued that it was much harder to electrify an existing railway than to build a new one such as the City & South London. At every annual general meeting the subject would be raised and then dismissed, with supposedly insuperable technical barriers given as the reason for the lack of progress. In fact, that excuse was mostly a cover for the lack of available finance.

The construction of the second deep tube railway, the Central, which ran parallel to the two main east–west sections of the Circle, together with increased competition from horse buses and the rising price of the high-quality coal which the Underground companies were forced to use in order to limit pollution in the tunnels, meant that by the turn of the century electrification could be put off no longer. The more affluent Metropolitan braved the issue first, installing two conductor rails as test track on a long siding in Wembley Park in 1897. More substantially, in 1898, the District and the Metropolitan made an agreement to conduct an experiment by electrifying the short section of track between High Street Kensington and Earls Court with power being supplied from a third rail. The line was opened to the public in May 1900, offering the chance to ride in the large and very heavy purpose-built six-car electric trains for a shilling. That was not a great bargain since for the past decade Londoners had been able to ride on the City & South London for a mere twopence and the following month the Central opened with the same fares. Perhaps the attraction was that the journey was in the open air, but it was unlikely there were many takers and the fares were quickly cut to the normal rates which prevailed until the service was withdrawn in November.

The District and the Metropolitan were still in a permanent state of conflict and therefore it was hardly surprising that they differed over the choice of means of electrification. London very nearly got an overhead system of electricity supply, a system that had been used on several early electric railways on the Continent, notably the small tram-cum-underground system in Budapest. Overhead electrification had the advantage of being easier to install on an existing busy railway compared with the extra conductor rails otherwise needed for the transmission of current. Moreover, Londoners would have been saved from the hazard of live rails which, over the years, has cost thousands of passengers and track workers their lives.

In 1901, James Forbes, still in control of the District, announced that he had raised £500,000 from shareholders for electrification without specifying what method was to be used. (The District, in fact, spent a total of £1.7m – say around £85m in today's money – in electrifying its lines over the following five years.) The Metropolitan, also cash-strapped but a little better-off, had the funds to proceed, and had selected a Hungarian system using overhead equipment. However, the Metropolitan was to be prevented from ever implementing its scheme by developments at the District.

Within weeks of Forbes announcing that he had the money for the District's electrification, the ageing magnate was finally ousted from his position as chairman when Charles Yerkes, an American businessman of dubious reputation, took over control of the company. Yerkes, who had experience of third rail systems in the USA, announced that he would have nothing to do with the overhead method of electrification. Now, after years of being the underdog, the District, under the control of brash American financiers, was calling the shots over the Metropolitan which was still seeking to press ahead with overhead line electrification. Clearly, even though competition rather than cooperation remained the driving ethic of the railway companies, no one was daft enough to suggest that two incompatible electrification systems could be built simultaneously. As Yerkes put it in a letter to *The Times*, 'Quarrelling over this matter will not build railroads.' With the railways, as ever, more interested in bickering than solving the problem at hand, the Board of Trade had to arbitrate through a judge who, in December 1901, pronounced in favour of the District.

So London got its electrification system using a third rail (and fourth, for the return current, allowing the track rails to be used for signalling circuits) thanks to the deliberations of the judiciary. And for once the Metropolitan got a bloody nose from its upstart rival, though the judge, Alfred Lyttleton, berated the District for the high-handed manner in which the company had treated the issue in simply announcing its intentions on electrification to the Metropolitan. In reality, overhead line equipment presented other sorts of problems that were at best costly and at worst insuperable. Principally, overhead lines were impractical for the relatively small tunnels of the District and the Metropolitan, let alone for the tiny deep tube tunnels of the City & South London, which would have been prohibitively expensive to enlarge. Moreover, there would have been the fear of overhead lines falling down on top of the trains in tunnels, a prospect so terrifying that it could well have deterred people from travelling on the system had it been used. Ultimately, the judge plumped for the third rail system because it had already proved itself on the City & South London while the overhead method was perceived as being more experimental.

Not surprisingly, the resolution of this issue did nothing to improve relations between the two railways, which were to remain as separate concerns for another three decades. While the District used a new stretch of line between Ealing and South Harrow to test the electrification equipment, it was the Metropolitan which managed to get electric trains in use on the existing railway a few months before its rival. After a number of trial runs, there was a press trip between Baker Street and Uxbridge in an electric train on 13 December 1904, about which *The Times*, pompous and banal as ever, wrote: 'Everything which took place conveyed the impression that those present were celebrating the beginning of a new era in the history of the old underground railways from which smoke, dirt and discomfort will be nearly banished.'[7] 'Nearly' was right. The first three electric trains which went into service on New Year's Day 1905 offered reasonable accommodation but were little different from their predecessors. Oddly, there was a first and third class but no second: the passengers in first sat upon green moquette in the non-smoking carriages but on green leather in smoking, because that was harder to damage with ash. The third class had to put up with sitting on buffalo hide, presumably because the Metropolitan had obtained a cheap consignment since this was the time when the poor beasts were being slaughtered in vast numbers in America.

The task of electrifying the existing lines on the inner Circle had been completed remarkably quickly. Just as today engineering has to be carried out while the system is closed between 1 a.m. and 5 a.m., work to install the equipment was limited to those hours. By early 1903 there were 400 men on the track working overnight laying the new conductor rails, and the number increased to 1,000 a year later. It is another tribute to the efficiency of organization in those days of little mechanization. Today, hamstrung by much more stringent safety requirements, expensive labour and heavy equipment, such a task would take far longer and cost much more.[8]

The Metropolitan had managed to complete its section of line rather more quickly than the District and was pressing to introduce trains on the inner Circle, but Yerkes insisted on waiting until through services could operate all the way to Whitechapel. When they did, however, it was a disaster. On the first day of the electric service, 1 July 1905, a cloudburst flooded Hammersmith station and a train was derailed at Mill Hill Park (now Acton Town). Then the dreaded lack of coordination between the District and the Metropolitan came into play. The latter's electrical equipment had not been properly integrated with the District's conductor rails and therefore the collector shoes – the metal blocks which run along the third rail to pick up the current – on the Metropolitan's trains, which were intended to operate all the inner Circle services, were knocked out of their mountings as soon as they reached the other company's tracks. It does seem remarkable that, even given the appalling relationship between the two companies, the Metropolitan equipment had not been tested on the District's tracks. Humiliatingly, steam engines had to be called back into service and the

Metropolitan's electrical equipment redesigned. Consequently, it was not until nearly three months later, in late September 1905, that a full electric service was run around the inner Circle. The rest of the District network was electrified remarkably quickly, with all steam trains removed by 5 November 1905. The Metropolitan retained steam locomotive services until 1963 on lines which extended furthest from London, such as Rickmansworth to Aylesbury from Baker Street, but all its services underground were soon using either electric locomotives or powered coaches, known as electric multiple units. That still left a few steam trains on the other services operated through the underground section of the network, but these were gradually phased out over the next couple of years and either replaced by electric trains or, in the case of the Hammersmith to New Cross service, withdrawn because the lessees of the East London line refused to meet the bill for the electrification, which was eventually carried out just before the outbreak of the First World War. The Great Western trains which ran from various suburban destinations through Paddington to Aldgate were the last to go, being replaced by electric locomotives from 2 September 1907 – which, of course, necessitated a quick engine change at Paddington.

At last, apart from a few Great Western steam-hauled freight trains which continued to run through to Smithfield goods depot near Farringdon until the 1960s, Londoners no longer had to endure the smoky tunnels that had characterized trips on the Underground since its opening in 1863. The achievement of changing from steam to electric power in barely six years since Judge Lyttleton's decision was yet another remarkable and largely unsung success of those running the system, made all the more amazing in that they worked for rival companies which were ever eager to pinch each other's market.

To provide the power for the trains, both the District and the Met set about creating their own separate power-generation plants. Cooperation, of course, would have been unthinkable! The District built an enormous power station at Lots Road on the Fulham and

Chelsea border, a site chosen for ease of access for the barges bringing coal along the Thames. Given that it was big enough to power several lines, this was a deliberate and powerful statement of Yerkes's intention to unite the underground network. The Metropolitan obtained most of its electricity from a plant at Neasden in north-west London, where the coal could be delivered easily by rail. While, for Londoners, the advent of electricity on the Underground must have come as a great relief, the fact that locomotives driven by burning coal in red-hot furnaces, and hauling wooden coaches, had operated with no major mishap for forty-four years in the cramped tunnels was in itself a cause for celebration.

It was only by the early years of the twentieth century that urban underground systems had begun to be built across the world in any number, and all were operated using electricity. A couple of minor exceptions were Glasgow where the underground system opened in 1896 using steam power but as fixed engines hauled a cable which pulled the trains, the tunnels were smoke-free; and Liverpool, where the trains of the Mersey Railway were steam-hauled from its opening in 1886 until electrification in 1903, but this was a four-mile-long line in a tunnel whose main function was linking Liverpool with Birkenhead, rather than a busy underground railway used by millions of passengers annually.

In Paris, the system which opened in 1900 was electrically powered, as was the new subway in New York. There, elevated railways built above roads had proliferated from 1872, being preferred to underground railways on the grounds of cheapness and because of the lack of historic buildings whose aspect would be ruined by unsightly railways. Certainly, the City of London would never have countenanced them. New Yorkers finally tired of the noisy, steam-hauled trains passing their second-floor windows at all times of the day, and work on a subway system, using electric trains to replace some of them, started in 1901. Britain, therefore, was the only country in the world to operate an underground train service using steam locomotives, an intuitively crazy idea necessitated by the particular history and circumstances of the city and created by the foresight and vision of its pioneers, notably Charles Pearson.

Surprisingly, despite the cleaner atmosphere, electrification did not attract the extra numbers which the railway companies had expected and on which their financial fate depended. The District had been so desperate for new business that in July 1903 it finally did away with the church interval (which like the Met, as mentioned in Chapter 3, it had felt compelled to obey) on Sunday mornings, which meant that at last trains were allowed to operate between 11 a.m. and 1 p.m. on the Sabbath. Neither the District nor the Metropolitan was in a healthy financial state. Both had been hit hard by growing competition: not so much, now, from the horse omnibuses as from the new tramways springing up in the suburbs and, in west London, the new Central London Railway, known as the Twopenny Tube because there was only one fare for any length of journey (see next chapter). Using a combination of tram and tube, it was possible to travel, for example, from Ealing to the City for just fourpence, half the third-class fare on the District. Hammersmith, served by both railways, was also reachable by trams which were cheaper. The Metropolitan had actually lost passengers, numbers falling from 96 million in 1899 to 88 million three years later, and it was only by slashing prices – the single third-class fare from Hammersmith or Shepherd's Bush to Aldgate was cut from sixpence to threepence – in 1902 that the number of passengers increased to 94 million in 1903. The District followed suit in 1904, cutting fares from Kensington or Earls Court to the City from fivepence to fourpence for third class, and while numbers grew modestly in response, it was electrification on which the two railways pinned their hopes.

A new signalling system had been installed, allowing for a closer interval between trains. Yerkes had proposed to run forty trains per hour, instead of the existing eighteen, an optimistic target both technically and commercially. His chairman, Robert Perks, optimistically forecast a doubling of traffic. It was not to be. Admittedly, the District did a bit better, attracting 55 million people in 1906 (the first full year of electric running), representing growth of 10 per cent, but it was nowhere near Yerkes's aspirations. Financial trouble was inevitable.

So, by the early years of the century, London had an extensive, mostly electrified overground network linking in with the Underground, which had contributed to the rapid development of large sections of the metropolis. But the real task was to improve services in central London, given its rapidly growing employment, and this could only be done through the new tunnelling techniques that had, at last, been developed, thanks to the heroic efforts of the Brunels, father and son. A decade before the start of the twentieth century, much was happening underground.

SEVEN

DEEP UNDER

LONDON

If it is scarcely believable that the concept of trains running under cities began to be considered in the early years of the nineteenth century, then it is even more incredible that the first deep tube line, powered by that newfangled invention, electricity, should have opened as early as 1890. Up till now, the story of the Underground had really been about a railway which happened to cross London in tunnels but which, in essence, was not very different from the network of suburban services springing up to serve London's burgeoning population. Now the focus changed completely, with not only the use of electricity but also the advent of tunnelling techniques that enabled deep level tube lines to be carved out of London's clay.

Just as the underground railway, particularly one operated by steam trains, was a concept that might never have taken root had it not been for the fortuitous juxtaposition of technological progress, government transport policies and the drive of its promoters, the deep tube lines would not have happened without an equally improbable set of circumstances. And Britain, again, was the pioneer. The appropriate technology came through at just the right time; rival forms of transport such as the motor bus were not sufficiently developed; and there were entrepreneurs ready to put forward schemes, though persuading investors to back them was always tough. Indeed, this part of the story has a strong American flavour, as not only did many of those putting up the money come from the USA, but so did one of the key players, Charles Yerkes, and much of the equipment and technology also came from across the Atlantic.

Like many Victorian inventions, the new type of railway relied heavily on previous failed experiments and errors. The key invention was the shield which the Brunels had developed to build the first tunnel under the Thames. While the tunnel itself was a financial failure, the engineering lessons derived from its construction were to be the basis of the creation of London's deep tube network. Another unsuccessful enterprise had taken Brunel's idea of a shield a step further. This was the Tower Subway, opened in 1870, which was built by an engineer called Peter Barlow beneath the Thames near the site of the present City Hall, downriver of London Bridge which was then the lowest bridge crossing. Barlow had used vertical cast-iron cylinders, which were driven down into the earth for the foundations for a suspension bridge further upriver at Lambeth, and had, in one of those brilliant bits of lateral thinking for which the Victorians were renowned, realized that the same technique could be used to bore horizontally through the ground to create a tunnel. Barlow adopted and improved Brunel's concept of a circular shield. It was pushed through the ground with jacks, allowing men to carve out and dispose of the earth with great efficiency. The other clever innovation was cast-iron circular segments which were bolted together to form the tunnel as the shield moved forward.

Barlow built an odd little railway with just a single carriage that was hauled through the tunnel by a cable powered by a fixed steam engine. The short journey must have been a pretty claustrophobic experience since the diameter of the tunnel was only 6ft 8ins, but at least lifts were provided to connect with the street level. There were slopes down at either end of the tunnel, partly to help the carriage gain momentum, with only a small flat section in the middle. Passengers, whose alternative was paying a bridge toll, were taken through for twopence first class and a penny second class. Having two classes was a bit of chutzpah on Barlow's part since the accommodation for the short ride was actually identical for both, the only difference being that first-class ticket holders gained priority in the queue.

It was to be a short-lived scheme. All the equipment proved unreliable and the venture was a commercial failure, going bankrupt in December 1870 a mere three months after opening. The train and other equipment, including the lifts, was removed and the fare slashed to a halfpenny for walking through the passage. Despite the fact that the pedestrians now had to tramp up and down timber staircases and through the tiny tunnel, lit by open gas jets perilously close to the handrail, a million people per year came through the turnstiles until the subway was put out of business by the opening of the Tower Bridge in 1894. It survives, prosaically, as a passage for power cables and water mains.

The brave experiments of Brunel and Barlow were to demonstrate that it was possible to tunnel under London, making the construction of deep tube railways feasible. Cut and cover railways in the central area were no longer realistic propositions for private developers. Not only were there simply not enough straight roads under which they could be aligned, but the first dozen feet below ground were becoming cluttered with all kinds of pipes and conduits as London now had a sewer system and increasing numbers of buildings connected to gas, water and electricity. Tube lines, on the other hand, could be hewn out of the soil deep under this complex of sewers and pipes. Developers were now in a position to suggest building railways virtually anywhere with the potential of attracting lucrative traffic. And they did.

The main difficulties encountered by Barlow with his subway had not been the failure of the tunnel technology but the cumbersome cable system of hauling trains. The solution, given that steam was out of the question in small deep tubes with no ventilation, was obvious: electricity. Nevertheless, it was to take twenty years after Barlow's experiment for the first tube railway to be built and, oddly, it would have its roots in a scheme for a cable railway. A couple of projects for electric railways had been put forward and rejected in the early 1880s, but there was great scepticism about the ability of electricity to power a major underground system. Therefore, the promoters of the line that was to become the first deep tube railway, the City & South London, originally envisaged a cable operated railway. The route of the City & South London, now part of the Northern line, was to go from the City, near Monument, to Elephant & Castle a mile and a half away. The Parliamentary powers were obtained on the basis of a cable railway and, after the finance of £300,000 was raised with less difficulty than usual, work started in October 1886. The technology of Brunel and Barlow had now been further enhanced by a former pupil of the latter, James Greathead, who devised a shield which not only enabled the earth to be cut out, but also allowed for a layer of concrete to be poured as the earth was dug, preventing collapses.

To the oft-asked question of why London has both the oldest and the most extensive network of deep level tube lines in the world, the rather banal answer is that the city has the right geological conditions, a factor which outweighs social, economic and political considerations. Nearly all the tunnelling for London's tubes has been driven through London clay, a yellow, brown or grey-green layer which lies above the chalk and sand that once formed a seabed. Most importantly, the tunnels burrow beneath the beds of gravel which, over thousands of years, the river has dumped on top of the clay. With the exception of a few parts of London where chalk is encountered, there is a thick layer of clay, up to 450 feet deep, which is relatively easy to cut through. Had there been rock, as under New York, London would not have had its tube network and, given the cost and disturbance of building low-level tunnels, the Underground map would be a much more sparse affair. Indeed, in south-east London the gravel goes deeper, which partly explains why no tube was cut there until the Jubilee Line Extension arrived in the late 1990s, by which time tunnelling techniques made it economically possible to dig through the more difficult geological terrain.

Even though the tunnels were bored at a depth of between forty-five and 105 feet, the promoters felt it was safest to follow the lines of streets wherever possible in order to avoid any potential conflicts with basements or old foundations. However, this was ultimately short-sighted since it meant that the line was designed with complicated curves and difficult gradients because, at times, the two tunnels were built on top of one another to avoid incursions under private property. That is why today's tube system has so many curves and climbs when, given the geological conditions, the routing should have been largely straight. While this did not pose any great problems for Greathead's brilliant shield during construction, it was to prove operationally difficult and, although the worst aspects have been rectified, continues to bedevil the running of the tube lines today. One far-sighted decision, however, was to use the standard 4ft 8½ins gauge for the track, the same as had been universally adopted on the main line railway. Had earlier suggestions for a smaller gauge been accepted, today's tube passengers would be travelling in even more cramped trains.

In 1887, a scheme to extend the City & South London line to Stockwell via Kennington was given Parliamentary sanction, representing a doubling of the length of the line as the promoters sought to tap into the relatively affluent suburbs of inner south London. An extra £300,000 was raised, which, together with borrowing of £175,000, meant that the total available to the promoters was £775,000, an amount on which it would always be difficult to obtain a decent return.[1] The other advantage of running further out was that it solved the thorny problem of how to get equipment and stock in and out of the railway. An inclined plane was built at Stockwell to connect the railway with the depot and workshops on the surface, where the power plant was also situated, but after an accident when the tow rope broke, allowing a carriage to escape down the main line, a lift was used despite the inconvenience.

It was only after construction had started that doubts began to be raised about the viability of using cables, especially as the line was now planned to be three miles long. The idea had been to have a cable travelling at ten mph on which the trains would clamp and unclamp at stations, but it was recognized that this would be impossible over the extended length. Having two separate cables each covering half the length was also briefly considered but then, mercifully, the cable contractor went broke. The obvious solution was to use electricity despite the earlier concerns about unreliability. After various experiments, a third rail system was adopted, a sensible decision given that the two separate tunnels were only a mere 10ft 6ins in diameter[2] and could not have accommodated an overhead system. Locomotives rather than powered coaches were purchased, and, to carry out test running, an engine and two carriages were dismantled and manhandled down one of the lift shafts because the tunnel to Stockwell had not yet been completed.

Despite the novel techniques being used, the digging proceeded without any major mishap and the work was completed on time. The line, which was the world's first major electric railway and the first deep tube line, was formally opened in November 1890, a month before the public was let in, by the Prince of Wales who switched on the current with a golden key. According to the *Daily News*, the Prince was a bit bemused by the ride in the large lift, capable of taking fifty people, which took him down at King William Street station and made a typically bad royal joke: 'It was quite pardonable that his Royal Highness should ask [whether he] was going down or the world going up.'[3] The reporter, too, found the experience strange and reveals just how innovatory the whole thing was: 'The sensation, indeed, of descending this lift of fifty feet to get below the level of the Thames is somewhat similar to a balloon experience. In a balloon, the earth seems to be sinking below you. In the King William Street lift, the world seems to be gently rising, the passenger all the while being pleasantly stationary.' The Prince, who would become Edward VII on the death of Victoria, was clearly an enthusiast for the railway and recognized its primary purpose of trying to clear traffic off the roads, as ever a forlorn hope:

> This railway today, this first electric railway which has been
> started in England will, I hope, do much to alleviate the congestion
> of the traffic which now exists, so that business men who have
> a great distance to go will find easy means of getting away from
> this great city and enjoying the fresh air of the country and
> I hope that it will also be a great boon to working men who
> are obliged to work in an unpleasant atmosphere, and who by
> its means will be able to get away for a little fresh air.

Clearly, the future king was not a frequent visitor to Stockwell which, at the time, was already a substantial suburb rather than the bucolic idyll he suggests.

The trains, each consisting of a little electric locomotive hauling three carriages with just thirty-two seats apiece, were short and designed with a fundamental flaw – they had no windows out of which passengers could see, merely narrow strips of glass above head height. This was based on the mistaken notion that the passengers would not mind since only the inside of tunnels and featureless stations would be visible. But that was to go against basic human psychology and not surprisingly the carriages quickly became known as the 'padded cells' and the line as the 'sardine box railway', a name quickly applied by *Punch* magazine. The passengers sat on benches running the whole length of the carriage which were indeed pleasantly padded, rather a luxury for the working men who travelled in the same carriages as their supposed superiors because, uniquely of any Victorian railway, there was only one class. In truth, the soft furnishings were a necessity since the ride was rough and bumpy, given the sharp curves and gradients and a track that was difficult to maintain. People were frequently hurled against each other, especially the standing passengers, who filled up every available space at rush hours but were not provided with any straps to grab. The small long windows above the seats were little more than ventilators but at least allayed the feeling of claustrophobia sufficiently to ensure that people were not completely deterred from using the line. The lack of visibility outside meant that the conductor on each platform between the carriages had to shout out loudly the names of each station. His job was also to open and shut the gated door at the end of each carriage and to help passengers on and off the trains.

One pleasant innovation was the installation of electric lighting in the trains, though as there was merely a handful of low-powered bulbs per carriage, only passengers fortunate enough to be sitting directly underneath them received enough light to read their newspapers. Nevertheless, it must have been an improvement on the gas lighting still endured by travellers on the Metropolitan and District, whose benches, too, were not so comfortably furnished. The stations, though, retained the dark gloomy atmosphere of their counterparts on the older underground lines because they were gas-lit: all the available electricity was needed to power the trains. That also explains why the huge lifts which transported the passengers to and from the platforms, and which the Prince of Wales found so odd, were hydraulically operated. The escalator had not yet been invented.

As well having only one class, another revolutionary innovation was the setting of a single fare, with no issuing of tickets. Passengers simply went through a turnstile after paying their twopence. *The Times*, having noted that the opening of the line marked 'an epoch in the development of the internal communications of London which may, perhaps, hereafter prove to have been even more important than the opening of the Metropolitan Railway in 1863', continued: 'All the complicated apparatus of booking clerks and tickets, first, second and third class, single and return and season, is swept away.'[4] There was one remaining form of discrimination: each train had a smoking car from which ladies were excluded. There was, too, some dissent stirred up by this new classless system. Some labourers were embarrassed about having to share carriages in their soiled work apparel with more affluent passengers whose clothes they might inadvertently dirty. A writer in the *Railway Times* suggested that 'we have scarcely yet been educated up to that condition of social equality when lords and ladies will be content to ride side by side with Billinsgate "fish fags" and Smithfield butchers'.[5] In a way, that missed the point. The fact that even for 'lords and ladies' the line was the quickest form of travel ensured that it would be well patronized. Strangely, those who made up the by-laws for this new system did not, perhaps, quite understand its nature. They had ensured that people travelling on the roof would be subject to a £2 fine, a penalty that clearly would only ever be levied posthumously.

On this occasion *The Times* was enthusiastic about the innovation even though its reporter was somewhat apprehensive when, coming out of the lift, he saw his train emerging from the tunnel 'with a roar, emitting sparks from the region of the wheels'. The new subway, he wrote, 'might be described . . . as a gigantic iron drainpipe, thrust by main force through the solid London clay, much in the fashion in which the cheesemonger thrusts a scoop into his Cheddar or Gloucester'. The journey from Stockwell to the terminus at King William Street, in the City, took about eighteen minutes, an average speed including stops of 11.5 mph, over twice as fast as the speediest surface transport.

The Times also dealt with the practical issue of fear about the newfangled invention. Would people fry to death if they had to disembark between stations in an emergency? No, came the answer which may seem obvious today, but must have been greatly reassuring for those Victorians who had not previously encountered electricity:

Will they have to walk through the tunnel with the knowledge that, if at any moment they should come into contact with the electric conductor, they will meet the gruesome fate which, to judge from American newspapers, seems to be the common lot of those who have to do with electric wires in the States? The authorities reply that, in the first place, directly a train breaks down the current will be cut off from the section entirely, and secondly, that even if any one did 'short circuit' the current through his own body, he would take no harm, beyond receiving a smart and confessedly disagreeable shock.

Hmm – while the first part of the answer was completely accurate, the second seems to be a bit of clever company propaganda swallowed by the gullible journalist. Given that the 450-volt system would have required around 160 amps to deliver the power to the locomotives, anyone rash enough to touch the rail would have been 'killed very dead' according to an electrical engineer.[6] Indeed, there was an early death when a foolish passenger persuaded one of the conductors to allow him to ride on the front platform of the coach immediately behind the locomotive and promptly fell off; but there are few reports of any subsequent mishaps, suggesting the system was very safe right from the outset.

As with the earlier underground projects, the line was a success in terms of transport, if not commercially, though there were all the problems associated with being a pioneer. The electricity supply was not sufficient to cope with several trains accelerating at once and the tiny tunnels proved inadequate for the demand. The locomotives, which had not been built to haul the weight of so many passengers as well as carriages which were heavier than originally designed, frequently suffered burnt-out engines. The trains struggled up the gradient to the terminus in King William Street, which also happened to be furthest away from the source of power, and consequently a maximum of a train every four minutes, rather than three, could be run. On occasion, the trains did not actually make it up the hill, and had to be allowed to roll back down again for a second attempt, an experience that must have been terrifying for the passengers. The City terminus had originally been designed for a cable railway which meant that only one train could be accommodated at a time.

On the first day, 10,000 people flocked to the line, again a tribute to Victorian hardiness given that descending deep under London into a gloomy tunnel to take a train operated by a little-understood method of traction would have taken more than a modicum of courage. But the regular use of the Metropolitan and the District must have inured most travellers to such considerations. Within weeks there were 15,000 per day using the line but the authors[7] of the standard work on the history of London's transport suggest that the line was a failure in relation to the early days of the Metropolitan.[8] That judgement of failure, however, seems a bit harsh. If the line did not have quite the impact of the first underground railway, the reason was partly geographical. The City & South London was only connecting a small section of south London with the City, a route on which there were many rival omnibus and tram services. In contrast, the Metropolitan had been designed as a link between major main line termini and the City. In fact, the City & South London was, from the outset, so crowded that initially the owners feared extending it southwards out of concern that the City terminus could not cope. There were certainly enough passengers to convince the owners that it was worth investing to make the line more viable. More locomotives and coaches were soon ordered, and the layout at the City end improved, but all of this was expensive, putting further strain on the benighted shareholders, who had not received any dividend in 1891 despite the high passenger numbers. Extensions were mooted, and eventually constructed in both directions, just as with the earlier underground lines, in the perpetual but forlorn hope that they would make the railway more viable. The shareholders of the City & South London remained long-suffering, with dividends rising slowly to a maximum of just 2⅛ per cent by 1898 but falling after that.

Despite the financial difficulties, the City & South London attracted a host of imitators promoting schemes for tube railways powered by either electricity or cable, though the latter all soon fell away. The first, the railway that was to become the Central Line, obtained approval in the summer of 1891. The Central London was to be a six-mile tube railway originally intended to run between Shepherd's Bush and Cornhill, in the City, but the plans were soon extended to reach Bank and Liverpool Street, giving it useful connections with the City & South London and the Great Eastern main line railway. A further spate of schemes was put forward in what became something of a tube mania. No fewer than six tube railway bills were put to Parliament in 1892 and, in a throwback to the early days of the development of the Metropolitan, a joint select committee was appointed to set out some principles for this type of development. Crucially, it agreed that tube railways could use the subsoil under public property without having to pay compensation, which made future developments economically feasible. Several schemes which were to form the basis of London's tube network were given the go-ahead following the committee's deliberations but all struggled to find money, notably the lines that were to become the Bakerloo and the Northern line's Charing Cross branch. As Hugh Douglas put it, 'Acts, acts, acts. They were everywhere in the nineties but where was the cash to implement them? . . . Commercial enterprises offered far greater returns to investors than railways.'[9]

There were all sorts of other barriers thrown in the way of promoters, which made it even more incredible that schemes ever managed to get off – or rather under – the ground. During the Parliamentary process, the promoters had to make concessions to the proprietors, both public and private, under whose land they were digging. Typically, the sewer authorities had to be kept happy with detailed plans while landlords had to be assured that there would be no deviation from the agreed path and be paid compensation for the slightest mishap. The bills were pushed through in a climate of antipathy to rail companies, engendered by their half-century-long domination of the transport market, and thus the parliamentarians were always ready to side with the objectors and doubters. All this created a bureaucratic minefield and a lack of flexibility which inevitably had the effect of pushing up the costs of schemes and deterring investors.

There was another barrier to attracting backers. The left-leaning Progressive members, who were in control of the newly created London County Council (LCC), lobbied hard and successfully for any new lines to be forced to guarantee that cheap working men's trains, like those pioneered on the Metropolitan and now standard on suburban services, would be provided. This was perceived, possibly wrongly, by prospective investors as further reducing potential dividends. A greater deterrent was the fear that the radical LCC, which was quite hostile to private enterprise, might eventually succeed in municipalizing the underground network, something that would not in fact happen until well into the twentieth century. Given all this uncertainty, it was hardly surprising that it would take a decade before the next major deep tube line, the Central, was opened.

The difficulties encountered by the pioneering City & South London were another deterrent to potential investors. In addition to the problems caused by the insufficient power, the major problem was the bottleneck at the King William Street station with its single platform. This was such a constraint on increasing usage of the line that the owners decided almost immediately to remedy the situation, but it took a decade before the work could be completed. They combined the construction of a northward extension to Moorgate with a realignment of the line, which included the abandonment of the troublesome King William Street terminus. It was replaced by Bank where the ticket hall sited in an enlarged section of the crypt of St Mary Woolnoth church, necessitating the payment of a whopping £170,000 compensation to the church authorities. With King William Street closed and extra power from Stockwell, trains could now be extended to four cars, which helped solve the rush-hour overcrowding. New stations, such as London Bridge, a strange omission in the original line, were built in cast iron like the tunnels, rather than brick which had occasionally been found to leak or partly cave in. The new lifts were electric instead of hydraulic, and therefore, as early as 1900, the system was beginning to contain almost all the features familiar to today's users. In most stations, the individual tracks ran parallel or above each other, although there were island platforms[10] at Angel and at the two new Clapham stations on the southern extension, also completed in 1900. At Moorgate the line was connected with the Metropolitan, the first interchange between two underground lines on a different level, a feature that was to become both common and essential for the creation of a network, rather than a haphazard spread of lines. The City & South London reached Angel in 1901 and was eventually extended to King's Cross and Euston in 1907.

The first line to receive Parliamentary consent following the partial success of the City & South London was to become London's only underground line that could accommodate full-size main line trains. Such large tunnels had been ruled out on cost grounds but the Great Northern & City from Moorgate to Finsbury Park was conceived as a bypass of King's Cross for the Great Northern's suburban trains and therefore it had to accommodate main line carriages. The line was authorized by Parliament as early as June 1892 but actually took a dozen years to build. Indeed, it was amazing that it was ever completed. Once the Bill had been passed, the Great Northern lost interest and became quite hostile to the idea because it was more interested in embryonic plans for the Piccadilly Line. The ball was picked up by the contractor, Sir Weetman Pearson, whose firm, S. Pearson, bought many of the shares and underwrote a 3 per cent dividend to get the railway built. By then, the Great Northern was so antagonistic that it would not even allow its abandoned fledgling to share Finsbury Park Station. Passengers had to use an inconvenient separate little underground station with a poor interchange and the line could not be used for its intended purpose of relieving pressure on Great Northern's suburban network. Here again the emphasis on competition rather than cooperation meant that valuable resources had been wasted. It was such a contrast to Paris where the first Métro lines were being built as a network of six lines conceived by the local municipal council.

The lack of any strategic planning for London's transport meant that the Great Northern & City was never continued through to south London from Moorgate and, as a result what could have been a major railway for London is merely a footnote in its history. Pearson[11] ran the line for three years but never made a profit. The railway subsequently passed first to the Metropolitan, which never knew what to do with it, and later it became part of the Northern Line.[12]

The Great Northern & City's story is one of those 'if only' tales with which London's transport history is so replete. If a couple of full-size tube lines had been built under the centre of London linking the suburban networks of south and north London, or indeed those of the east and west, as the RER does in Paris today, the whole of the capital's transport system and indeed the very nature of many of London's outlying areas would have been transformed. But such an enterprise was impossible to carry out with private capital. In Edwardian times, the estimated cost per mile of building a tube line was reckoned to be £370,000 (say, £18.5m in 2004 prices) for the little 11ft 6in tunnels that became standard; and nearly double that, £650,000 (say, £32.5m) per mile for a full 16ft tunnel able to take a main line train. The finances, therefore, simply did not make sense without state support, and the concept of a mixed economy had not yet been devised. It was only in the 1920s and 1930s, when cheap government loans or subsidies became available for job creation schemes, that underground railways would be built with state support – and even then only relatively cheap extensions into the suburbs rather than new through routes under London.

The other new tube railway which obtained Parliamentary permission quickly was the Waterloo & City, another little stub of a line which, like the Great Northern & City, has never reached its potential. This was London's second tube railway to be built and was the realization of a long-term aim of the London & South Western Railway to run services into the City from its terminus at Waterloo. Over the years, there had been various plans to connect the two which had come to nothing. Instead, passengers were forced onto a heavily overburdened omnibus service, or had to transfer to a separate Waterloo station run by the rival South Eastern Railway to reach London Bridge and Cannon Street, necessitating the hassle of a walk and the purchase of a second ticket. Originally, the London & South Western had hoped to extend its main line across the Thames and into the City, but the success of the City & South London suggested a simpler and much cheaper solution, a direct underground connection.

The backing of the London & South Western, which was so desperate to see the line built that it guaranteed returns of 3 per cent, ensured that raising the capital of £540,000 for construction of the one and a half mile line was easy and work started in 1894. The line has no intermediate stops, being a simple shuttle between Waterloo and Bank, near the Bank of England, and thus is aimed almost exclusively at the commuter market of people working in the City. Unusually, therefore, it only operated during the week and was shut in the evenings and at weekends. As on the City & South London, a turnstile system was used for the twopence fare, with tickets only being issued to those making the return journey which cost threepence. After 1900, conductors with bell punches sold the tickets on the trains, a task that must have been nigh impossible in the rush hour.

With tunnels that were slightly bigger than those of the City & South London, the Waterloo & City was built to a high standard, except for the way those using it had to enter and leave the system. For reasons of economy lifts were not built and, instead, passengers had to walk up to ground level. This required a considerable effort, particularly at Bank where the line was nearly sixty feet below the surface and the poor passengers had to negotiate a steep incline which was fitted later with several sets of five steps to make the climb a bit easier, rather like the alleys one often finds in hilled towns in France and Italy. This lasted until 1960 when a flat escalator, a novel idea called a Trav-o-lator, was installed to relieve the feet of the City gents. There was, though, right from the beginning a huge hydraulic lift at Waterloo to haul the coaches in and out of the system for maintenance.

The most innovatory aspect of the Waterloo & City was that the trains were operated by powered motor coaches at each end rather than a separate locomotive, a system that was common in the USA. There were four, later five, cars, including the two powered coaches which, apart from the section occupied by the motors, could be used by passengers. This was the first use of such electric multiple units in the UK and it meant that the trains were much lighter, and consequently cheaper to operate. Painted in a chocolate and salmon livery, they looked elegant and were so robust that they lasted forty years. Another innovation was sliding doors which gave access to platforms between the coaches that were protected by folding iron gates. The lessons of the padded cells had been learnt, too, as there were windows despite the lack of views; but the seats were wooden, perfectly reasonable given the shortness of the journey.

The trains had been designed to travel at a maximum of thirty-five mph, far faster than the City & South London, but the Board of Trade, then responsible for safety, would only allow the trains to go round the curves at fifteen mph, which increased the journey time to more than six minutes, rather than the originally planned four. Trains were frequent, though, every five minutes and later four.

Despite the hassle of the inclines and steps, passengers took to the line (which soon became known as The Drain, a name it retains today) in large numbers because it fulfilled such an obvious need. Daily weekday ridership quickly reached 17,000, most of it at peak time, and, cleverly, the company bought single-carriage motor coaches to run during the quieter midday hours.

As mentioned above, the most important schemes to emerge from the Parliamentary committee in 1892–3 were the routes of the embryonic Bakerloo and Northern (Charing Cross branch) lines but these would take some time to get under way. It was the Central which made the most rapid progress, because it had obtained the support of various Establishment figures who managed to raise the capital quickly – or at least faster than any of the rival schemes – albeit not without the usual difficulties. The railway clearly fitted a major need since it would provide an efficient route along London's major east–west artery. According to evidence given in support of the Bill, 6 million people annually travelled along that transport corridor on the 239 omnibuses which worked it. The scheme had a much grander feel to it than its predecessor, with longer and heavier trains – though they were still smaller than those on the Metropolitan, which partly ran in parallel with the new line and consequently objected to the Central's plans.

The funding was obtained through a complex mechanism which enabled the promoters to tap into the huge pool of capital available in the USA. Indeed, this was to be repeated with the funding of the tube lines built by Yerkes a few years later and it is no exaggeration to say that London's tube system owes its existence almost entirely to American finance. A syndicate to promote the Central London railway was formed and included such luminaries as Ernest Cassel (later Sir), one of a group of bankers who helped manage the finances of the Prince of Wales and later went on to become an adviser to the King; Henry Oppenheim, another well-connected banker; and the American philanthropist and banker Darius Ogden Mills. The promoters worked through the Exploration Company, which was backed by the Rothschilds. Once a second Bill, allowing the extension to Bank and Liverpool Street, had been passed in 1892, Cassel spent a long time persuading Henry Tennant, the former general manager of the North Eastern Railway, to became chairman in June 1895 of a revamped board, which included more members of the Prince of Wales's circle. When the company sought to raise nearly £3m in shares soon afterwards, the public, having had their fingers burnt with these schemes once too often, only took up 14 per cent of the stock – although this time they were wrong: uniquely of major new underground lines, it would have earned them a good rate of return. Instead the Exploration Company, thanks to Cassel and his rich friends, bought most of the rest of the shares. As well as Americans, the major shareholders included many prominent Europeans and a few notable investors from outside London. Among the smaller shareholders with at least one £10 share, there was a plumber from West Hampstead, a signalman from Northants, a pig keeper from Berkhamsted, a piano tuner from London and 'a great number of clerks in holy orders' who must have been rather more affluent than their peers today.[13] The remainder went to the contractor, the Electric Traction Company, a financing method that was becoming almost the norm for underground lines. In fact, the contractor was also owned by Cassel and his associates and it was able to start work in the spring of 1896.

As with the City & South London, huge shafts were dug down to where tunnelling using the Greathead shield method could begin. The Central had the advantage of being straight for long stretches but, as with its predecessor, at various places the tunnels were routed to run on top of each other – at Notting Hill Gate and Chancery Lane, for example – in order to keep the line under roadways and therefore avoid having to pay compensation to private landowners. In a way, this was ridiculous. The tubes were being dug out at such a deep level that it did not really matter what was above them in those days long before skyscrapers, and in any case the Parliamentary Committee had recommended that compensation need not be paid. However, the promoters were worried about causing damage and they put in far more curves and gradients than necessary, which greatly reduces operational efficiency to this day. One clever innovation did, however, save considerably on energy and running costs. Stations were built at the top of slight inclines which meant that trains automatically were slowed down by the gradient as they approached the station and sent faster on their way on departure.

The original completion date was to have been 1896 but inevitably delays over obtaining the finance meant that it was only by the end of 1898 that the tunnelling, nearly all through London clay, was complete. Extensions for the work had to be sought from Parliament but, in retrospect, it is not the fact that there were delays which is remarkable but rather that the line was finished within four years.

At Bank, the City had insisted on a major bit of planning gain. The railway was forced to build a complex system of seven interconnected subways which not only gave access to the booking hall but also had to be accessible to the public seeking to cross the congested roads around the Bank and Mansion House. It was one of the trickiest parts of building the railway, involving twenty-four-hour working by teams of labourers, and nearly bankrupted the company, helping to push up the eventual cost of completion to nearly £4m. As a result, Bank was to become the first major interchange of the Tube system as it was the terminus of the Waterloo & City and also became an intermediate station on the City & South London after its extension was completed in 1900. However, passengers had to buy separate tickets for each part of the journey as the two companies did not allow through bookings, yet another consequence of the emphasis on competition rather than cooperation.

To fulfil the conditions of the latest Extension granted by Parliament, the line had to be completed by the end of June 1900; but only a ceremonial opening was possible by that date. The Prince of Wales, who had taken a personal interest in the scheme as a result of the involvement of his advisers, headed a glittering guest list which included all the bankers who had made the project possible and the author and journalist Mark Twain (Samuel Clemens), then a London resident. The Prince's train went all the way to Shepherd's Bush where, just beyond the station, the line surfaced and ran into the depot. There, after brief speeches, the Prince returned on the train for lunch in Mayfair, while the waiters apparently snaffled all the food and were found lying around drunk by the poor staff of the Central who had been promised the leftovers themselves.

The Central was opened to the public in August and caught the imagination of Londoners to a much greater extent than City & South London a decade earlier. It was fitting that the Central, the first modern tube railway, should open at the start of 1900, the dawn of the twentieth century. The long stations, each with platforms over 100 yards long, were Spartan but smart affairs with white tiling throughout – a brave decision given the dust – and lit by electricity. Initially the platform floors consisted of wooden planks, but these were replaced by stone slabs after the disastrous fire on the Paris Métro in August 1903. The Central served fourteen stations between Shepherd's Bush and Bank, a journey that according to the early publicity was supposed to last twenty-one minutes, the same as today's schedule, but seems to have taken around four minutes longer because of the difficulties of getting people on and off the trains. The *Railway Times*[14] blamed the passengers: 'The prevailing impression seems to be that they are walking slowly out of church or assisting at a funeral,' it wrote. To ensure that the trains were ready for departure, the seven-car trains had a crew of six to operate the gates between each pair of cars, in addition to the driver and his assistant. At every station, there was a procedure which required 'each gateman facing the front of his car [to hold] up his hand when his gates were shut. When the front guard saw the correct number of hands, he showed a green light to the rear, to which the rear guard responded by showing a green light forward to the driver or his assistant, and the train could start.'[15] With this complicated rigmarole, it seems amazing that the trains ever left on time. The crew, incidentally, worked ten-hour shifts without a meal break. The driver and his mate brought sandwiches and left supplies of tea and sugar with the signalmen (there were seventeen signal boxes, mostly at the end of platforms), collecting their brewed beverage when they next passed. Working all day in the tunnels was harsh and by the end of the day the crew's faces were black from the metal dust given off by the motors and brake blocks. Indeed, the conditions were so onerous that the Central employed 'call boys' to knock on the doors of the crew in the Shepherd's Bush area to ensure that the men got up in time for their shifts, a practice that was otherwise confined to main line railways. Despite the hardships, the workers received just thirty shillings for a sixty-hour week.

While the stations themselves had none of the style of the dome-capped edifices which graced the City & South London, below ground the sound financing had been used to ensure that conditions underground were much better than on its predecessor. As O.S. Nock put it, 'Where the City & South London displayed remarkable ostentation above ground, and the most dismal cramped conditions on the railway itself, the Central London did almost exactly the reverse. The surface buildings were simple and business-like, but underground there was plenty of space and light.'[16] The stations themselves were built in a style described as 'a kind of Renaissance carried out in terra-cotta'.[17]

The carriages, too, were totally unlike the claustrophobic monstrosities of the City & South London. The *Daily Mail* was perhaps waxing a little bit too lyrical when it called the coaches palatial and luxuriously upholstered, but there was no doubt that they were a great improvement on the 'padded cells'. The trains, six cars at first but soon expanded to seven, each had forty-eight seats, both lining the sides and at right angles to them, and could accommodate over 400 people, including standing passengers, at busy times. The Central's carriages were longer than on the City & South London and also had gates at each end. They had a stylish modern appearance as they were painted in purple, brown and white, again a brave choice given that the tunnels, though not smoke-filled, still generated considerable amounts of dust. Indeed, as with the Metropolitan nearly four decades previously, ventilation was a major concern. While *The Times* had also been excited by the new line, referring to 'ample accommodation, the spacious lifts, the pure air, the uniform temperature, the convenient stopping-places, the good light and the rapid movement',[18] a reader wrote to complain that he had been stuck for half an hour in a train at Marble Arch.[19] He expressed concern that the air became 'exceedingly oppressive' and wondered what would have happened if the lights had gone out as well. He asked for more information to be passed on to passengers by the guards, a complaint that will have great resonance for today's rail travellers.

Another correspondent to *The Times*, a barrister,[20] suggested rather sensibly that smoking should be banned from the lifts which gave access to the stations. These were built to carry up to 100 people and were clearly not a pleasant experience as not only were they tightly packed but, according to the lawyer, 'add to this, workmen smoking clay pipes, or would-be gentlemen smoking bad cigarettes or rank cigars, accompanied with spitting, and you have an unmitigated nuisance, which will tend to prevent many persons from making use of this new means of locomotion'.

The Central Railway responded to these criticisms with a typical bit of Victorian pseudo-scientific mumbo-jumbo, reminiscent of the Metropolitan defending itself against similar charges: 'Numerous experiments on a scientific basis,' a director wrote to *The Times*, 'have proved that the oppressive condition of air sometimes complained of in railway carriages above or below ground is related to the temperature and not to the purity of the air.' He went on to use a not entirely reassuring analogy: 'It has been practically demonstrated by physiological and chemical experiments that a live man might be sealed up in a lead coffin for half an hour without any resultant feeling of oppression – I say nothing of depression – provided he were treated as frozen mutton in a cold store, so that the air he breathed might still remain cold.' He concluded that the worst that could happen in a prolonged stoppage is that 'some of the passengers might get warm'.[21] In fairness, the Central, like its predecessors, proved extremely safe with no major mishap – a remarkable achievement given the experimental nature of the technology and the inexperience of most Londoners in using this new form of transport.

Initially, the Central had hoped that the piston action of the trains as they sped through the tunnels would be sufficient to keep the system ventilated, but this proved wildly optimistic because it was the same air that was simply being shunted around a virtually closed system. One suggestion, from a botany professor, George Henson, was that the smell could be alleviated by placing evergreen shrubs such as holly and rhododendron on the station platforms. The line's manager, Granville Cunningham, was enthusiastic, but seems not to have pursued the idea, which presumably would have resulted in a lot of dead foliage. The Railway was forced into more concerted action when London County Council chemists, alerted by a series of complaints about the malodorous fetid air – including one from a civil servant in the Sudan Political Service who likened the atmosphere to a crocodile's breath – were called in to investigate pollution underground. They found that the evil-smelling atmosphere was caused by excessive dryness, with an average humidity of 45 per cent, compared with the normal street level of 76 per cent,[22] and an excess of sulphur and nitrogen oxides. The answer was to install fans, one at Bond Street in 1902 and another larger one at Wood Lane, but complaints persisted. It was not really until filtered and ozonized air was injected into the Tube system, a process that started in 1911 but was not completed until the 1930s, that the atmosphere really started to improve. Nowadays, the air in the tunnels is controlled by 130 fans which are supposed to keep the temperature at around 21°C (73°F), rather warmer than the 13°C (55°F) which prevailed in Edwardian days and which actually was perceived as fairly reasonable. People in those days tended to dress warmly to go out, which meant that 55°F never felt cold and, in the hot weather, was reckoned to be pleasantly cool – especially during that first summer when there was a heatwave with temperatures regularly hitting 90°F.

The *Daily Mail*, led by its proprietor Alfred Harmsworth, an enthusiast for all newfangled gadgets, gave much more positive coverage. The paper was founded in 1896, after the opening of the City & South London, which therefore missed out on having such a strong supporter in the press. By 1900, it was already selling half a million copies daily and Harmsworth used the paper to promote inventions such as the telephone, motorcycles and, in particular, motor cars. *Mail* reporters were therefore expected to be enthusiastic about a new development such as the Tube, but this means that their reporting has to be viewed somewhat circumspectly today. At the opening, the *Mail* front page read 'if this kind of thing goes on, London will come to be quite a nice place to travel in'. The staff were commended for their coyness and the conductor was singled out for being 'all of a quiver of joy and pride. But there was no indecorous exhibition of emotion; every man was resolutely British'.[23] It was the *Daily Mail*, as early as 4 August 1900, just five days after the opening to the public, which first dubbed the line the 'Twopenny Tube'. The *Railway Times* made the outlandish claim that motorists and cyclists were calmer as a result of the opening of the line and even suggested that an anorexic, who had not eaten for eighteen months, suddenly developed a ravenous attitude as a result of a journey on the line.[24] As O.S. Nock accurately points out, this favourable coverage was rare indeed among newspapers: 'The "Twopenny Tube" got a most enthusiastic reception in the English press, which has never in its history been very well disposed towards railways of any kind.'[25] Perhaps this positive coverage was a counterpoint to all the bad news in the papers, which were full of harrowing tales about the casualties in the Boer War and, on the day after the opening, news of the death of the Prince of Wales's younger brother, Alfred.

Unlike the poor gloomy City & South London, the Twopenny Tube caught the public imagination. People flocked to the line. Within weeks, 100,000 were travelling on the railway daily. On the day of the triumphal return from the Boer War of the City Imperial Volunteers, who made a state entry into the capital, a staggering 229,000 travelled on the Central. During the early 1900s, the annual total was around 45 million annually, nearly 125,000 daily.[26]

There were several reasons for this success. First, the line was on a transport artery and took a lot of existing business off both buses and the underground lines. According to one newspaper report, 'The busmen are in despair. "Six of my regulars went by it today" growled a Bayswater conductor'.[27] As its directors had feared when they objected to the building of the Central, the Metropolitan, still steam-hauled, lost out heavily to the new line with its modern electric trains. Secondly, the Central had been built to a high standard. Even the Board of Trade inspector reckoned the stations and passageways were 'commodious'. Access to the trains was by lift and the bigger stations had three or four – there were forty-eight in the whole system. Thirdly, the line benefited from the growing economy which boosted not only employment but travel to the growing number of shops in Oxford Street; when, in 1908, Harry Gordon Selfridge was building his eponymous store, he wanted Bond Street station to be renamed Selfridges and tried to connect it with a passage under Oxford Street, but in the end was unsuccessful in both enterprises. And finally, the supportive press coverage provided free advertising for the line.

Unlike on the City & South London, the carriage manufacturers had anticipated that there would be standing passengers and fitted straps to the roof for them to grab, thereby creating 'straphanging', the long-suffering Londoners' expression for commuting. The railway was rather more stylish and comfortable than its predecessor, yet still kept the same cheap fares with everyone travelling in one class, a real bargain as it was for a much longer journey. Originally the promoters, put off by the bad publicity engendered by the cheap and nasty City & South London, had inserted in the Bill that there would be two classes – first and third – costing twopence and a penny respectively per mile. But the manager, Granville Cunningham, suggested the uniform fare that was to be important in creating the popular image of the line as a 'people's railway'. Moreover, workmen could get cheap early morning tickets, allowing them a return journey for the normal single fare of twopence. As a result, the name of Twopenny Tube quickly became widely adopted, and began to appear in songs. Gilbert & Sullivan hastily changed their reference for the 1900 revival of

Patience from a man travelling on a threepenny bus to 'the very delectable, highly respectable, Twopenny Tube young man'. A more substantial recognition came in a song in a musical, *San Toy*, then playing in the West End, which contained a verse about the fears of a Chinaman travelling on the line, expressed in the racially stereotyped language of the time:

Me goes out, come on to rain
Me tink me go by low down train,
Climbee in bus seem too much fuss
Me hearee talk 'bout tupn'y drain
Me getee in, me takee seat
Lift go miles down underee street,
Me very frightee where me go
Me hearee place much hot below
Me tink maybe me meet Old Nick –
Me hopee out dam quick, quick, quick![28]

Blessed with such good patronage, the Central, uniquely of the major underground lines, paid good dividends right from the start. There were such large numbers travelling on the line that the operating expenses only represented just over half the revenue, even with the large crew on each train. Consequently the company managed to pay a healthy 4 per cent dividend in each of its first five years, and 3 per cent until its merger into the Underground Group shortly before the outbreak of the First World War.

This was in spite of the cost of rectifying a very major mistake which was beginning to attract unfavourable coverage in the newspapers: rather than following the successful example of the Waterloo & City and using motor coaches, the trains were hauled by locomotives, which, though bigger than those on the City & South London, were still an unsuitable form of traction for an underground line. Greathead had originally intended to have a locomotive at each end, which would have avoided the complication of having to shunt the locomotive round at the termini, but this would have required connecting the two with a large electrical cable running under the train, an idea vetoed by the Board of Trade because of the fire risk. Consequently, the single locomotive, using a relatively new and untried technology,[29] had to be very heavy to haul the train and the vibration caused by the forty-three-ton locomotives with only a rudimentary suspension had a devastating effect on buildings on the surface. There were so many complaints from proprietors fearing a collapse that the Board of Trade was forced to appoint a committee of three scientific experts to examine the issue. They were told that when the trains passed, buildings shook so that it became impossible for draughtsmen in Cheapside to draw straight lines. To alleviate the problem, some of the locomotives were modified and fitted with gears which made their passage a bit smoother; but the Central's management had the wit to realize quickly that the only long-term solution would be the use of motor coaches.

The change was effected remarkably quickly, pre-empting the inquiry report which did not appear until February 1902. By August 1901, only a year after the opening, the company had already introduced two experimental six-car motor coach trains on the line and this trial proved successful. As a result, a whole set of motor coaches, built in Britain but using American motors, was ordered. They began to be phased in from April 1904, and by 8 June that year the remarkably swift and successful changeover was complete. The move to motor coaches had the added advantage of reducing the time needed at the termini from five to just two minutes, alleviating the other great problem facing the line in its early days: overcrowding. One daft wag suggested in *The Times*[30] that the solution would be to run trains on both tracks eastwards in the morning to take people into the City and in the opposite direction in the evenings. Subsequent correspondents sensibly pointed out that there would be no way of bringing the rolling stock back to carry more passengers. Another correspondent, Janet Hogarth, who had been forced to resort to using an omnibus because the rain had brought a surfeit of people onto the Central, made a plea for ladies' coaches, as she was at a loss to know how to deal with the issue of mixed travel because of the chivalry of her fellow gentlemen travellers: 'The man travelling habitually to the City between 9 and 10 a.m. naturally wishes to keep the seat he has secured; the woman, also travelling habitually, is most loath to deprive him of it. But what is she to do? She cannot always see if a car is full before entering, she feels it ungracious to refuse his chivalrous offers, and she is made painfully conscious of the inconvenience she has unwittingly caused.' Her suggestion for a ladies-only coach, like those segregated compartments which survived on British Rail suburban trains into the 1960s, was not taken up by the Central.

Other suggestions to tackle the overcrowding included raising the fares by using 'the old fashioned rules of political economy' in order to 'stop killing with kindness this boon for Londoners'.[31] In fact, the single fare was to survive until 1907 when competition from motor buses and the opening of other Tube lines reduced the numbers travelling on the Central. Fares of threepence were introduced for longer journeys and, two years later, the fare for shorter trips was reduced to a penny.

Having achieved such immediate success, the owners of the line quickly put forward plans for expansion. Their big idea was to create a loop, essentially a kind of circle line, that would have included stations at Mansion House, Hyde Park Corner, High Street Kensington and Hammersmith, but this was only one of a plethora of ideas for new tube lines which the success of the Central had stimulated. So yet again, as happened virtually every time there was a major new underground development, Parliament took over, creating a joint committee which had the task of evaluating the various proposals and assessing which best met present and future traffic requirements. The Parliamentarians were not to know it, but this was an incredibly small window of opportunity. Within a few short years, the competition from motor buses, trams and, soon, motor cars, would make any privately funded line impossible to finance. The Parliamentary joint committee rejected the Central's scheme, in favour of the rival plan to build a railway from Hammersmith to Palmers Green which had been partly approved as far back as 1897.

The Central was therefore left with tacking on short extensions at either end but was not able to do so until several years later. Spotting that an exhibition site was being developed at a huge site at Wood Lane, just north-west of Shepherd's Bush, the Central directors obtained permission to extend the line and create a loop at the western end. The opening of the extension in May 1908 coincided with the start of the exhibition, a celebration of Franco-British achievements intended to cement the four-year-old Entente Cordiale. The site took over from Earls Court as London's main exhibition centre and large shows were held there every year until 1914. The Olympic Games of 1908 (and, incidentally, those of 1948) were held in the adjoining stadium and the area acquired the unofficial name of 'White City' because the concrete buildings, which supposedly included 'twenty palaces' for the inaugural exhibition, scattered among miles of artificial lakes and canals, were covered with white stucco.[32]

One slightly desperate attempt to boost revenue by the Central at that time was the introduction of a parcels service. A 'Lightning Parcels Express' service was started in 1911, using men on tricycles to carry packets between stations and nearby offices, but like the similar one on the District (Chapter 6) it was short-lived. It closed down in 1917 through shortage of manpower, never to be resumed.

At the east end of the Central, the line was eventually extended to its initial intended terminus at Liverpool Street. This had been part of the original plans but powers to carry out the work had lapsed because the Central's directors had concentrated on other investments, such as replacing the original locomotive fleet. The station, which also covered the adjoining main-line terminus of Broad Street, was opened in July 1912 but plans for further extensions westwards were shelved with the outbreak of the war. As a history of the line puts it, 'the opening to

Liverpool Street was the swan song of the Central London as an independent enterprise'.[33]

While both these extensions and the various exhibitions provided a welcome boost to the Central's traffic, the line was facing increased competition and numbers of passengers were on a downward curve. This was partly the result of an economic recession and increased competition from motor buses, but, most importantly, because no fewer than three other tube lines had been taking shape under London, all supported by the mysterious American, Charles Yerkes.

E I G H T

THE DODGY
AMERICAN

London had no strategic plan to create a coherent network of underground railways, and yet today has a reasonably integrated system. There are obvious deficiencies and lacunae, such as the lack of a connection between the Circle and the Northern Line at Euston, but in many ways it is impossible to detect the haphazard way in which the system was developed. This has been more the result of luck than design. And it is also thanks to the efforts of Charles Tyson Yerkes, the American who quickly gained control of much of the underground network, both existing and under construction, in the first few years of the 1900s. Few Londoners realize, however, that the very shape and extent of the underground network in London was not determined by planners, or even Parliamentarians, but – as this chapter shows – as the result of a battle between two American magnates.

Of the pantheon of Underground heroes, the people who created and ran it, from Charles Pearson to Lord Ashfield, Yerkes is the most controversial and, arguably, the man who had the most influence in ensuring London obtained a large network of lines. Yerkes only showed an interest in London in the final decade of his sixty-eight years and his earlier life was, to say the least, colourful; so much so, indeed, that many of the stories about him have been told and retold so often that there are considerable discrepancies between the various accounts. Accuracy is further confounded by the three-volume epic[1] based on Yerkes's life by an American novelist, Theodore Dreiser, who liberally mixed reality with fantasy.

Yerkes was born in Philadelphia in 1837, into a banking family of Welsh ancestry and Quaker beliefs, not a creed to which Charles ever seems to have subscribed. He set up a brokerage office at the age of twenty-two thanks to a legacy, and made a fortune through his ability to read the bond market better than his peers. He created a bank but soon lost all his money: a fire in the commercial heart of Chicago in 1871 caused waves of losses throughout the Eastern United States, and the collapse caught out Yerkes who was unable to pay interest on money he held for the City of Philadelphia. He was sentenced to thirty-three months' imprisonment for 'technical embezzlement' of $400,000 and spent seven months in jail, during which he showed his self-belief by telling a reporter: 'I have made up my mind to keep my mental strength unimpaired and think my chances [of] regaining my former position financially are as good as they ever were.'[2]

Pardoned by the state governor, apparently for political reasons because he knew where too many bodies were buried, he set about making a second fortune. After helping to finance, very profitably, the Continental Passenger Railway Company which, despite its grand-sounding name, was Philadelphia's local rail network, in 1882 he moved to Chicago where he hoped to set up another bank but instead took an interest in the horse-drawn tramways springing up throughout the city.

How he managed to gain control of this extensive network remains something of a mystery. His modus operandi was to borrow money – on dubious security – to obtain stock and gain control of companies, offering dividend guarantees which he would then have to pay out of capital – not a sustainable practice. He would then create holding and subsidiary companies, juggling the accounts in a way that ensured no one would be able to trace precisely what was happening, and then he would issue further 'watered down' shares to raise more money. While similar complex arrangements are made today by big businesses in order to avoid taxes and prevent scrutiny, the difference is that Yerkes frequently strayed onto the wrong side of the law. As a business biography of Yerkes puts it, 'his bookkeeping methods and business tactics were so complicated that a clear account of how he captured control of Chicago's street railways can scarcely be made'.[3] The *Dictionary of American Biography* said his rail empire had become known as the 'Chicago Traction Tangle, a network of construction companies, operating companies and holding companies, of interlocking directorships and friendly contracts, of financial manipulation and political corruption'.

Financial opaqueness characterized all his empire-building, and some of his deals stretch credulity. He electrified the Chicago tramways by awarding the contract to a company he had incorporated the day before, and then charged the tramway more than $10.7m for work which should have cost $3m. He also made money out of property speculation around transport developments which he was carrying out, a method he appears to have attempted to use in London.

In Chicago, he was also helped by the depth of the corruption of government, particularly at a local level. Between the end of the Civil War and the turn of the century, the USA was expanding rapidly and government, at all levels – federal, state and municipal – had a wide variety of favours at its disposal such as franchises for bus and tram networks or utilities. These could, generally, be bought by those businesses prepared to pay the price in bribes. Yerkes took full advantage of this system and used his dubious financial methods to gain control of a large chunk of the antiquated tramways in the windy city by the mid 1880s. Borrowing money from his former partners in Philadelphia, he acquired a majority shareholding in one of the three main tramways, the North Division, and a second, West Division, followed soon after.

It would be simplistic to suggest that Yerkes's motivation was simply to make money, though he accumulated enough to buy a mansion on

Fifth Avenue in New York and fill it with old masters including a Rembrandt and luxurious furnishings such as a gold bed reputed to have belonged to the King of the Belgians (or mad King Otto of Bavaria according to a different account). He was also motivated by a desire to create transport networks for which he would be remembered. In fact, apart from the Tube, his most lasting memorial is the Yerkes Observatory at the University of Chicago, where he seems to have been the victim of the sort of sharp practices which were his trademark. A couple of canny academics approached him, suggesting that a large endowment would salvage his poor reputation in Chicago and they managed to persuade him into stumping up half a million dollars, leaking the news to the local papers before Yerkes could reconsider the offer.[4] The *Chicago Times* was not impressed: 'The astronomical beneficence of Mr. Yerkes does not excuse his street railway's shortcomings any more than the educational liberality of Mr. Rockefeller justifies the methods of the Standard Oil Company.' At least Yerkes can be grateful that his generosity bought him a measure of immortality, as the Observatory still bears his name whereas few Tube users today have heard of him.

Yerkes consolidated and improved the tramways, replacing horses with electric power and bringing two abandoned tunnels under the Chicago river back into use. He disguised his substantial holdings through a complex system of nominees but the local press, which was generally hostile, pilloried him as the Mr Big of the local transport system whenever complaints were made. And there were lots of them. His trams were badly lit, dirty and unventilated, and services often ran infrequently and irregularly. They were awfully overcrowded in rush hours because there was insufficient stock, but Yerkes was unrepentant. His motto was 'It is the straphanger that pays the dividend', and his other favourite dictum for success in the tramway business was 'Buy up old junk, fix it up a little and unload it upon other fellows.'[5]

Yerkes was both clever and ruthless, using all available methods, legal and illegal, to see off competitors and maintain a monopoly.

Bribery was simply routine and on occasion he used blackmail, reportedly sending women to compromise rivals and politicians. He was, predictably, a notorious womanizer himself, with a string of mistresses. Yerkes finally overstretched himself when he tried to obtain a 100-year franchise for his street tramways, his usual bribes to the local City Council and the Illinois state legislature proving insufficient even though they amounted to $1m. The arrangement, which astonishingly provided for no payment to the City, was passed by these two bodies but the governor vetoed the deal. When Yerkes tried again, this time for fifty-year deals, local people staged demonstrations against the plan, frightening the aldermen: 'On the night the vote was taken in December 1898, mobs with guns and sticks paraded the streets and a hempen [hangman's] noose was lowered from the gallery of the City Hall.'[6] Tammany Hall politics was coming under greater scrutiny, even if it flourished in that most corrupt of cities for another couple of generations.

Realizing that he could progress no further in the USA with his reputation ruined, Yerkes looked to Britain for what he saw as an untapped market. He sold out his Chicago interest for a sum variously estimated at $10m or $15m, but it is unclear whether any of that was left to invest in London given his propensity for extravagant spending – he had, for example, just bought another New York mansion for his favourite mistress.

The exact date when Yerkes first came to London and began to team up with his partner, Robert (later Sir Robert) Perks, is not known. There is some evidence that he sailed to the UK in 1896 and even suggestions that he had a conversation on the boat with Dame Henrietta Barnett, the founder of Hampstead Garden Suburb, during which she outlined her plans: 'Gazing into her eyes, he confessed his own plans – to "convey all London about in tunnels and this system of underground travelling would cause the erection of a station on the western edge of Hampstead Heath".'[7] But quite apart from the obviously fictional romantic nonsense, there is no firm evidence that this meeting ever took place, as the Dame herself reported only that she had had a conversation with a gentleman whose identity she never ascertained and she did not mention that he was American. Moreover, Yerkes was very unlikely to have known in such detail about the proposals for a Hampstead line to which he is supposedly referring. It is certain, though, that he came to Britain two years later, as he then began to show an interest in the District Railway in which Perks had a substantial holding.

As we have seen, Yerkes quickly took control of the line and electrified it, as he had done many of his Chicago tramways, and appointed Perks as chairman of the District. Perks, a devout and upright Methodist, whose main claim to posterity is that he raised the funds for the erection of Westminster Central Hall, was a railway company solicitor, a former colleague of Edward Watkin and a major shareholder in the District. Given his strong religious beliefs, he was the most unlikely partner imaginable for Yerkes, but clearly this pairing of the Good and the Sinful worked. Within a couple of years, Yerkes had gained control of three other Tube lines, the embryonic Northern Line (Charing Cross branch), Bakerloo and Piccadilly, all then unbuilt but which together form the basis of London's Tube system today. Remarkably, all three were to open their initial sections in a short period between March 1906 and June 1907, and it would take another sixty-one years for another deep tube line, the Victoria, to be dug under central London. Indeed, between 1903 and 1907, if one includes the Great Northern & City and the Angel to Euston extension of the City & South London, a staggering twenty-six and a half miles of tube railways were built under London. The construction of each of these railways is a complex and intertwined story of Parliamentary bills, heroic efforts to raise capital, opaque financial deals and amazing feats of engineering and construction, most of which passed off with remarkably few mishaps.

The first of the three lines on which construction got under way was the embryonic Bakerloo, known originally as the Baker Street &

Waterloo Railway, which had obtained an Act of Parliament in 1893 to run between the two stations in its name. There had been several previous incarnations of this idea because of the inconvenient location of Waterloo, the London & South Western Railway's London terminal which, as we saw in Chapter 7, had already stimulated the construction of London's second deep tube line, the Waterloo & City. As far back as 1865, a scheme to connect Waterloo with Whitehall using pneumatic power, near Scotland Yard, had obtained Parliamentary sanction and even been partly built. The plan collapsed as a result of a financial crisis but would probably not have been technically feasible in any case, given the problems encountered during construction of Brunel's Thames tunnel. Another proposal, for a half-mile-long Charing Cross & Waterloo Electric Railway, was also sanctioned by Parliament. It was to have been a cut and cover railway, with a deep tube section under the Thames and a northern terminus near Trafalgar Square, but again lack of money, together with the untimely death of its electrical engineer, Sir William (Wilhelm) Siemens, in 1883, killed off the embryonic railway shortly after the start of construction.

The Baker Street & Waterloo was a much more ambitious scheme since it was scheduled to be three miles long with several intermediate stations including Oxford Circus and Piccadilly Circus, which would become major hubs of the tube network. The main purpose of the railway was to create a link between north and south which, given all the concentration on east–west lines, had been rather forgotten. But the promoters also sold their project on the basis that the line would allow business people in the West End to go to Lord's Cricket Ground in time to see the last hour's play without leaving the office early. The Bill also specified that the railway could be used for carrying mail and small parcels as well as passengers.

As usual, the developers failed to attract the necessary capital and the scheme remained dormant for a couple of years until a supposed white knight, the London & Globe Finance Corporation, came to the rescue in November 1897. The company was owned by Whitaker Wright, yet another of the disreputable businessmen with which the story of the Underground is so peppered. And like so many of them, Wright had both US and UK connections. He was an Englishman who had made his fortune in the USA by mine prospecting and returned to Britain to live in 'mildly eccentric affluence'.[8] He had created a small empire of diverse companies which were 'characterized by the existence on their boards of various dignitaries of whom few, if any, took part in their activities'.[9] He was passionate about all things subterranean: he built a huge estate at Lea Park in Surrey which included a vast lake and, beneath it, a smoking room reached by tunnels in the form of an underground conservatory so that his guests could watch fish or swimmers disporting themselves overhead. Another tunnel led to a large room under the artificial lake where tea could be taken.[10]

Whether the Globe company ever had sufficient finance to complete the line is doubtful, but it became the main contractor as well as developer, and construction started in August 1898. The rather ingenious method used was to have the main worksite as a pontoon stretching far out into the Thames, from which shafts were sunk and spoil removed straight onto barges. The digging under the river had to be undertaken with the aid of compressed air to prevent water leaking in but occasionally some would escape, creating an enormous bubble that made a huge splash when it reached the surface. One such waterspout upset a boat involved in a race and the company had to pay damages to the owner. The Greathead shield method, which had now become standard, was used to dig out the two tunnels, but the line was expanding on paper almost as fast as underground through a succession of Acts of Parliament which granted extensions to Marylebone, then to Paddington, in the north and to Elephant & Castle in the south where the line could connect with a network of tramways.

Substantial work on the tunnels had been completed, at a cost of £650,000,[11] when, after eighteen months, the Globe's funds ran out. Wright's little empire of intertwined companies sustained heavy losses and collapsed as a result of financial irregularities which forced several into insolvency. When the problems spilled over into the railway project Wright desperately tried to talk up the value of the shares in the Baker Street & Waterloo, and even started buying up stock in the company to create a buoyant market, but to no avail. At the end of 1900, the London & Globe was declared bankrupt and most of the work on the line ceased. Suddenly, Wright found himself being pursued both by creditors and the criminal authorities. He attempted to flee, first to Paris and then to the USA, where he was unceremoniously put on a boat back to England. He was arrested on arrival and prosecuted for publishing false balance sheets and accounts. In January 1904 he was found guilty of defrauding investors to the tune of a staggering £5m and sentenced to seven years' imprisonment. But the case was being heard in the Royal Courts of Justice, rather than the Old Bailey, and before he was taken to prison he was allowed to meet his advisers in a private room where he dropped dead, having swallowed a cyanide capsule. A revolver, clearly a back-up method of suicide, was found on his body.

Yerkes managed to acquire the moribund line cheaply early in 1902. He merged it with the rest of his burgeoning empire of underground railways to create the Underground Electric Railways Company of London Limited (UERL), which was to run much of London's transport network until the creation of London Transport in 1933. The UERL gained control of the other two big tube projects: the Great Northern, Piccadilly & Brompton Railway, the central section of the future Piccadilly Line; and the Charing Cross, Euston & Hampstead Railway, which would become the Charing Cross branch of the Northern; as well as the District Line. That left only the Central, the City & South London and the Metropolitan outside UERL control and before the start of the First World War the first two of these would be incorporated into the empire created by Yerkes.

Having bought these virtual railways – in reality little more than planning permissions for putative lines without any source of finance – Yerkes set about raising the money to build them. He was astonishingly and rather inexplicably successful. He teamed up with the international family banking firm of Speyers, which had offices on both sides of the Atlantic – London, New York and Frankfurt – and was headed, in London, by Sir Edgar Speyer who agreed to help Yerkes raise £5m for the construction of the tube lines. The precise arrangements, which involved the same kind of complex financial engineering that Yerkes had used in the USA, were unfathomable even to Sir Harry Haward, the financial comptroller of the London County Council, which kept a close eye on transport developments in the capital.[12] Shares were sold in the USA, France, Germany and the Netherlands, as well as in the UK where, in general, people were sceptical about US financial methods which were generally thought to be dubious and, on occasion, corrupt. This was, indeed, a period in which large amounts of American capital were moving into Britain in a variety of industries as there were more opportunities for profitable investment than in the USA, but as one history puts it, 'all this rustling of commercial paper was taken rather coolly in London'.[13] Nevertheless, without US investors, the Tube network would have never been built. The London Stock Exchange had simply refused to invest in the various plans for tube lines which had been drawn up over the previous decade and, as we have seen, the Central only received funding thanks to US investors and the involvement of Establishment figures able to call on sources of 'old money'.

There is little doubt that Yerkes and Speyer really believed that, as Yerkes put it, the enterprise of building tube lines under London 'cannot but be profitable'.[14] Speyer, indeed, claimed later that he only agreed to help raise the money after the most careful scrutiny. But he also profited personally from the deal. Two of the Speyer companies, together with Yerkes's old bankers in Boston, the Old Colony Trust, were to receive £250,000 each on the formation of the UERL, 15 per cent of the capital raised, and a considerable burden on the future profitability of the enterprise.

Speyer's scrutiny, however, must have included some great leaps of faith. Basically railways are fairly simple businesses, but predictions on both lines in the accounts are difficult to make. On the expenditure side, it was possible to devise a fairly robust assessment of the cost of tunnelling, but the bill for stations, which required the acquisition of potentially very expensive sites, was more difficult to calculate. On revenue, predicting numbers was – and indeed remains – a mug's game. In the event, all the predictions for the new tubes were massively optimistic and the investors never made any money. The number of passengers travelling on these railways was dependent on many factors, notably the state of the economy and competition from other railways, trams and, increasingly, from the most modern form of transport, the motor bus, which Speyer and Yerkes could not easily have predicted.

The investors approached by Speyer and Yerkes seem to have been convinced that the potential returns in investing in the expanding London underground network were considerable. The Americans, principally from New York and Boston, bought nearly 60 per cent of the shares, with the British taking a third and the rest mainly being purchased by Dutch investors.

The £5m, though, was nothing like enough to fund the three new tube lines and the electrification of the District. A further sum of around £10m was needed and when an attempt to raise money for the Piccadilly was made in 1903, only 40 per cent of the shares were taken up. Here, Yerkes devised his master plan, an Edwardian version of junk bonds. The reasoning was that the tube lines were bound to make a profit and the price of the shares would go up. Therefore, he would raise money through what he called profit-sharing secured notes, a concept halfway between equity and debt. The notes, of which he sold £7m worth, would be redeemable for their value – which ranged between £100 and £1,000 in either dollars or pounds – in 1908 and would pay interest of 5 per cent. But they would also, crucially, go up in value with the shares on which they were secured, ensuring that the investors would see their capital value enhanced if the tube lines were as successful as predicted. The investors could, therefore, hedge their bets by getting a guaranteed rate of return as well as sharing in the profits. Amazingly, despite the scepticism over UERL's share placings, this scheme, together with a successful rights issue to the original investors, brought in all the money Yerkes required. Needless to say, it was a decision that the investors would greatly regret. In total, with various other issues of debenture stock, Yerkes raised £18m to invest in London's Underground.

But was there a more cunning plan behind Yerkes's thinking, related not to railways but to property? Did he really expect to earn a fortune through railways or were they a device to make money through increasing land values? Yerkes had always taken a great interest in the property served by his railways. There are several versions of the story of how Yerkes made field studies of the area around Hampstead and Golders Green. The best account describes how, in autumn 1900,

> two men drove in a hansom cab over the lofty heights of
> Hampstead Heath high over London. From time to time, the
> driver drew in his reins, allowing the men to leave and walk
> over the open spaces. Barely a rooftop could be seen. Later they
> took the cab down to see the level fields north of the hill. The
> only feature here was an isolated crossroad, fringed by a couple
> of old houses and some farm buildings. They had reached the
> rural hamlet of Golders Green, not far from Hendon.[15]

One of the men was Yerkes and his companion, who is the source of this tale, was Harley Hugh Dalrymple Hay. Other accounts suggest that Yerkes actually sent an agent and only visited the site later, but whatever the precise details, Yerkes chose the bleak land over the hill from the Heath as the depot and terminus for his new railway, the Charing Cross, Euston & Hampstead line. Quite possibly, too, he invested considerably in the land, something he had done before in

Chicago, to profit from the development. The principal historians of London's transport postulate that Yerkes profited in this way, though their evidence is thin: 'many eligible building sites had been acquired by an American-sounding concern calling itself the Finchley Road & Golders Green syndicate'.[16] Certainly, if this is the case, Yerkes might have made a lot more money from these property interests than from the building of the line itself.

The Hampstead line, however, had to wait rather longer to be revived than the Baker Street & Waterloo, where work soon restarted after Yerkes took over and had raised the money. Construction proceeded smoothly, apart from the odd glitch such as the Board of Trade requiring enhanced standards of access and safety which forced the company to rebuild Oxford Circus, 'making it the only tube station to be substantially rebuilt before it even opened'.[17] Various additional stations such as Regent's Park and Lambeth North, allowed by the constant stream of new Acts which enhanced the scheme, also had to be accommodated at a late stage, but towards the end of 1905 empty trains were testing out the system. The Edwardians took as much trouble as their Victorian predecessors to 'sell' the new railway to the public. Just before the opening ceremony in March 1906, teams of journalists were given free rides along the line, lunched at the Great Central Hotel at Marylebone and left 'happily clutching their [publicity] hand-outs',[18] probably not very different to those given to their successors when the Jubilee Line Extension opened in 2000.

The journalists were informed about the host of innovations – all of US origin – which helped improve both performance and safety, such as automatic signalling using track circuits to indicate when a train was in a particular section of the line, a system that became universal throughout busy sections of Britain's railways; and a train stop system, a mechanical device which stopped trains automatically if they went through a signal at red.[19]

There were clever little innovations for passengers, too. One was the use of compressed air to allow lift operators, who also collected tickets, to open the gates at the far end so that there could be a one-way flow, with people using different sides to enter and exit. While such 'people management' concepts may seem trivial, they were the kind of improvement which made a tremendous difference to the everyday operation of a system that had to cope with massive numbers at rush hours.

The lessons of the Central had been learnt and the rolling stock consisted of multiple units, rather than carriages hauled by heavy locomotives. The cars, a term which betrayed their origins in the USA where they were built, were assembled in Manchester, then taken by rail to Camden Town in north London and then onto the tracks near Elephant & Castle after being hauled, partially dismantled, through London by horses in the early hours of the morning to avoid disrupting the traffic.

The first section of the line, between Lambeth North (then called Kennington Road) and Baker Street, opened on 10 March 1906 with a standard speech, this time from Sir Edwin Cornwall MP, the chairman of the London County Council.[20] There was little ceremony, except a luncheon at the Great Central at Marylebone, 'served in faultless style in the charmingly decorated dining-hall' according to a contemporary account. Sir Edgar Speyer, who had replaced the ailing Yerkes as chairman of UERL, must have thought that the Progressives, who had been swept out of office by the Conservatives, were still in power at the LCC because his speech was clearly geared to their agenda. He told the audience in offering the Loyal Toast to the King and Queen: 'This line will furnish great advantages to the poor people of this great metropolis, and I think it will be the first step towards the solution of the problem of the housing of the poor which the Queen has so much at heart.'

The London *Evening News* called the line 'Baker-loo' in one of its early stories about the new railway and the moniker caught on quickly, but the precise authorship of the first use of the name remains one of those little mysteries which historians of the system love to debate.

Other suggestions, such as the 'Loo' proposed by the rival *Star* newspaper, were ignored and 'Bakerloo' was adopted officially by the railway in July 1906. This incurred the wrath of the haughty editor of the *Railway Magazine*, G.A. Nokes,[21] who complained that 'the announcements placed outside the stations of the Baker Street & Waterloo Railway that it is the Bakerloo Railway are not likely to increase the popularity of this struggling concern. Some latitude is allowable, perhaps, to halfpenny papers, in the use of nicknames, but for a railway to adopt its gutter title is not what we expect from a railway company. English railway officers have more dignity than to act in this manner.' This was a thinly disguised attack on the Americans who clearly were not going to receive any gratitude from the likes of xenophobes such as Nokes for having financed and built a railway which the British had singularly failed to support.

The stations were the first built to a design pattern created by Leslie Green which was used on all the new Yerkes tubes, a style familiar to any Londoner today who looks above the fascia of many central Underground stations where the ruby-red glazed tiles characteristic of Green's designs can still be observed. They were nearly all originally two-storey buildings with arched windows at mezzanine level but the flat roofs were designed to allow future development. The colour was deliberately chosen to make the buildings stand out from their neighbours, but one history suggests, rather unfairly, that 'their art nouveau and sombre dark rhubarb [sic – the colour has been given various descriptions] elevations soon palled'. Not so. While not as striking as their art deco 1930s successors and, indeed, rather restrained, they are a dignified and elegant early example of branding, and their uniform appearance helped to create an identity for the Underground system.

Down below, there was the clever device of using different colours for the patterns of tiles in each station, perhaps to help illiterate passengers identify their stop. The station names, too, were marked out in coloured tiles, set against the mostly white background. It was neat and unadventurous but effective styling. Green, who designed all the stations on the three tubes, died aged only thirty-four in 1908, just a year after the completion of his last one.

For Londoners, the line was a boon. The journey from Piccadilly Circus to Baker Street cost just twopence and took seven minutes. On a horse omnibus, the fare was the same but the minimum journey time was twenty minutes. The horse cab took fifteen minutes for a fare of one shilling and sixpence. Yet, despite this advantage, the Bakerloo, the first of Yerkes's new lines, proved an unhappy but accurate augury for his other schemes. Ridership was well below expectations: although 37,000 travelled on the first day, in subsequent weeks the line appeared almost deserted. In April, the *Daily Mail*[22] recorded that only eighty-six people were on a train leaving Baker Street in the evening rush hour and other newspapers seemed to take a delight in publishing photographs of empty trains. These numbers suggested that the investors were never likely to get the promised returns and, indeed, would be lucky to receive any. Yerkes had decreed that there should be a single flat fare, as when the Central opened, of twopence. This was part of a much wider concept espoused by Yerkes, who argued that flat fares had an important social effect. In terms which suggest that Yerkes was something of a transport visionary, and not just a rather money-grabbing entrepreneur, he had told the Royal Commission on London Traffic which sat between 1903 and 1905 that 'the acme of railway transportation in the City of London and its suburbs would be that a person could travel from any one point to any other point, making connections from one line to another, all for a single fare. That would be the perfection of travel and it will never come about unless there is an amalgamation of the railways.' Yerkes argued that until then, people were confined to one particular zone or line, whereas on the lines he controlled in Chicago, 'a person could travel from the heart of the city five blocks away where the well-to-do people lived for twopence halfpenny and for the same fare could continue his ride further, which took him out on the prairie'. His aim, he said, 'had always been not only to build up the suburbs, but to induce the working classes to go there' and his vision for London was the same: 'What London needs for its working classes is fresh air and green grass, and they will never get either with the railways and tramways in the condition that they are, at the present time, or being run as they are.' Maybe one has to take all this with a pinch of salt, given Yerkes's past, but there is a well-articulated philosophy here not that much different from the one espoused by the first underground pioneer, Charles Pearson. Indeed, the journalist R.D. Blumenfeld confirms that Yerkes was always forward-thinking. In his diary for 1900, Blumenfeld says of Yerkes: 'he predicted that a generation hence London will be completely transformed; that people will think nothing of living 20 or more miles from town owing to electrified trains. He also thinks that the horse and omnibus is doomed.' Blumenfeld was not convinced, adding: 'Although he is a very shrewd man, I think he is a good deal of a dreamer.'[23]

The second of the Yerkes tubes to open was the Great Northern Piccadilly & Brompton railway, an amalgam of a series of schemes conceived in the five years before work started in 1902. The first outline for this route had been put forward by the perennially broke District as a way of relieving traffic on its busy section between Earls Court and Mansion House. It was to be an underground express line, with just one stop at Charing Cross, and it obtained Parliamentary approval in August 1897, despite the District showing no ability to finance it. On the same day, Parliament also approved plans for a more conventional tube line between South Kensington and Piccadilly Circus, which included stops at Knightsbridge and Hyde Park Corner, under the name of Brompton & Piccadilly Circus. The latter tried to raise capital the following year, but failed and was taken over by the District which obtained powers to connect the two schemes in August 1899. The various sections of the line began to coalesce into a coherent concept but still without any sign of finance being available. Simultaneously, an entirely separate tube railway system, the Great

Northern & Strand, had obtained parliamentary powers and it was intended to stretch between the Aldwych and Wood Green, via Finsbury Park. Despite its name, it was not promoted by the Great Northern although that railway appears to have been supportive of the idea. Merging these two proposals created what would be London's longest tube line but inevitably the proposals for the termini varied. The section to Wood Green from Finsbury Park was dropped but the western section from South Kensington was extended to Hammersmith, providing extra connections. All but a tiny section, at the western end, was to run underground.

The man who pulled these disparate schemes together was, of course, Yerkes. And, as with the Bakerloo, it was Yerkes who managed to get work started, some five years after the idea had first been approved by Parliament. But first, this time, he had to beat off a fiercesome opponent, no less than John Pierpont Morgan, the greatest financier in the USA. And amazingly, because he was prepared to play it dirty – even more so than J.P. Morgan who himself attracted considerable opprobrium for his business methods – Yerkes, a small-time hustler in comparison with the great financier, won. Predictably, the way Yerkes achieved this victory attracted controversy and criticism.

Morgan, like many US financiers and industrialists, had begun to look east for business opportunities and spent some time in the UK in 1902, including attending the coronation of King Edward VII. Morgan had made his banking fortune during the American Civil War by continuing to do business while many rivals did not dare, but also later specialized in rescuing and amalgamating bankrupt railroads. Most famously, he bailed out the US government when it found itself short of reserves and he organized the United States Steel Corporation, the largest combination in the world, with a capital of $1,300,000,000, a staggering sum. He also established the shipping combine in the North Atlantic trade, including the White Star Line, and his reputation for being able to make money was such that 'peddlers on the London

streets were selling for a penny a "licence to stay on the Earth" signed
J. Pierpont Morgan'.[24]

When Morgan backed a scheme for about forty miles of tube railway
in London, including a line from Tottenham and Southgate in north-
east London to Hammersmith in west London, pretty much the same
route as the two main proposals which constituted the eventual
Piccadilly Line, he expected to get his own way. But Morgan and
Yerkes were not the only ones with an interest in this route. A third
player was London United Tramways (LUT), a company which was
keen to run a line through Kensington and Westminster, the two
snobbish boroughs which had banned tramways from their streets and
were therefore ripe markets for underground lines. In order to smooth
the Parliamentary process, Sir Clinton Dawkins, the man leading
Morgan's bid, agreed to share with LUT a section of the planned
railway between Charing Cross and Hammersmith, on the
understanding that LUT would have a 50 per cent stake.

Morgan promised trains which would travel at an average of
eighteen mph while Yerkes's were to be slower, at sixteen mph. Asked
about this, his engineer James Chapman showed the extent to which
Yerkes's team were prepared to be economical with the truth. In reality
the slower speed was due to the lack of power in the motors but
Chapman, in evidence to the committee, claimed that the matter was
'not a question of engineering or the manufacture of apparatus, it is a
question of the endurance of the passengers. A passenger cannot be
handled like a bullet in a gun.'[25]

Both sets of plans were accepted by Parliament, even though the
peers appointed to scrutinize the bills must have realized that there
was no chance of two such similar routes being built. Indeed, they
imposed a condition that was to be fatal to Morgan – the schemes had
to be completed in their entirety or else Parliamentary approval was
not valid. But even they probably had not realized that Yerkes was
prepared to play quite so dirty in order to scupper his rival's scheme.
Yerkes and Speyer found a weak point in Morgan's plan, the link with

LUT. Speyer approached LUT, which apparently could not reach a final agreement with Morgan over the finances, and bought a controlling interest. The reasons for LUT betraying its partner are unclear, though there is speculation that the directors were keen to cash in their shares at a good price. Once Speyer had acquired control, the LUT/Morgan plans were doomed because the part of the scheme for which that consortium was responsible, Hammersmith to Hyde Park, would not now get built and thus their Parliamentary powers fell. Morgan's other tube plans swiftly collapsed and he withdrew from the scene with a bloody nose. From the USA, he telegraphed his British partners: 'deeply sympathetic with you in your bother over Tubes. Would seem to be the greatest rascality and conspiracy I ever heard of . . . '26 As the authors of the history of London's transport suggest, 'a weighty comment indeed coming from the man who was then the world's leading authority on such matters'. MPs were infuriated by the underhand move by Yerkes and Speyer and there were several pained speeches in the Commons in a debate in October with much talk of a 'dirty transaction' and 'a scandal which had probably no precedent'.27 But by then, work was well under way and there was little that could be done. In any case, there is a hint of cant about the MPs' readiness to criticize Yerkes, prompted by a xenophobic attitude towards the American financiers who were pressing to develop railway lines in the capital.

Certainly, the history of London's Underground would have been very different had J.P. Morgan triumphed over Yerkes. There would have been a whole different set of stations on what is now the Piccadilly and there might well have been a line from Clapham Junction to Marble Arch and possibly one from Charing Cross to Acton, both ideas for which Morgan's team sought Parliamentary approval. Perhaps, too, London would have had an all-night underground service, as New York does, since this was one of the innovations put forward by Morgan which particularly pleased the Parliamentary scrutineers. He suggested that trains would run every

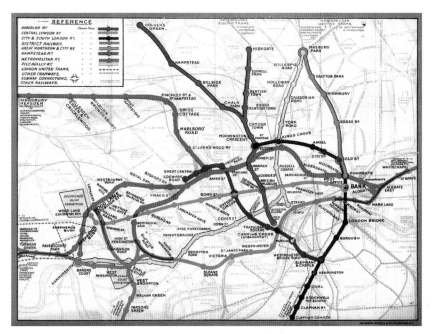

This 1908 map is the first to show all the Underground lines. It is largely geographically accurate, except for the Metropolitan, which, oddly, has been bent towards the west, presumably to accommodate the key above it.

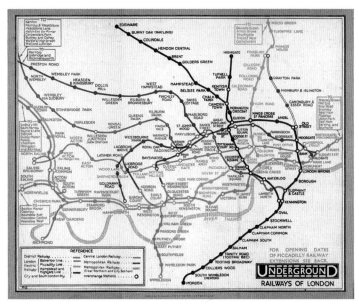

By 1932 the system had expanded into the suburbs, and the map had become a chaotic representation of the system. Many passengers, particularly those unfamiliar with London, must have been bewildered by its complexity.

© Transport for London

The modern version of the Harry Beck map demonstrates the flexibility of the design as it incorporates several extra lines and many more stations but still follows the principles he first set out, such as using only 45° and 90° angles and eschewing geographical accuracy in favour of clarity.

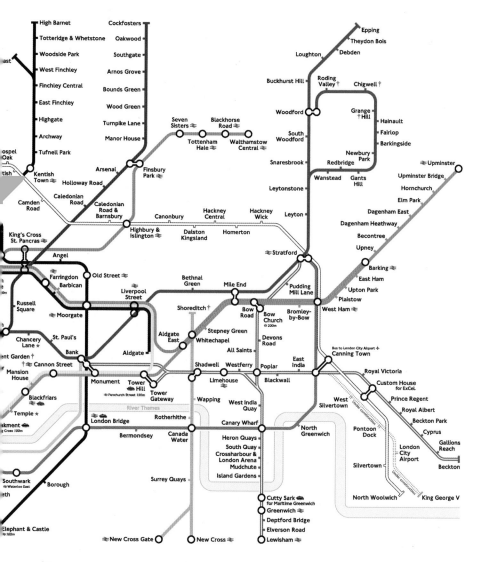

High Barnet
Totteridge & Whetstone
Woodside Park
West Finchley
Finchley Central
East Finchley
Highgate
Archway
Tufnell Park
Kentish Town ⇌
Holloway Road
Caledonian Road
Camden Road
Caledonian Road & Barnsbury
King's Cross St. Pancras ⇌
Angel
Farringdon
Barbican
Russell Square
Moorgate ⇌
Chancery Lane ★
Bank
Cannon Street †⇌
Mansion House
Blackfriars ⇌
Temple ★
London Bridge
Bermondsey
Southwark
Borough
Elephant & Castle

Cockfosters
Oakwood
Southgate
Arnos Grove
Bounds Green
Wood Green
Turnpike Lane
Manor House
Seven Sisters
Tottenham Hale ⇌
Blackhorse Road ⇌
Walthamstow Central ⇌
Arsenal
Finsbury Park ⇌
Highbury & Islington ⇌
Canonbury
Dalston Kingsland
Homerton
Hackney Central
Hackney Wick
Old Street ⇌
Liverpool Street
Bethnal Green
Mile End
Shoreditch †
Bow Road
Aldgate East
Stepney Green
Whitechapel
Devons Road
All Saints
Aldgate
Shadwell
Westferry
Poplar
Limehouse
Blackwall
Monument
Tower Hill
Tower Gateway
Wapping
West India Quay
Rotherhithe
Canary Wharf
Canada Water
Heron Quays
South Quay
Crossharbour & London Arena
Mudchute
Island Gardens
Surrey Quays
New Cross Gate
New Cross ⇌
Cutty Sark
for Maritime Greenwich
Greenwich ⇌
Deptford Bridge
Elverson Road
Lewisham ⇌

Epping
Theydon Bois
Loughton
Debden
Buckhurst Hill
Roding Valley †
Chigwell †
Woodford
Grange Hill †
Hainault
South Woodford
Fairlop
Barkingside
Snaresbrook
Newbury Park
Redbridge
Wanstead
Gants Hill
Leytonstone
Leyton
Stratford
Pudding Mill Lane
Bow Church
Bromley-by-Bow
Devons Road
East India
Canning Town
Bus to London City Airport ✈
Royal Victoria
Custom House for ExCeL
Prince Regent
Royal Albert
Beckton Park
Cyprus
Gallions Reach
Beckton
North Greenwich
West Silvertown
Pontoon Dock
London City Airport
Silvertown
North Woolwich
King George V

Upminster ⇌
Upminster Bridge
Hornchurch
Elm Park
Dagenham East
Dagenham Heathway
Becontree
Upney
Barking ⇌
East Ham
Upton Park
Plaistow
West Ham ⇌

River Thames

UNDERGROUND

Reg. user No. 04/E/1453

A 1905 poster demonstrating that the 'Twopenny Tube' was used by all classes.

two and a half minutes during the rush hour, every five for the rest of the day, and that there would be a half-hourly service in the small hours. Since the Underground, with the odd exception such as New Year's Eve, has never run all night, would Morgan have been able to deliver on his promise? Had he reckoned on the need for engineering work? Perhaps. Such a service can only be offered if there are sufficient crossovers between the two lines for sections to be closed while still allowing a shuttle service in both directions on the same track, as happens with the Channel Tunnel. New York can run services all night because many lines are four-track and two can be closed without shutting the whole route. Morgan, with his millions, probably would have managed to get his schemes built, but, on the other hand, would he have matched Yerkes's amazing achievement in building three lines and electrifying another all in the space of half a decade? Unlikely.

After his victory, Yerkes's joint proposal melding the various sections of the Great Northern and Brompton schemes into what became the Piccadilly – no nasty amalgamated names to antagonize the *Railway Magazine* here – was given the go-ahead by Parliament in August 1902. Various other rival schemes for parts of that route failed to get Parliamentary approval, leaving Yerkes a clear field. Indeed, so confident was he of victory that work had already started at Knightsbridge the previous month, before the formality of Parliamentary approval.

As with the Bakerloo, work proceeded without major mishap, using the now well-tried technology of the Greathead shield. Officially the contractor was the UERL itself, and the work was then divided up between several subcontractors, an arrangement which made the finances of the company even more opaque. The line was effectively complete by the autumn of 1906 and, after the usual test-running by empty trains and a press run with a good lunch for the journalists at the Criterion, it was opened by the President of the Board of Trade and future Prime Minister, David Lloyd George, on 15 December. This was deliberately timed to cater for the Christmas shopping rush, seen as a lucrative market particularly as, in those days, it was squeezed into a much shorter period than today.

Given that the line was eight and a half miles long, there was no attempt to have a unique fare; but there was only one class. Passengers were charged between a penny and fourpence and one innovation was that they could buy strips of six tickets at a discount between two specified stations. There were season tickets, too, for regular commuters. Since the stations were designed in the same way as those on the Bakerloo, by Leslie Green, and the cars were also similar, there was little new of note for Londoners to see. With one exception. At Holloway Road station, a circular kind of Trav-o-lator had been built which, the engineers promised, would deliver people up at a rate of 100 feet per minute. This was a heroic failure and was never put into service. Nor, unfortunately, do any drawings of how it was intended to work survive. The remains of the system, a mess of steel chains and decaying wooden steps, were found at the bottom of the lift shaft a few years ago and sit, forlornly, in the London Transport museum depot at Acton, with a sad little notice saying that the idea was 'not a success and was quickly abandoned after the station opened in December 1906'.

In fact, the first functioning railway escalator in London was opened on 4 October 1911 at Earls Court, between the Piccadilly and District line platforms. A man with a wooden leg, 'Bumper' Harris, was reported to have been employed to travel up and down all day to give passengers confidence that they could use it safely, but in fact this oft-told story is a myth.[28] Generally, the new device was accepted by the public but its name, 'escalator', incurred the wrath of a correspondent to *The Times*,[29] a Mr E. Anton, who wrote: 'you announce the instalment of an "escalator"! Pray save us from such a barbarism.' He went on to suggest that 'not one person in 20' will have an idea of its meaning which, he said, was taken from the French *escalier*, combined with the Latin *ator*, meaning doer. Instead, he suggested it should be called a 'stair lift', 'simple familiar understood [*sic*] of the people'.

The Piccadilly had one curiosity: the branch between Holborn and the Strand (later called Aldwych), a legacy of the fact that the line had been conceived as three different schemes which were somewhat untidily patched together by Yerkes. The Strand was opened in November 1907 and mostly operated as a shuttle between the two stations on which few people ever travelled. In fact the first few trains attracted no passengers apart from a labourer who travelled 'in lonely grandeur to the Strand'.[30] However, there was a junction with the northbound main line which enabled a 'theatre express' to be run through to Finsbury Park at precisely 11.13 p.m. on every weekday. Aldwych, at the time, was very much the heart of theatreland and, at least initially, the trains were 'thronged with appreciative customers'; but the more popular playhouses gradually became those nearer the Piccadilly's main line, and the service was withdrawn. In truth, the small branch line hardly seemed long enough to make it work bothering to wait for the shuttle service and throughout its life the service to Aldwych was sparsely patronized but it is frequently used today for filming scenes of the Tube.[31]

Another innovation of the Piccadilly was the decision that some trains should skip some of the less-used stations in order to reduce running times. Passengers were warned that the train was 'passing' the next station, which inspired the title of a 1928 play by Jevan Brandon-Thomas, *Passing Brompton Road*, a mildly successful West End farce about a socialite who thought this was the reason for her poorly attended parties. Brompton Road, always too close to its neighbours, South Kensington and Knightsbridge, in any case closed permanently six years after the play opened and the habit of 'passing' stations was quietly dropped. Such anomalous stations built too close to their neighbours have mostly been closed over the years, even though in Paris the distance between Métro stations is much less and there has been no such similar rationalization. The reason is simply that the London lines are on the whole much longer than the Métro and therefore, to keep running times reasonable, stations had to be kept well spaced, apart from the rare exception, such as Covent Garden, which is separated by a mere 280 yards of track from Leicester Square.

The tube line which had first attracted Yerkes's attention, the Charing Cross, Euston & Hampstead railway, was the last to be completed, as a result of planning delays. The line, as first conceived, was to go from the Strand via Tottenham Court Road to Euston, Camden and Hampstead and, with the usual changes – for example, ensuring a connection with the London & South Eastern railway at Charing Cross – had been approved by Parliament in 1893. However, raising the capital had proved even more difficult than for the other tube lines being promoted at the same time. Perks, Yerkes's strange bedfellow (there were jokes about the machinations of Yer-kees and Per-kees in business circles), had become involved in the line in 1897 but the directors' energies were mostly devoted to keeping the powers alive rather than raising funds to build it. Even though a contractor had been appointed in 1897, no start had been made by the time Yerkes took an interest. Perks acted as intermediary when the company was bought by Yerkes in October 1900 for £100,000, paid by a syndicate dominated by American interests including Marshall Field, the Chicago store magnate.

Before starting work, though, Yerkes was intent on changing the route to accommodate his ideas of stretching into the green fields and had to obtain Parliamentary powers for the new route terminating at Golders Green, where there was also to be a depot. The extension to Golders Green was strongly opposed by Hampstead residents who, aroused by sensationalist press reporting, feared, no less, that the whole Heath risked being damaged by the tunnelling underneath. *The Times*, again ready to stimulate fears about the possible effects of any modern invention, ran a story from 'a correspondent' on Christmas Day 1900, presenting an imaginary picture of the possible consequences as if it were a factual news report: 'A great tube laid under the Heath will, of course, act as a drain, and it is quite likely that the grass and gorse and trees on the Heath will suffer from lack of moisture . . . Moreover, it seems established that tube trains shake the earth to its surface; the constant jar and quiver will probably have a serious effect on the trees by loosening the roots.'

It was the kind of stuff that may have been reasonable when the first underground trains were being mooted in the 1860s, but *The Times* seems not to have noticed that this was the dawn of the twentieth century. Nevertheless these fears were taken seriously. Eventually, sense prevailed and Hampstead Borough Council, which had originally opposed the line, gave its support provided an intermediate station between Hampstead and Golders Green were built.[32] As for the 'jarring', the line was to be operated using multiple units, not the heavy locomotives originally used on the Central, and the Heath has survived intact. In fact, the line is 250 feet below the surface at Hampstead Heath, the deepest tunnel in the whole system and as far below ground as Nelson stands above Trafalgar Square. Even the nearby station is 192 feet below ground, necessitating the longest lift journey on the network.

The Bill for the amendments was passed by Parliament in November 1902 but preliminary demolition and preparation had already been started in July. Tunnelling began in September 1903 and was complete by December 1905. There were very few problems with tunnelling, except at Euston where watery sand proved an obstacle. There were, however, greater difficulties with the stations, notably at the original Charing Cross terminus. Again, the lack of coordination between railway companies caused unnecessary difficulty because the South Eastern Railway, rather than seeing the arrival of the Tube as a great boon, was more concerned with ensuring that there would be no interference to the cab traffic at the front of Charing Cross. But fate intervened. The arched roof of Charing Cross collapsed on 5 December 1905, killing six people[33] and wrecking the adjoining Avenue Theatre. The terminus was closed for more than three months and in the meantime the builders of the Hampstead tube took full advantage by digging up the station forecourt and covering it over with steel girders, allowing the contractors to build their station by digging downwards, rather than upwards as they would have had to do had the accident not occurred.

The final route approved by Parliament allowed for a split into two branches at Camden Town, with the eastern section, originally planned to go only as far as Kentish Town, stretching as far as Archway. On the western side, permission had been obtained to continue another four miles to Hendon and Edgware, but that extension was not built until the 1920s; a plan to reach Watford never materialized. The Hampstead tube would remain as a separate railway to the City & South London until after the Great War and the name 'Northern line', by which both routes are now known, was not used until 1937.

Since this was the third tube line opening within a year, the lucky Londoners might have been a bit blasé about these events – but not enough to eschew a free ride. After Lloyd George, again, had performed the opening ceremony on Saturday, 22 June 1907, travel for the rest of the day was free and *The Times* estimated that 127,000 people used the line. This generosity was not appreciated by everyone. A letter to the *Hampstead & Highgate Express,* written just before the opening, warned that

> as this offer is sure to be chiefly taken advantage of by the great unwashed of St Giles's and the equally hydrophobic denizens of the 'Dials' [Seven Dials, then still a slum], not to mention tramps, outdoor dossers of St James's and Hyde Parks with other germinals, let us hope, for our peace of mind, and body, that the trains will be thoroughly fumigated and disinfected before the railway is opened to the paying public.[34]

This curmudgeonly fellow's heart may not have been warmed by the report in the following week's paper which said that 'among the Hampstead youngsters who enjoyed themselves in the Tube on Saturday was Ernest Thrush of Wildwood Grove, aged eight years. His final ride landed him at Charing Cross after the last return had left that station. He had never been to London before that Saturday.'

The *Ham & High* itself was more sanguine than its mean-minded correspondent, recognizing in its editorial that the arrival of the Tube had begun to attract development to the area even before its completion, bringing great changes to Hampstead 'which have begun in the erection of a considerable number of large, first-class houses in the neighbourhood, as well as a terrace of villas adjacent to the Tube station. Shops are to be erected on the North End road, while one block of flats, with a shop underneath, has already been built at the corner of the lane which leads to the Crematorium.'

The terminus, Golders Green, was an interesting portent for the future in showing how the Tube helped the expansion of London. It was the first station on the Yerkes tube lines built in the open air and it showed that such new transport links could quickly transform sleepy outlying villages into thriving London suburbs. Indeed, Golders Green had not even been a village when the Tube arrived, merely, according to contemporary photographs, a farm with a crossroads and a wooden signpost. The first house was only completed in October 1905, less than two years before the station opened, and in the following year the place was already a boom town according to a visitor: 'Within sight of the Golders Green terminus of the Hampstead Tube, half a dozen estate agents' pavilions may be counted dotted about the fields.'[35] Once construction of the Hampstead line started, the value of the land went up from between £200 and £300 per acre to between £600 and £700. By the end of 1907, six months after the opening, there were seventy-three houses in Golders Green, and by the start of the war this had mushroomed to 471. Nearby, too, Dame Henrietta Barnett's dream of Hampstead Garden Suburb, where 'poor shall teach the rich and where the rich, let us hope, shall help the poor to help themselves' was being realized and made possible by the easy access into town for work.[36]

These opening ceremonies had all become rather routine, and so were the new lines. Fundamentally, they were all based on the same concept with the same style. The lifts serving every station were provided, as on the other two Yerkes tubes, by Otis, the US company; and the cars were, like most of the others, made in America and assembled at Trafford Park in Manchester. This reliance on American equipment did not endear Yerkes and his successors to many Parliamentarians and industrialists but its use was for practical rather than sentimental reasons. The Americans had greater experience of dealing with electrical equipment and the company defended itself, arguing that English equipment was priced much higher when quotes were sought. In fact, barely 10 per cent of overall purchases were made abroad and the picture, even with the cars, was a mixed one: the District, for example, bought 280 in Europe and half that number from the UK, which the management complained was an unreliable source because of strikes. The Piccadilly used all European cars, half from France and the rest from Hungary.

The labour to run the system was, of course, all British and there was plenty of it. Drivers were the elite with the top grade receiving, in 1909, seven shillings and a penny per day compared with a porter's mere two shillings and tenpence and four shillings and sixpence for a booking clerk or guard.[37] Conditions were onerous, with a ten-hour day as the norm and just six days paid holiday a year. Time and a quarter was paid for working on Sunday, Christmas Day or Good Friday. Train crews carried meal baskets while station staff had a mess room and booking clerks gas rings where they could cook or brew up in their ticket offices. Staff discipline was strict, along the traditional quasi-military lines adopted by the railways, with workers being dismissed for such minor offences as smoking on duty, overshooting stations or having altercations with passengers. The uniforms had to be worn buttoned to the neck, even in hot weather, and black boots were de rigueur as brown ones were thought to look untidy.

With all these tube lines now open, Londoners were having to learn how to use them. Passengers were used to sedate overground trains where there was always time to get on and off, helped in by polite porters and train dispatchers, but the experience on the Tube was very different. There were plenty of staff: a guard at the front of the train between the first and second cars, and a gateman on the gangway platform between each car and the next. But the trains had to keep time and the staff were ever ready to hurry passengers along with a judicious push or shove, and much shouting: treatment that attracted complaints in newspaper letters columns from aggrieved travellers. The job of the gatemen was made more difficult by the fact that passengers were allowed to travel on the small outside platforms on each car. Indeed, it was probably a pleasant alternative to the crowded insides in the heat of the summer when gatemen were encouraged to leave the bulkhead doors open for ventilation purposes.

Essentially, Londoners had to be educated the hard way in how to use a mass transit system. In particular, they had to be made to realize that, in the rush hour, they could expect another train within a couple of minutes if they could not get on the first one, rather than twenty or even thirty minutes later as on the suburban overground services. Therefore, it was not worthwhile trying to cram onto an overcrowded train.

On the Yerkes tubes, instead of hand signals like those on the Central, the rear man sounded a bell through to the next gateman once all his passengers were safely on or off the train. The bell ringing travelled up the train until the guard sounded his to inform the driver that the train was ready to depart. This cacophony of bells was a characteristic sound of travelling on the Tube in its early years, until the next generation of trains, with compressed-air-operated sliding doors, began to be introduced in 1919 and became universal in the interwar years. These did not require gatemen between each set of cars, an added advantage at a time when labour was in short supply after the carnage of the Great War.[38]

Another source of complaint was the poor accent of the gatemen who, despite the name plates and differently coloured tiles at each stop, were required to shout the name of every station, turning

Tottenham Court Road into *Totnacorranex*, Hampstead into *Ampstid* and Highgate into *Iggit*. It was, though, the perception that the staff were discourteous which attracted the most criticism. The *Railway Engineer* used it to further its campaign against all things American: 'Such methods [of dealing with customers] are only importations from America, where rudeness and noise from railway servants are meekly tolerated, if not appreciated.'[39]

Such comments were part of a concerted campaign against the Underground by a largely hostile press. Every little incident was picked up, in a not dissimilar way to the rough ride given to the railways in the UK especially since privatization in 1996. Like Nokes's remark about the name 'Bakerloo', much of the coverage was anti-American, a criticism of 'their' methods of doing business and treating customers. The District, too, attracted considerable negative coverage with various mechanical failures and, in particular, its primitive air-operated doors which apparently had a tendency to tear off ladies' skirts, something particularly shocking to the Edwardian psyche.

The coverage of what were often simply teething problems in a remarkable new system of electrified railways was so negative that Sir George Gibb, the managing director of UERL, wrote to the papers complaining of 'a perpetual shower of virulent and premature criticism'. To no avail. He failed to stop the flow of negative coverage, not least because at root there was a fundamental problem: as soon as numbers on the Bakerloo failed to meet expectations, the company was permanently at risk of going bust and the press picked up on this financial weakness.

Indeed, in financial terms, unlike the Central, the three Yerkes tubes were a flop – the *Railway Engineer* in July 1906 was ready to write off the Bakerloo, observing, somewhat prematurely, 'this tube railway may now be regarded as a beautiful failure'. The passenger figures for all three lines were nowhere near expectation, nor indeed close to the levels needed to give the kind of return which Yerkes had promised. Yerkes had procured the services of Stephen Sellon, a tramway expert, and used his figures gaily to predict annual passenger numbers of 60, 50 and 35 million respectively for the Piccadilly, Hampstead and Bakerloo as well as a massive increase for the District, which, following electrification, was projected to attract 100 million users annually. In reality, in the opening full years of each of these lines, the totals were respectively 26, 25 and 20.5 million, around half the totals predicted, and the District carried just 55 million passengers in 1906.

In fairness, there is a long tradition of railway passenger predictions being over-optimistic and such errors are still commonplace today.[40] It is a necessary game to go through because the railway promoters, whose motive is often more complex than simply to make money, know that their projects will benefit society and be impressive memorials even if they don't stack up economically. But nowadays, governments pick up the tab for such schemes, as half-built infrastructure projects are too much of a political embarrassment, whereas poor old Speyer had to battle with shareholders in order to keep the companies solvent. Modern projects, too, are invariably dogged by cost overruns, whereas, to his credit, Yerkes seems to have built his lines on schedule and on budget, though the opaqueness of the contracting arrangements means it is impossible to verify that absolutely.

The timing of the building of the tube lines was fortuitous and Londoners owe Yerkes rather more than may be apparent. Just as Pearson's foresight ensured the construction of underground railways long before any other countries were considering such schemes, and otherwise they might never have happened at all, so, too, did Yerkes ensure that London had a tube network. It is no exaggeration to say that, without him, many of the tube lines might never have been built. As we have seen, while the plans to build them had been given Parliamentary sanction, they were all stalled by planning and financial difficulties.

Had there been a delay of even as little as ten years, the competition from the motor bus would have deterred investors. The idea of the motor bus began to be considered in the late 1890s, and after various failed experiments with electric and steam vehicles, the first one ran on London's streets before the century was out. In October 1899, the Motor Traction Company started running two twenty-six-seater buses, powered by Daimler engines, between Kennington and Victoria, later extending the route to Oxford Circus. The service lasted just over a year and there was a smattering of other efforts, but fortunately for Yerkes, at the time when he was seeking capital for his various railway enterprises, in 1901–2, the motor buses had not managed to get a toehold in the market, nor to present a convincing case for potential investors despite the fact that the petrol engine technology was becoming more reliable. It was not, in fact, until 1905 that motor buses began to be used in any great numbers and start to displace the horse buses which, while cheaper to purchase, were much more expensive to run, oats being more expensive than petrol.

Therefore Yerkes had sufficient time to obtain capital and, crucially, start building his railway before the arrival of the much less capital-intensive and potentially profitable motor buses. It was just in time given that the war would have stopped the construction of any planned railways, and the technological developments it engendered gave motor transport even more of a competitive advantage compared with rail. Yerkes's amazing feat in raising the vast sum of £18m to push through the construction of these lines was crucial in ensuring that London got its Tube network. Given the crucial role these lines played during the interwar years in fostering the growth of the northern suburbs, it could be argued that much of London owes its existence to the early failure to take advantage of the internal combustion engine.

The depth of Yerkes's achievement is made greater, too, by the fact that he built the central parts of the system, which were the most expensive and technically difficult, rather than bringing in a semi-suburban railway to meet the Circle line at the edge of the capital in the hope of raising revenue to continue work. Moreover, Yerkes bravely raised all the funds in one huge deal. What he told the investors to persuade them to stump up the money is unclear, but the poor souls did not make any money.

Yerkes never saw any of these tube lines open. Like Pearson before him, he died before seeing the fruits of his efforts. In ill-health, he had chaired a meeting of the UERL where he had to calm down irate directors representing worried shareholders, and the following month he returned to the USA where he died of kidney disease on 29 December at the Waldorf-Astoria hotel, a few blocks from his own mansion where his estranged wife was living. His debts ate up most of his intended bequests, but his great legacy, the Underground Electric Railway Limited, survived, with Yerkes's banker, Sir Edgar Speyer, as chairman. When the UERL took over two more tube lines just before the Great War, the City & South London section of what became the Northern and the Central, it would become known as the Combine, controlling all major underground lines apart from the Metropolitan. Thanks to Yerkes, London had its tube system. Melding it into a coherent network was the task of his successors.

NINE

BEGINNING TO

MAKE SENSE

The pattern of London's Underground network was now set. It was not to be until the late 1960s that another tube line under the centre of London would be opened but, for the time being, there was plenty of spare capacity and some duplication, where lines competed against each other, in a system which had expanded at such a breathtaking pace. The haphazard method of development was partly the price London had paid for being a pioneer, and partly due to the refusal of the government to engage with the planning of the system, leaving it all to the capricious Parliamentary process. The French system of central planning was not the British way, which was still dominated by its emphasis on entrepreneurship and a disdain for government involvement, notably the refusal of the state to pay for these railways.

However, the system could not continue as a random collection of uncoordinated lines, and the next two decades of Underground history were more about consolidation and creating a coherent administrative structure following the exciting Edwardian period of development. That does not mean that this era was either dull or unadventurous since there were, after the war, significant extensions into the suburbs and the establishment of the London Transport Passenger Board at the end of the period was a ground-breaking triumph. And just as the physical creation of the network required pioneers and heroes such as Pearson, Watkin, Forbes and Yerkes, so did its melding into the most famous and respected transport system in the world. Again, it was two very different men who achieved that success, this time working together, even though at times their relationship was difficult: Frank Pick who joined the Underground Electric Railway Limited at a junior managerial level in 1906 and became chief executive of London Transport on its creation; and Albert Stanley (later Lord Ashfield) who joined the UERL in 1907 and eventually became chairman of London Transport.

The years before the Great War were the start of the consolidation and integration of London's transport system through a concentration of ownership and the creation of links, both physical and practical, such as the use of through-ticketing between lines. But it was to take twenty years, interrupted by the world's greatest conflict, to knit the disparate bits of London's transport system into London Transport. First there was the issue of saving the Underground from bankruptcy, which was the responsibility of Speyer and his new managing director (later Sir) George Gibb. The parts played by both Speyer and Gibb in this story may be minor when set against the likes of a Pearson or Pick but they are nevertheless highly significant. Speyer took on Gibb because he realized he needed an experienced railway operator following the departure and death of Yerkes. Gibb, a Scottish solicitor, was what we would now call a moderniser – broad-minded and accessible – traits rarely found then in the rail industry. He had previously been general manager of the North Eastern Railway where he had reformed the administration, notably making use of statistics to inform business decisions, which may sound obvious but was innovatory at the time and became the basis of his efforts to simplify the Underground structure. Unlike many railway operators, who tended to be insular, he learned from the experience of a visit to the USA and attempted to apply ideas from there. He was also unlike his peers in being friendly towards the press, despite its overall hostile attitude towards the railways, and even took an interest in transport economics. Gibb's most outstanding but unwitting legacy was that he appointed both Pick and Stanley, the men who were to shape London's transport for a third of a century.

There had been several missed opportunities to create a more coherent structure for the Underground, rather than allowing it to be at the mercy of free market forces. Private ownership of such a metro system is not sensible given the central role it plays in a city's life, the impossibility of making even well-used lines pay for themselves without subsidy let alone provide a decent return for investors, and the need to develop the network in the way that maximizes social benefit. The left-leaning London County Council had realized this as early as 1902, when it sought to obtain overall control of the network by becoming a traffic authority with powers to plan and control all London's Underground railways like the New York Rapid Transit Commission on the other side of the Atlantic. But no Edwardian government was going to agree to that, and instead, in the traditional way of British politicians seeking to defer decisions, it announced a Royal Commission on transport in the capital.

A more concerted attempt to take over the Underground was made in April 1906 by Sidney and Beatrice Webb, the illustrious socialists who founded the Fabian movement. Sidney sat on the LCC for all the Edwardian years and Beatrice, in her diary, recalls a meeting with Sir Edgar Speyer and Gibb who wanted the LCC to raise £5m for the UERL to become a sleeping partner – an early version of a public private partnership – with the right to take full control twenty-one or forty years later. However, the Progressives soon lost power and the Conservatives who replaced them were not interested in such municipalization.[1]

At the opening ceremony of the Hampstead tube, both Gibb and Speyer pleaded publicly with David Lloyd George, the president of the Board of Trade, to help their dire financial situation, arguing that the level of losses by the Underground companies was unsustainable and that London was alone among major cities in not subsidizing its transport system.[2] They wanted the government to help either through financial support or regulation of the rival bus and railway companies. It was not to be. Lloyd George fobbed them off by remarking that he was not going to come to the rescue with any 'socialistic legislation'.[3]

Unable to seek government help, Speyer and Gibb had to persuade their shareholders to allow them to restructure the company's finances. Not an easy task when, essentially, investors had been sold a pup. The crisis was brought to a head by the promise Yerkes had made to redeem his £7m worth of junk bonds, the 'profit sharing notes', on 30 June 1908. By the time the three tube lines had opened, the value of the £100 notes had fallen to a third of their sale price and Speyer had to bail out the company with his bank's money by paying off shareholders who were threatening to launch bankruptcy proceedings. The solution put together by Speyer and Gibb was the only one available – to convert the notes into long-term debt, redeemable in 1933 and 1948.[4] The shareholders reluctantly accepted the arrangement, realizing, as in all such situations, they had little choice since bankruptcy would have left them with nothing.

Why had it proved impossible to run the fantastic tube network and District line at a profit? At one of a series of acrimonious meetings, in May 1908, Speyer outlined what had gone wrong: unfavourable money markets (in which to redeem the profit-sharing notes); delays in completion (though, in reality, that was merely a result of over-optimistic scheduling without contingency plans since the lines were built remarkably quickly and with no major problems such as tunnel collapses or unexpected geological conditions); bus and tram competition (fair enough, as both were expanding); late changes required by Parliament (changes in scope are always a difficulty with big schemes); fares which were too low (a criticism of Yerkes's strategy of flat fares); and the burden of taxes and rates (highly predictable and a lame excuse). Speyer did have the grace to admit that mistakes had been made by his traffic experts and, in truth, the failure to attract numbers to match those over-optimistic predictions was the major cause of the company's parlous state.

Gibb endured an awful first year in the job, trying to stave off bankruptcy and boost passenger numbers. Even by the time of the debt rescheduling, Speyer and Gibb were making progress on a programme to improve the financial situation of the business, both by reducing costs and increasing revenue. On costs, Gibb tried to bring together the various lines under one management but this was thwarted by the American interests who were worried about losing potential capital gains on what were virtually worthless shares. It was only when Stanley took over in 1910 that the change was pushed through.

On the revenue side, the company moved away from the idea of flat fares which Yerkes had always supported. Uniform fares had made travel too cheap and, more important, were not compatible with encouraging through bookings with other transport systems. If passengers were to be allowed to buy tickets which involved the use of more than one line, there had to be differentiation between short and long journeys as London's system was simply too large to set a single fare that was a fair average for all travellers. However, introducing gradations of a halfpenny went too far in the other direction and the system could have been simplified, something that did not happen until Ken Livingstone introduced his Fares Fair system, based on zones, in the 1980s. The non UERL lines such as the City & South London and the Central, which had started with single fares, had also gradually moved away from the concept as their lines lengthened and competition from bus and trams forced them to try to maximize revenue.

For a brief enlightened moment in 1907, there were efforts by the majority of transport undertakings in London, both rail and bus, to coordinate their fares policies. The process started with an agreement between the various operators of east–west services which resulted in the Central increasing fares for longer journeys to threepence and the Metropolitan making corresponding increases on the Hammersmith.

Following this agreement, a meeting was held involving bus and tram as well as Underground interests, and even the North London Railway, which also managed to agree a series of coordinated fare rises. But ultimately these companies were private concerns in competition with one another, and without any legislative backing their cooperative efforts were bound to peter out.

While the bus and tram operators soon withdrew, the various Underground operators decided to form a joint committee to discuss fares and related issues; they realized that there was more to gain through coordination than through cut-throat competition, given the growing threat from motor buses. A meeting of all the underground line owners, including the Metropolitan and others not controlled by the UERL created a joint booking system allowing through journeys without having to buy a second ticket, and this was gradually introduced throughout the system and parts of the main line railways. The underground line owners also agreed to install illuminated signs outside each station with the word 'UndergrounD', with the familiar capital first and last letters replacing the rather more prosaic but handy word 'Tube', favoured by the Central.

This branding was the brainchild of Albert Stanley who was already working behind the scenes in bringing together the disparate transport methods in the capital. The beginnings of an integrated London Transport system were being created, fittingly, by the man who would eventually lead it. Stanley was first appointed at the instigation of the US investors who wanted to prevent the merger of the management of the lines in order to protect their investment but, ironically, was soon to recommend the same strategy. Born into a humble Derbyshire family, Stanley[5] had gone to America with his family as a small child and worked on the railways from the age of fourteen, starting as a messenger boy with the Detroit tramways company. His obvious administrative and strategic talents must have been immediately apparent, as by the age of eighteen he was made a divisional superintendent and two years later overall superintendent responsible for the opening of many new lines. He moved to New Jersey where again promotion was rapid, and he was given responsibility for the state's tramways in 1904 and for all its transport operations three years later. But he spent little time in that job as in 1907 Gibb, who had become aware of Stanley's talent on his 1901 visit to the USA, invited him to return to Britain as the general manager of the UERL.

Stanley, who of all the Underground pioneers probably achieved the most simply because he was to work for the organization for over thirty years, said later that he had been reluctant to leave New Jersey, in view of his recent promotion, and only came on the understanding that he could return within a year. Stanley is also reported[6] to have told his senior managers that the UERL was bankrupt and he wanted resignation letters from all of them post-dated six months ahead. He then borrowed £50,000 from the banks to pay for publicity but soon found that the local London press was amenable to publishing news about improvements to the system. In that sense, Stanley, amongst all his other talents, was a pioneer of PR techniques, as well as a brilliant operator of railway systems.

For instance, until Stanley's intervention, the Yerkes tube lines had each produced their own publicity literature, a wasteful duplication.[7] Now, a huge publicity campaign was launched, involving the production of 6 million free leaflet-sized maps of the system, showing each line in a different colour, which could be picked up at stations or hotels, restaurants and even ocean liners. It was a breakthrough in showing integrated information, although it was still fairly confusing compared with the simple brilliance of the version Harry Beck designed in the 1930s.[8] Large enamelled copies of the map were displayed at stations and outside there were illuminated versions under the slogan 'Anywhere Quickest Way Cheapest Fare'. This slogan was the idea of a fourteen-year-old boy who had entered a competition organized by the Evening News on the instigation of Stanley, another example of his talent at dealing with the press. There was even a game called 'How to get there?', based on Ludo, with various penalties and obstacles for lost tickets or signal stops, which the *Railway Gazette* ribbed mercilessly by suggesting further forfeits such as 'Breakdown on District, proceed on foot', 'City & South London closed for cleaning, retire from game' and, best of all, 'polite conductor on Hampstead Tube – miss eight moves through shock'.

Most importantly, this was the period when the roundel, the bar and circle sign, one of the world's most famous early corporate symbols, was developed for station names. There is confusion about the precise origin (although a similar device had been used by General Buses from around 1905). The elegant tiles of the stations were becoming messy as advertisements proliferated, and the printed strips bearing the station names were difficult to distinguish from the other displays. To deal with this, from 1913 the names started being shown on signs with a bar across a red circle. The Metropolitan used a diamond instead of a circle and several other versions of the basic idea were tried until Pick, after a lot of experimentation, chose the current design.

Again, Stanley was behind the idea and he introduced several other innovations to improve what would now be known as 'the passenger experience'. These were simple, such as 'next lift' indicators; ensuring that line diagrams were placed inside trains; coordinating lift departures with train arrivals; and timetabling the trains to run at regular intervals. Stanley realized that however good the marketing, to attract and retain passengers, services had to improve; and he devoted a lot of energy to reducing journey times and delays, and increasing frequencies. On the overcrowded District, for example, he managed to increase the number of trains from a maximum of twenty-four per hour in 1907 to an amazing forty per hour – i.e. just ninety seconds apart – by the end of 1911, rather more than today's maximum of thirty per hour, albeit today's trains are longer.

On the tubes, too, there were improvements, with the time between Hammersmith and Finsbury Park on the Piccadilly cut from thirty-eight to thirty-three minutes. Express trains were introduced on the Hampstead branch, with some trains not stopping between Golders

Green and Euston, and although this could hardly have pleased the residents near intermediate stations, the experiment was judged a success. A system of alternate trains stopping at every other station was introduced on parts of both the Hampstead line and the Piccadilly, which meant the fastest trains on the latter covered the distance between the two termini in just twenty-eight minutes. Frequencies on the tubes were increased with the Bakerloo running thirty-four per hour and the Hampstead, south of the junction at Camden Town, by September 1909 reaching forty-two per hour, with the claim that it was 'the most frequent train service in the world'. Hours of running were extended, too, with the last trains leaving central London at 1 a.m., again rather better than today's service.

The rival Metropolitan also got in on the act of making improvements, by running more trains on the Hammersmith & City after it was electrified in 1907, increasing frequency from six to eight per hour and cutting the journey time between Hammersmith and Aldgate from thirty-nine to thirty-two minutes. The Metropolitan's most luxurious innovation, though, was the introduction in 1910 of a Pullman service on its Aylesbury to Liverpool Street service. Two coaches, *Mayflower* and *Galatea* (named after the two yachts which competed in the 1886 America's Cup), were each fitted with nineteen upholstered armchairs at which meals were served. The 8.30 a.m. from Aylesbury reached Liverpool Street at 9.57, suggesting that those who could afford such luxury did not have to be in the office as early as their underlings, who would have started at least an hour before that. People who had been to see a play in London could enjoy a late dinner on the theatre special which left Baker Street at 11.35 p.m.

Another development on the UERL lines which made passengers' lives slightly easier was the introduction of strip tickets (now called carnets), which were later dropped and not revived until the late 1990s. This allowed regular passengers to buy a strip of half a dozen tickets at a small discount, enabling them to avoid the rush hour queues at booking offices. These were an instant hit. *The Times*[9] reported that 100,000 such tickets had been sold in the first week 'and they were increasing in popularity every week'. The tickets were transferable and meant that three people travelling together could buy a strip of six and save a bit of money, and avoid having to queue. In fact, the tickets were not an entirely new idea, having been tried out for a while on the Piccadilly, as mentioned in Chapter 8. Therefore, the coverage in *The Times* is again testimony to Stanley's PR skills, as the article is little more than a puff culminating in the very complimentary statement that 'The object of the Underground is expressed in the words "no waiting". The lifts work in conjunction with the trains, and the trains run at such frequent intervals that a passenger never has to wait above a few seconds, therefore the object of the strip tickets is to eliminate the only other possibility of delay – namely, that of waiting behind a *queue* at the booking office for the issue of tickets.'

All these measures, together with a growth spurt in the economy up to 1909, led to a significant rise in the number of passengers. On the Bakerloo, for example, by 1909 there were frequent complaints about overcrowding. There were irate letters in *The Times* during the first two months of that year – but, to put matters in perspective, one correspondent was shocked at finding twenty-five straphangers standing in his carriage.[10] One passenger even wrote in to say that he had been unable to alight at Regent's Park and had been carried on to Oxford Circus, and when he complained the guard merely told him that he had no right to stand so far down the carriage if he expected to get off at the next stop. As a result of the increased traffic, the three UERL tube lines managed to pay modest dividends of between 0.75 to 1.25 per cent to their shareholders by 1910. This was nowhere near a decent rate of return as investors could get far more by simply lending to the government, but it was better than nothing, which had been their lot for several years. Despite the shareholders' initial misgivings, Stanley managed to push through the merger of the three tube lines so that they all came under his management, which saved costs; but the District remained, for the time being, separately run.

Stanley's agenda was always to unify and integrate all of London's transport and in early 1912 he took a giant step towards that goal by gaining control of the largest bus company, the London General Omnibus Company, which had, after a series of mergers, become the capital's dominant operator and thus created what became known as the Combine. This acquisition not only allowed Stanley to integrate the services in such a way that direct competition against his own underground lines was reduced, but also ensured he could weaken the remaining three lines outside his control by using buses to run against them. It was a clever move:

> By this shrewd and far-sighted manoeuvre, the Underground
> Company had neatly removed a most dangerous source of
> competition and brought into its family a lusty profit earner
> which could support the poorer relations; it had avoided the
> otherwise inevitable establishment of its own bus fleet and could
> now contemplate the prospect of a vast integrated transport
> system based on through bookings and connected services.[11]

The bus company had paid dividends of 18 per cent the previous year, as it exploited the attraction of motor buses which, together with its monopoly position, created a period of super-profits. After the merger of the two companies, the hidden subsidy from buses underpinned the economics of London's transport system and protected the much weaker finances of the Underground network.

Not surprisingly, the various other underground lines in London were struggling too. The Central, for example, which had boasted 45 million passengers in 1903, carried just under 36 million in 1912 as a result of bus competition. Its ridership had been boosted in 1908 by the Franco-British Exhibition, but it was now declining and the company could only muster a 3 per cent dividend for its shareholders. The City & South London was now over twenty years old, and in need of major investment. The parlous state of these two companies left them ripe for takeover, especially now that the Underground Company could run buses against them. In November 1912, after a series of secret talks, plans to acquire the two lines were announced by Stanley. Neither was in a position to demand a big price for acquisition by the Underground Company. The shareholders of the Central, which was in a healthier state, got a much better deal, receiving the equivalent value of stock in the new company, while the owners of the City & South London had to settle for a mere two thirds of the value of their shares. The Underground Company's own weakness meant it had to offer shares rather than cash but nevertheless both deals went through on New Year's Day 1913, the shareholders presumably realizing that it was the best they were going to get. At the same time, the full gauge Great Northern & City was bought by the Metropolitan with the intention of integrating it into its system, but various attempts to link up with other railways, notably the Waterloo & City, failed. It remained a white elephant, although passengers numbers increased marginally as a result of the introduction by the Metropolitan of faster and more frequent trains. The one curiosity of the line was that in 1915 the Metropolitan introduced first-class accommodation on the Great Northern & City trains, making it the only tube railway ever to offer more than one class, a provision which remained until 1934. Meanwhile the Waterloo & City itself had an uneventful time, remaining in the ownership of the London & South Western Railway and enjoying a separate but successful existence.

The Central was immediately tarted up, stations were cleaned and equipped with the standard roundels. The maximum fare on the Central was reduced from threepence halfpenny to threepence and more through tickets to connect with other transport routes were made available. Other minor improvements included converting lift gates to compressed air and speeding up services through resignalling. Escalators were already becoming the norm. The Central, which had extended to Liverpool Street in 1912, used escalators at the new station and they were also installed when the Bakerloo was pushed out to Paddington in 1914. Indeed, from 1913, all new deep-level stations were fitted with escalators rather than lifts. These extensions to Liverpool Street and Paddington were good for business by making up for the original failure of the tube lines to connect with main line stations, unlike the original Metropolitan and District railways which had been built with the specific aim of creating such links.

During this pre-war period, there were several other improvements and brief extensions to improve connections on the system, with the main line railways as well as with other underground lines. Both Gibb and, particularly, Stanley understood that there was a great need for better interchanges, which would improve the service for passengers and boost revenue for operators. This was to be the start of a long process of knitting together the disparate lines, which often ran over and underneath each other without connection or were linked only at the surface level so that passengers had to leave the system, walk to the other station and probably buy another ticket. Oxford Circus, for example, was served by two different stations on the Bakerloo and Central, which, as one history puts it, 'frowned at each other across Argyll Street'.[12] No longer. In November 1912, work began on a new concourse and a subway connection between the two lines. On the Central, a new interchange with the Piccadilly was planned to be built at Holborn, replacing the old British Museum station, although the scheme was delayed by the war. The most chaotic situation was at Charing Cross and Embankment, where the Bakerloo, Hampstead and District lines all had separate stations within a couple of hundred yards of each other despite being owned by the same company. In 1914, the Hampstead line was extended underneath the District and the two lines were connected by escalators. A further set of escalators was built to link the District with the Bakerloo, reducing the time to make a connection from three minutes and fifteen seconds to one minute and forty-five seconds. A new station – then called Charing Cross but now Embankment – was built on the surface; John Betjeman described it as 'the most charming of all the Edwardian and neo-Georgian

Renaissance stations'.[13] The Hampstead line retained a station underneath Charing Cross station, and over the decades the various stations around Charing Cross have been called Embankment, Strand, Charing Cross and Trafalgar Square, with the same name on occasion being transferred from one station to another in a way that has confused many Londoners.

The other major pre-war change was on the Bakerloo which, after reaching Paddington, was extended further outwards. This is the first example of a tube line expanding far out into the open air in order to generate traffic and was to become a model that was later widely adopted, creating a dual role for London's tube railways as an underground system in the centre and a suburban one outside. Outside the centre, construction, which was mostly on the surface, was, of course, much cheaper and the tube lines were in many respects following in the path of their sub-surface predecessors.

The District in particular made good use of its extensions by running a variety of innovative services, especially excursions which proved popular – not least because journeys on the electrified lines were comfortable and smooth. The longest service went all the way from Ealing to Southend and included a stop at Barking to change from an electric to a steam locomotive. These day trips to the seaside stimulated the opening of resort cafés which were entirely dependent on this trade. During the summer, Ealing, Ruislip and Osterley were popular destinations for school trips and families to get out of the polluted capital. The wildlife, however, was rather taken by surprise by the quiet electrified trains. According to a history of the line, 'so many birds and beasts were killed by District trains on the countrified South Harrow branch that the District set up a natural history collection of stuffed creatures in glass cases, which was displayed at Charing Cross',[14] including an otter killed in April 1911.

Stanley's policy of expanding the tube lines outward did not really get under way until after the First World War, with the exception of the Bakerloo's incursion into the countryside. Once the Bakerloo had reached Paddington, it was always envisaged that the line would break out of the tunnels into the suburbs. However, that extension required a joint project with the country's most profitable and dynamic railway, the London & North Western, alongside whose lines it was planned to run. The North Western had been disdainful of suburban services because its main line traffic to Birmingham and the industrial towns of the north-west, together with highly lucrative freight business, were profitable enough to satisfy the shareholders. The company felt it did not need the complication of running a lot of stopping trains which would clog up the lines at the entrance to Euston. Therefore, unlike on the other main London railways, particularly those south of the river, there were few stations on the North Western in the outskirts of London, a mere eight between Willesden and Tring, twenty-six miles away – more like the pattern on a meandering country railway. To its credit, the North Western provided an excellent service from those stations, which all quickly became the hubs of growing developments stimulated by the railways' policy of cheap season tickets. Watford, notably, was the biggest of these new towns and grew rapidly.

From 1910, the far-sighted London & North Western, which never did things by half, decided to step up the level of services in order to boost its income and embarked on an ambitious plan of development. An entirely new two-track line was to be built solely for the suburban services, with extra intermediate stations and electrification installed. Stanley saw this as an unprecedented opportunity to take part in a scheme that was to play a key role in the development of north-west London. The Underground Company negotiated an alliance with the North Western to adopt the same electrification technology as the Yerkes tubes and to allow Bakerloo trains to operate out to Watford after emerging from the tunnel at Queen's Park to join the main line railway three and a half miles out of Euston. The North Western reckoned it would benefit from being able to offer services that ran right through to Elephant & Castle from Watford. Work on the scheme was already well under way when war broke out in August

1914, by which time the new suburban line between Willesden and Watford had opened, and, amazingly, was seen as such a priority that construction continued with virtually unimpaired progress during the hostilities. By May 1915 Bakerloo trains were running to Willesden and two years later through to Watford.

There is still something incongruous about seeing tube trains, with their flat fronts designed to push the air through the dark tunnels, out in the open. Those on the Bakerloo must have been a particularly strange sight when running alongside the huge steam locomotives operating the main line services out of Euston. However, these tube trains were going to become an increasingly common sight in London's suburbs. But first there was the Great War to endure, which halted most development on the Underground and, importantly, led to a hiatus in the planning process.

TEN

THE UNDERGROUND

IN THE

FIRST WORLD WAR

While the story of the Underground as air raid shelter during the Second World War is part of British folklore, it is much less well known that, briefly, thousands took refuge there during the First World War. The number of passengers using the system also went up sharply and the war marked the point at which both government and Londoners recognized the vital role of the Underground in moving people around the capital.

London suffered its first aerial bombardment on 31 May 1915 when a Zeppelin airship suddenly appeared over north-east London and dropped a ton of bombs, killing seven people and wounding thirty-five. A succession of raids continued through that summer. The orders of the Kaiser were that attacks should be targeted only at naval military installations, but dropping ordnance out of Zeppelins or primitive aircraft was a crude business and most of the damage was caused to civilian targets and population.

It was, perhaps, unsurprising that people assumed the Underground system was the safest place to be during such raids. The irony was that at the onset of the war, in August 1914, there had been a scare prompted by G.A. Nokes, the critic of 'Bakerloo' and by then the editor of the *Railway and Travel Monthly*, suggesting that the system was being used as a store for German armaments.[1] Nokes was such an eminent railway journalist and author that his ridiculous allegation resulted in a fruitless search by the police of the disused section of tunnel on the City & South London. Once the raids started, people began flocking to the Underground, either riding around on the trains or sitting at stations.

Unlike at the outset of the Second World War, both the Underground Company and the authorities were happy for people to use the system as a shelter. Antwerp had been bombed from Zeppelins as early as August 1914 and this had raised the notion that London could be attacked in a similar way. Even before the first attack, the Underground Company had responded with publicity deliberately designed to encourage people to seek protection in its system from the bombing. In October 1914, one advertisement read: 'It is bomb proof down below. Underground for safety; plenty of bright trains, business as usual'. Another said:

Never mind the dark and dangerous streets
Underground
It is warm and bright
Be comfortable in well-lit trains and read the latest war news.

The Zeppelin raids were very sporadic and though, for a while, people sought shelter in the Underground, the attacks ceased and the issue did not become a problem. During those first raids, there were as many as 12,000 shelterers at Finsbury Park and 9,000 at King's Cross, many of whom had simply been held up when train services stopped, as initially all trains were halted until the 'all clear' was sounded, although this was later relaxed. The bloodiest raids by the Zeppelins were on two nights in September 1915 when forty people were killed, but aircraft attacks proved more destructive. It was not until a concentrated bombing by aircraft in September 1917 that the masses began to use the Underground system to shelter regularly. On hearing of a raid, the police, some on bicycles, would carry round 'Take Cover' signs and encourage people to head for the Underground. The Underground Company allowed its station passages and platforms to be used and was compensated by the Home Office with a mere £130 per week to pay for the extra personnel and lighting required. The company provided eighty-six stations for the shelterers, with an estimated capacity of 250,000. When there were successive raids on the 24th and 25th, which suggested that the attacks might be nightly, an estimated 100,000 people started sheltering and the authorities became concerned about the problem.

The original idea had been that only people caught inadvertently in the streets should shelter in the Underground there, but instead the system began to fill up with frightened crowds even before any warning had been sounded. And they brought everything with them. They ignored the posters which stressed that 'people sheltering are not allowed to take birds, dogs, cats and other animals on to the Company's premises' and came ready to spend the whole night, taking bedding and food as well as their pets. Some started travelling round in trains, the Circle being a favourite, 'partaking of refreshments' they had brought with them, according to the *Railway Gazette*,[2] because it was less boring than staying in the same place and the trains continued running as long as a warning had not been sounded. It was, the *Gazette* stressed, principally 'people of the poorer classes, mostly aliens, women and children' who used the system during raids. As a result, travellers going about their normal business were allegedly being inconvenienced, especially since, as we see below, record numbers of passengers had started using the system. In many ways it was a prelude to what was to happen a quarter of a century later during the Second World War, and indeed set the tone for the authorities' opposition in 1939 to the use of the system as a shelter. In fact, according to a police memorandum[3] little inconvenience had been caused to passenger traffic by the shelterers, who remained 'orderly and obedient' throughout.

Concerned that people would expect nightly raids and therefore block the system by heading down there every night, the authorities decided that only ticket-holders should be able to go down into the system except when an air raid warning had been sounded. Yet on the very night these restrictions were imposed, on 28 September, a Russian woman was killed in the crush at Liverpool Street station, again a portent to much more serious incidents in the Second World War.

The report into the use of the Underground as a shelter during the First World War estimated that in response to the thirty-one attacks, some 4,250,000 people had used the system. That would suggest around 140,000 every night of a raid, though fewer if the figures included nights in which there were no attacks. The peak was on 17 February 1918 with 300,000 crowding into the system, well above its official capacity. This prompted enquiries in Parliament about hygiene and disease, but the Home Secretary, Sir George Cave, allayed fears by announcing that the stations were in every case thoroughly cleansed and disinfected by the management before traffic was resumed – a claim that was probably more propaganda than substance considering the task faced by the Underground Company, which had lost many of its staff to the war effort.

Indeed, the greatest social impact of the war on the Underground was the employment of women for the first time in the history of the system. They took over the men's jobs in large numbers and were essential in keeping the network running. At the height of the war, half the 3,000 District's employees were women, and a third of the 4,000-strong Metropolitan workforce. Whole stations came under the control of women, with the newly opened Maida Vale leading the way, though it shared a male stationmaster with three neighbouring stations. The *Railway Gazette* grudgingly recognized this as 'preferable to employing hobbledehoys' and women continued to take on new tasks, replacing gatemen on trains in 1917, but the roles of guard and driver remained the preserve of men. Women received the same wages as men, which, given the gender inequalities in other industries between the two, was a remarkably enlightened policy, forced on the management by the trade unions. However, the women were displaced by men returning from the war and the system reverted to being run entirely by men.

It was not only people who found shelter in the Underground during the Great War. Sections of the tube system were used for the storage of museum treasures and paintings, clearly a sign that the authorities were concerned about widespread bombing, even though, in the event, that particular threat never materialized. The disused platform at Aldwych was sealed off, and in September 1917 over 300 pictures from the National Gallery, about one tenth of the collection, were housed there until December 1918. The miniature post office railway, being built to transport mail between sorting offices using automatic trains, was used to store parts of the collection of the Tate, the National Portrait Gallery, and the Public Record Office.[4] The Victoria & Albert used a nearby spare station tunnel at South Kensington, shared with cases of china from Buckingham Palace. All these precautions were carried out too late in the war to be useful and proved unnecessary since, after that damaging raid on 17 February 1918, there were only two further attacks, London had strengthened its air defences and the Germans had largely lost faith in their ability to win the war.

When the attacks ended, the *Daily Mail* published a map of where bombs had fallen; there was a clear pattern of attacks along main arterial routes and in the centre of London. The final toll was 670 deaths and nearly 2,000 wounded. The Underground was not a specific target but the railways had been and several stations and lines were attacked, though damage was fairly minimal. Indeed, more disruption was caused by the authorities' decision to suspend all underground and main line railway traffic during raids than by the consequent damage. This rule was later relaxed and trains were allowed to proceed slowly during attacks, which was a sensible compromise between safety and the need to keep transport links functioning in wartime.

The war highlighted the vulnerability of the system to attack. Indeed, to protect the system itself, the Underground Company had wanted to install flood doors in case bombs caused a breach. In response to the outbreak of war, four temporary timber baulk barriers were created. They consisted of steel framework supports in which heavy timber baulks could be dropped to seal the twin tunnel mouths at the south end of Charing Cross station and the north end of Waterloo on the Bakerloo. Each barrier would take almost an hour to install and they were only designed to check immediate flooding. Nevertheless, this rather crude system required the constant allocation of 100 men on stand-by in case of a breach. A more permanent solution of steel doors was suggested by the Underground Company but as this would have required 170 tons of steel that could otherwise be used for ammunition, the Ministry of War rejected the idea. Even when it was pointed out that sixty-five miles of tunnel could be flooded, with massive loss of life, the Ministry only relented enough to discuss the issue more urgently; and it was not until after the war that a lining of armour plate was installed on the Bakerloo Line either side of the river. To this day, flooding remains probably the greatest risk of a major catastrophe in the tube system, although much stronger defences have been built.

Apart from the use of the Underground as a massive air raid shelter, the Great War had two long-term effects on the Underground: a move towards integration which became irreversible and a massive rise in usage which was to create both problems and opportunities.

Although the Underground Company controlled most of the lines, each one still had separate accounts and shareholders, resulting in complex calculations to allocate revenue. To make matters even more complicated, the District line had been taken under direct control of the government, along with most of the main line railways, while management of the tube lines had been left with the company. This meant that District staff would receive a war bonus, but their counterparts on the tube lines would not. A strange consequence of this anomaly was that Stanley devised a plan to establish a common fund for receipts from the various lines, which convinced the government to pay the bonus to all the company's staff, including those working for the London General Omnibus Company. More importantly, this was the beginning of the kind of pooling arrangement which was essential to create an integrated transport system for the capital, towards which Stanley seemed always to be working. The arrangement protected the less profitable parts of the Combine, the rather Orwellian name increasingly used for Stanley's ever-growing empire, and meant that the shareholders' rates of return were equalized. Consequently, the owners of the bus company received less than under the previous arrangement, and the Underground stockholders more.

The overcrowding was also to have long-term consequences. At the beginning of the war, as mobilization resulted in hundreds of thousands of new recruits heading to training camps and to southern ports for transfer to France, the Underground Company allowed all uniformed men to travel free until 1 October 1914. But even after the soldiers had to pay, the Underground system had to cope with vastly increased traffic – in contrast with the Second World War when numbers were to go down. There were a variety of causes: the massive troop movements, leave travel, cutbacks in road services as vehicles were used for war and their drivers sent to the front, and the greater affluence that accompanied the high employment levels resulting from the conflict. The major history of the tube network suggests another reason: 'Another contributory factor [to the growth] was the dim-out enforced after dark as a precaution against air attack – people naturally preferred travel in the well-lit tube cars to slow bus and train journeys through darkened streets.'[5] Clearly the Underground

Company saw the war as an opportunity, too. For Easter 1915 the company issued a poster using the war in a ironic way to boost passenger numbers: 'Why bother about the Germans invading the country – invade it yourself by underground and the motor bus', a testimony to the confidence and courage of those running the company who were not scared of making light of a very sensitive subject.

The growth continued throughout the war and by 1917 was causing such overcrowding on the tube system that it engendered widespread criticism in the press and even Parliament. The limitations of the technology as originally designed were beginning to be felt. The attendant-operated lifts were slow and there was a shortage of rolling stock, exacerbated by the difficulty of getting spares during the war, which meant many trains were shorter than normal. Although some improvements were being made, such as controlling the lifts from landings (which was faster as well as saving labour), and replacing hydraulic operation with electric lifts or escalators, these were long-term investment programmes which would take decades to complete and had little short-term impact. The overcrowding problem was exacerbated when in May 1918 the government, through the Board of Trade (whose president was now none other than Sir Albert Stanley)[6], ordered a cutback in services because of concern over coal shortages, and several stations had to be closed early or on Sundays. Despite all the problems, overall use of the Underground increased by two thirds during the course of the war, and by the end of the conflict half of all passenger journeys in the capital were on the Underground system.

In terms of the numbers of trains, the busiest section was the Metropolitan's City widened lines, the link built fifty years previously to allow trains to go from Farringdon across the river and into the overground rail network. This was still one of only three rail connections through London, and the most direct. Therefore it had carried an extraordinary number of troop and other special military trains, a total of 26,000 during the war, an average of sixteen trains per day. At peak periods, in a build-up to an offensive, the traffic was much greater than that, reaching, for example, 210 daily for the first fortnight of 1915.

To cope with the crowds on the tube lines, various short-term measures were introduced, including barriers at platforms which slid open once the alighting passengers had left and queuing systems at the busier stations, but in reality little could be done to improve the situation except to increase the overall capacity. It is no exaggeration to suggest that the war made both government and the population realize the extent to which the Underground system was a vital part of the infrastructure of the capital – and even of the nation. The increased usage was so great that, together with a rise in fares of one third, it enabled modest dividends to be paid to all the various shareholders of the companies making up the Combine – with the exception of the District which was still unable to provide its owners with any return whatsoever. The Underground system came of age in the Great War, and now, with Stanley back at the helm after his stint in government, the stage was set for expanding and consolidating the network.

ELEVEN

REACHING OUT

While the short-term effect of the war had been to halt progress on a number of planned developments on the Underground system, the increase in passengers strengthened the case for these extensions to be built. Stanley understood that it would always be difficult to justify these new sections stretching far out into the suburbs and countryside in purely economic terms. Of course, they would generate additional traffic, but that would not be enough to compensate shareholders adequately for their investment and risk. The war therefore marked the end of the pretence that the Underground could be a solely private enterprise; all future work would have a public component in its funding.

Stanley had returned to the Underground after resigning as President of the Board of Trade in 1919 and became Lord Ashfield of Southwell in the 1920 New Year's Honours list. The two years at the Board of Trade proved to be vital experience for Ashfield, giving him the opportunity to see the world from the other side, an insider in government moving freely among civil servants, MPs and ministers. Previously, Ashfield had been a hands-on manager, wheeling and dealing and outwitting opponents by the sheer vision and clarity of his thinking. Now he became even more impressive, using diplomacy and charm as well as sheer force of intellect. His talent was always obvious but he was a complex character who did not give away much even in his personal writing. He was, therefore, a somewhat unfathomable genius who confused those who worked with him as they could never quite suss out his aims and motives. Ashfield, on the other hand, was very perceptive, with a sharp intuitive understanding of his fellow men, and he had that indefinable quality, presence, which allowed him to dominate meetings effortlessly. He inspired loyalty, devotion even, among his staff and he had a quality that was rare in those class-ridden days, the 'common touch'. There is no doubt that without this formidable character at the helm, the Underground would not have developed so comprehensively and extensively over the next two decades.

The Bakerloo's expansion to Watford having been completed despite the war, the next proposed extension was for the Central to run out to Ealing Broadway. That line had been opened without electrification to carry freight during the war, but now it needed intermediate stations and electrification to be integrated into the tube system, a task that was carried out quickly with services inaugurated on 3 August 1920. There were also well-developed plans for two extensions: Golders Green to Edgware on the Hampstead railway; and Shepherd's Bush to Gunnersbury on the Central, which in fact was never built. Ideas for several more were being floated, such as extending the District out to Sutton, linking Highgate with Muswell Hill and extending the Piccadilly beyond Hammersmith, only the last of which was ever realized. Before the war, as we have seen, the economics of such schemes made it impossible to provide adequate returns for shareholders. Now, with both labour and materials more expensive, the price of building a mile of fully equipped tube railway had risen from £600,000 in 1914 to £1m five years later (around £25m in today's money). The cost of borrowing capital for a private company was around 5½ per cent, while the deep tube lines were returning, even after a strong period of growth, a mere 2 per cent. The basic economics thus demonstrate why the building of lines and extensions on the basis of private capital was coming to an end.

The Underground, therefore, needed to obtain cheap money to fund these schemes. While the Victorian attitude of minimal government involvement was beginning to soften, obtaining direct grants to fund major infrastructure projects was not yet on the political agenda. However, underpinning such schemes with low-interest loans from the state was made possible by the need for Lloyd George's coalition government to tackle the growing unemployment problem. The post-war boom quickly turned into a major recession, with almost 2 million unemployed by 1921, and the government brought in legislation, the Trade Facilities Act, to encourage public works that would relieve unemployment through Treasury guarantees. Ashfield jumped at the chance and produced a £5m scheme for a variety of works including the extension to Hampstead, 250 new tube carriages and the linking of the Hampstead and City & South London lines at Euston to create what was to become the Northern Line.

The extension to Edgware marked a new departure for the tube railways, the first journey deep into the countryside without an existing main line railway to run alongside, in contrast to the Bakerloo's line to Watford which ran beside the London & North Western. At last Ashfield was beginning to achieve his ambition of enabling London to grow by creating lines which stimulated development. The section of line marked, too, the start of the new Underground policy which was to allow people to travel from the outer suburbs directly by train, rather than having to change at overcrowded interchanges from trams or buses. Since the Combine now controlled many of these bus and tram routes, it was in a position to run down services when they were in competition with new rail extensions, and ensure that they fed into the Underground rather than competed with it. The concept of 'integrated transport', a fashionable term among transport experts today, had not been developed, but Ashfield, more than many of today's planners, understood precisely what it meant and in a way can be said to have invented it.

Reaching Edgware involved building a viaduct over the Brent Valley, passing over what is now the North Circular – an impressive edifice for the little flat-fronted trains which spend most of their time in dark tunnels. The ten-year delay between the original approval for extending the line beyond Golders Green and the start of work as a result of the war meant not only a doubling of the cost but also, rather embarrassingly for the Underground company, demolishing some of the very houses which the company had encouraged to be built, because of a change in the northward route.

The open-air stations on the Central's extension were modest affairs that were little more than shacks, but Pick, who was now assistant managing director of the company, wanted something rather more permanent and stylish for the Edgware extension. The stations at Hendon and Brent were an attempt by the architect, S.A. Heaps, to develop a new suburban type of station. Clearly the late Green's dark ruby tiled walls would have looked incongruous in suburban and rural settings. Heaps went for a rather conventional classical style, with Portland stone porticos of large Doric columns and spacious but simple brick booking halls. At the centre were oak passimeter ticket offices, which had previously only been installed at Kilburn Park in 1921. Passimeters, an American concept, were free-standing booths, fitted out with modern ticketing equipment, which allowed passengers' tickets to be both issued and checked without having staff at the barriers. They were an ideal labour-saving device for lightly used stations as they enabled the booking clerks both to issue and check tickets from the comfort of their booth. Their awful name, derived from the devices which counted the passengers as they passed through turnstiles on either side of the booth, belied their elegant rectangular shape. Similar booths became fairly standard at outlying Underground stations, but the name, fortunately, did not pass into current usage.

In contrast, Burnt Oak only had a small shed as a ticket office, and no accommodation for passengers as there were none! The station was entirely surrounded by fields, linked to the Edgware Road by an expensive new approach road that foretold of further development. It was only in 1926 when the London County Council starting building the Watling Estate around the station that traffic picked up, and in 1928 a Heaps Georgian-style building was erected. Fortunately, thereafter Pick did not persevere with Heaps, turning instead to Charles Holden, who, as we see below, built a series of futuristic stations which remain today the only notable buildings in most of the districts they serve.

By the time the Edgware extension opened in the summer of 1924, the village of barely 1,000 souls had a fast and frequent train service to Charing Cross, with a train every ten minutes taking just half an hour to reach the West End. Clearly, the provision of such a good service was predicated on the expectation of rapid growth.

The line that was to become the Northern was beginning to take shape. A link between Kennington and Charing Cross was built, which, together with the new Camden Town to Euston section, created a loop which allowed trains from the south to go on either the Bank or Charing Cross branches. However, to integrate the Hampstead tube fully with the City & South London required the difficult task of enlarging the older section's tunnels, by replacing all 22,000 supporting rings which had been built to a slightly smaller gauge. The platforms also needed lengthening so that the whole route could take seven-car trains. That was not only an expensive operation which caused major disruption during 1922–3 but also resulted in one of the rare major tunnel collapses in the history of the Underground.

On 27 November 1923, a train hit a wooden board used to shield the work from the passing train and when the driver stopped to remove it, his guard informed him that there was water and gravel coming into the tunnel behind the train. With great presence of mind the driver managed to get to nearby Borough station, and within fifteen minutes an estimated 650 tons of gravel had collapsed into the tunnel. A huge crater opened up in Newington Causeway, forty feet above the rail line, causing a massive gas explosion when the main broke – but fortuitously a water main also cracked, dousing the flames. Amazingly, there were no casualties; but the brave attempt to run a partial service through the building work had to be abandoned and a full train service was not restored until a year later.

Meanwhile, work had begun on the extension to Morden, deep in the Surrey countryside, but still, until just before the terminus, in deep tube tunnels. This extension was aimed at tapping into the lucrative markets of Balham and Tooting, and here the Underground was in direct competition with the suburban network of what was now the Southern Railway, one of the four new consolidated railway companies. There was a trade-off, with the Southern agreeing to the extension to Morden provided the Underground Company abandoned plans to extend the District from Wimbledon to Sutton. That deal partly explains the Underground's absence in much of south London, which, as explained before, is also a result of the geological conditions. The attention to detail was demonstrated by the way the Underground Company built an entire mock-up of Morden station inside an exhibition hall to assess the suitability of the design. Morden was in the open air, just below street level, but all the other new stations were connected to the street by escalators.

The Morden section was opened on 13 September 1926 by the junior Transport Minister, John Moore-Brabazon.[1] The minister made clear in his speech that while he was delighted to be opening the extension and to drive the first train, he stressed that it would only be possible to build further extensions if the railway were well supported and earned the required dividends. Ashfield, standing next to him, said that 14 million extra passengers were required to make the extension pay, but, of course, the complex finances of the company with its hidden subsidies between buses and trains meant that such figures were difficult to verify. Ashfield, naturally, knew such lines could never pay for themselves out of the fare box. By then there was a sixty-year body of evidence (since the completion of the first section of the Metropolitan) to that effect.

The opening marked the end of the first post-war Underground expansion programme funded on cheap government money. While London Underground would benefit three times in the inter-war period from government measures which encouraged such expansion and allowed the network to expand considerably, these policies were always a result of a wider macroeconomic strategy designed to reduce unemployment. They were not what they should have been: a recognition of the fundamental benefits of having an efficient and cheap transportation system in a city like London. Indeed, this is a characteristic of the whole history of the Underground which Brabazon's ill-informed comments illustrate well. Successive government have failed to recognize the intrinsic value of the system not just for Londoners but as part of the lifeblood of the whole nation. Investment has always been a balancing item in the national accounts or a bauble thrown to London Underground in furtherance of wider economic objectives.

An average of thirteen trains per hour were run from Morden to Golders Green via Charing Cross but at peak times some went on the other section via Bank. The railway, which was effectively today's Northern line, with the exception of the extension out to High Barnet and Mill Hill East from Highgate, still did not have a proper name. There was no easy way to identify it as there had been with the Bakerloo. *The Times* tried valiantly with ghastly suggestions such as Edgmor, Medgeway, Mordenware and even Edgmorden, but none had the simple ring of its predecessor. It was not until 1937 when work started north of Highgate that 'Northern line' was adopted as the official title, a confusing choice to people unfamiliar with the system since it is the only tube line that penetrates into deepest south London.

The Underground Company, far-sighted as ever, created what was effectively the first 'park and ride' station at Morden. An extensive network of single-decker buses from such places as Cheam, Sutton, Mitcham and Banstead took passengers to the station, and the company built a huge shed opposite the Underground terminus to house both cars and cycles for those arriving at the station under their own steam. At the time, Morden was a mere village, with barely 1,000 inhabitants. As one history describes it, 'Clustered around the new terminus were three streets of cottages, three or four large villas and the Crown Inn. All around, as far as the eye could see, were fields and parklands.'[2] That soon changed. Within five years, according to the next census, there were 12,600 residents.

The Piccadilly was the other tube line to be extended during the inter-war period and that was prompted as much by 'people power' as by the grand visions of Ashfield and Pick. A campaign for a tube north of Finsbury Park had started as early as 1919 when the local 'Advisory Committee of the Labour Exchanges' suggested an extension right out to Hertford. Finsbury Park was a particular bottleneck since two railways terminated there. The photographs of rush-hour scenes, with people crowding for trams and buses in the small area outside the station, suggest that every night there was the risk of a major disaster due to the bustling crowds. Since Finsbury Park was the end of the line, it was the same kind of transport interchange as, say, Morden or Edgware, but it was much busier. This was not only because the station was much closer to central London than those others, but also because the outer suburbs it served, such as Harringay and Wood Green, were already well developed with high concentrations of terraced housing. The local press frequently highlighted the issue, reporting, possibly with a little tabloid exaggeration, that 'men and women fight like rugby players for means to reach their homes' and 'clothes are torn, and fainting girls and women are so common as to pass almost without comment'.[3] Such was the public outcry that the *Daily Mirror* ran a series of stories during 1922 pushing for an extension. The paper quoted doctors who described the terrible state of women's nerves after a struggle to get home and even suggested that one survivor of the trenches of Flanders had perished of a chest disease as a result of the crush. The pièce de résistance was when an MP was reported to have been knocked down in an attempt to board a tram at Finsbury Park.

Yet it would take more than a decade for the extension which would relieve this chaotic state of affairs to be built. The usual rivalries between the rail companies stymied the initial plan, with the Great Northern opposing the scheme, having been given a veto on such extensions as part of its 1902 approval of the Great Northern & City line. By 1923, however, pressure from outside was mounting. The Middlesex Federation of Ratepayers' Associations, headed by an indefatigable general secretary, J.W. Pardoe, collected a 30,000 strong petition to present to the Minister of Transport, stressing the 'grave menace' of overcrowding at Finsbury Park. The petition had been timed cleverly for when the London & North Eastern Railway – which had taken over the Great Northern when the railways were consolidated – needed Parliamentary approval for a scheme to electrify its suburban routes. The LNER was forced into the position of either agreeing to the tube extension or proceeding with its own electrification scheme. However, it did not have the money and dropped the electrification plan, prompting an inquiry into the Piccadilly extension which resulted in a compromise by allowing the Underground to extend to Manor Park with the possibility of further expansion later. Pick, however, had told the inquiry that the Underground wanted the extension to reach out into the open air where costs of building a railway were one fifth those of tunnelling, making the overall scheme more economic in relation to the numbers of passengers it could be expected to attract.

There was no money to build the extension even as far as Manor Park, and here Pick and Ashfield showed their political acumen. While publicly continuing to stress that the organization had no funds for investment, they bought various houses on the proposed route and had detailed discussions with the Ministry of Transport over their plans. Rescue for the people of North London came in the form of another recession, which prompted a further bout of spending by the government in order to stimulate the economy and reduce unemployment. The Depression was at its height in July 1929 when the new Labour government brought in the Development (Loan Guarantees and Grants) Act. This went further than its predecessor of 1921 by guaranteeing the payment of interest on capital raised for major works, effectively underpinning the private sector to build new infrastructure. The interest on the loan for the first fifteen years was a grant rather than a loan, an unprecedented measure of state support for public works projects.

That was all Ashfield and Pick needed to ensure that the Piccadilly extension could get under way. With the kind of panache that TV chefs demonstrate today when presenting 'one I cooked earlier', they put forward a ready-made scheme to stretch the Piccadilly line right out to Cockfosters, seven and a half miles beyond the Finsbury Park terminus, and, at the opposite end, four and a half miles out to Northfields, alongside the District's tracks. The massive programme of work, finally agreed in 1930, also included several major station reconstructions.

With a speed that seems almost miraculous today, the extensions were opened in stages during 1932–3 with the usual fanfare and distribution of free tickets. The Prince of Wales even drove one of the early trains, breaking a long run of royal absence from Underground openings. The Piccadilly became the Underground's premier line, its new stations emblematic of the growing self-confidence of the organization, even though they were built at a time of slump and economic depression. They were the work of Charles Holden, an architect who had toured northern Europe with Pick in the summer of 1930 to look at the modern styles emerging abroad, which were clearly a powerful influence on his designs. While each station was different – unlike Leslie Green's standard ruby-red design – they had a generic theme which made them recognizable. Notably, the most prominent feature of each station was a tall ticket hall, usually circular, and with a simple lining of red-brown bricks broken by sections of steel-framed cathedral glass. Everything was blended into a consistent design, from the design of the ticket offices and wooden telephone booth doors, to

Yerkes used his architect Leslie Green to design his stations to a set formula, using the characteristic ruby-red tiles that still adorn many of them. This one at Down Street, Mayfair, was closed in 1932.

(Left) Charles Yerkes managed to obtain finance for the creation of three new Tube lines and built them in just seven years, an almost miraculous achievement of which few Londoners are aware.

(Right) A scene from Queens Park station in 1917 with a station assistant putting up a poster for an event at the Royal Albert Hall below one for a football match presumably at Chelsea's Stamford Bridge ground near Walham Green station, now called Fulham Broadway.

During the First World War, men called to the Front were replaced by women in many of the jobs on the system, including the opening and shutting of the gates at the end of every carriage which, in the early days of the tube trains, had to be hand operated.

Lord Ashfield and his daughter on the day of the reopening of the City & South London Railway following work to amalgamate it with the Hampstead section to create what would later become known as the Northern line.

Stations such as Sudbury Town designed by Charles Holden and opened in July 1931, were often the first substantial buildings in the districts they were intended to serve.

The Underground tried to create its own market, with posters such as this one encouraging people to move to the suburbs and selling season tickets which were cheaper, per mile, than those from stations nearer the centre.

Why not live at Sudbury Hill?

Small, modern, labour-saving houses with garages and gardens. Live in the country where you will have room to breathe. 40 minutes to Charing Cross. 50 minutes to Mansion House.

SEASONS		1 Month	3 Months
	Charing Cross . .	24/6	67/6
	Mansion House . .	26/6	72/6

UNDERGROUND

METRO-LAND

PRICE TWO-PENCE

The cover of the 1930 *Metroland* booklet was still selling the suburban rural dream.

Animals killed by trains, as lines expanded into the rural surrounds of London, included otters and owls, displayed here at Charing Cross station in 1929.

The Film-lover
travels UNDERGROUND

Piccadilly, Oxford Circus,
Leicester Square, Strand
Stations

Frank Pick, the administrative genius
behind London Transport, using his famous
green-ink pen.

A 1930 poster encouraging people to
go to the cinema. The Underground
was careful not to give free promotion
to any particular venue or film.

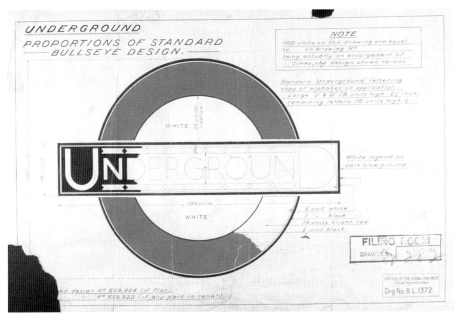

A 1925 redesign of the famous roundel by Edward Johnston, with the characteristically
expanded capital U and D.

Between the wars, air displays at RAF Hendon attracted huge crowds, most of whom travelled there on the Underground to nearby Colindale station.

(Left) At the height of the Blitz, the stations became so crowded that people had to spend sleepless nights on the escalators – the deep stations proved to be 'the best shelters of all'.

(Right) Special refreshment trains were run to provide basic food such as buns and tea to thousands of shelters.

Thousands of West Indians were encouraged to come to Britain to take up vacancies on the Underground and the buses. Here, London Transport's recruitment officer Charles Gomm signs up the first batch of applicants in Barbados, 1956.

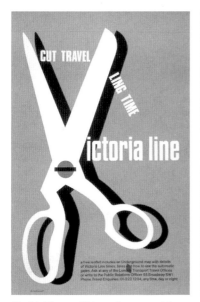

(Left) The tradition of eye-catching posters on the Underground continued with the opening of the Victoria line, the first new tube line in central London since Edwardian days.

(Right) Several of the stations on the Jubilee Line Extension are architectural masterpieces like this one at Canary Wharf but, unlike those built by Green and Holden, are characterised by their contrasting styles.

The subterranean railway beneath Piccadilly Circus.

the smallest detail such as stair rails, clocks and signs. They were neither designed nor built on the cheap: bronze was used for the ticket office window frames and for handrails, while elegant lamps, mounted on columns with bowl-shaped reflectors, shone their light upwards to the ceiling, providing a comforting warm mood.

Holden's modern, elegant stations gave the Underground a cachet which helped attract people to the burgeoning suburbs. Pick intended them to be 'inviting doorways in an architectural setting that cannot be missed by the casual passer-by'.[4] In essence, they were designed as a means of facilitating a smooth transfer from street to platform with as few obstructions as possible. Their ticket machines would be set slightly to the side, for convenient use by purchasers while not disturbing the passage of the season ticket holders bustling their way through. The stations were, indeed, cathedrals for the places in which they were situated, a magnet which helped to attract people to what were otherwise featureless, though comfortable, developments. Most stations had a few shops, but they were principally intended to be places where passengers did not linger. One exception was Enfield West, which had a buffet. It was well over two miles from Enfield town centre and the authors of the history of the Tube suggest that the provision of the café may have been 'a *douceur* for those taken in by the station name'.[5] Eventually, following protests from the local council, the station was renamed Oakwood.

The remoteness of the areas where these tentacles of the Underground were stretching is demonstrated by the reaction of local residents. One old lady reported that 'she had never ridden on a tram or a bus and when interviewed just before the opening of Southgate station, said that her last wish would be to see the great new architectural wonder before she was "taken"'.[6] The Piccadilly's extensions transformed the districts they served even more rapidly than older lines because the transport and economic pre-conditions happened to be just right. By the time they opened, the London Transport Passenger Board (which almost immediately became

known as London Transport or LT) had been created and its control
of buses and trams ensured the provision of a more coherent and
comprehensive network of other transport services linking into the
Underground stations. The LT's dominance also allowed it to set
fares which were not as expensive, per mile, as stations which were
further away from central London, and this increased the
competitive advantage of the more distant suburbs in relation to the
ones closer to town. Given that land prices were somewhat cheaper
in those areas, LT's policy meant that these suburbs grew much more
quickly than would otherwise have been the case. How much,
ultimately, that benefited London and Londoners is debatable. It
could be argued that this policy ensured even more urban sprawl
and, moreover, the faster dispersal of the tightly knit communities
characteristic of crowded inner-city life. Nevertheless, Pearson would
have been pleased.

The gradual climb out of the Depression also provided the ideal
economic conditions for the rapid growth of the suburbs. The stock
market crash, and the low returns on government securities, meant the
building societies were awash with cash and eager to lend to house
purchasers. The pool of unemployed workers who had moved to
London to seek work meant labour costs were low, and building
materials were also cheap. All this ensured that the supply of houses
grew rapidly, with the private housing boom peaking in 1934. The
houses were cheap. House prices were at their lowest-ever levels, an
average of just £500 with some smaller ones costing less than £400.
Pick's insistence that the line stretched as far out as possible paid rapid
dividends. At Arnos Grove the Piccadilly reached undeveloped areas
whose transformation into suburbs, thanks to the fast twenty-four
trains per hour service to central London, was incredibly rapid. As a
history of the line puts it, 'After a slow start, the builders were hard at
work on landed estates and parkland, laying out roads and building
houses on every acre of spare land north of Arnos Grove, around
Southgate station and east, south and west of Oakwood.'[7]

To the west, too, there were massive developments because of the fortuitous timing, in terms of the economic cycle, of the completion of a new section of the Piccadilly line which had been extended to supplement existing services on various sections of the District and Metropolitan. Rayners Lane saw the construction of hundreds of new houses on both sides of the line, which included a particularly large estate called Harrow Garden Village, developed by the Metropolitan's related but legally separate company, Metropolitan Country Estates, where in 1932 houses could be bought for between £895 and £1,350. Other new stations such as Ruislip, Ruislip Manor, Eastcote, Hillingdon and Ickenham would all see enormous growth stimulated by the Metroland developments (see Chapter 12). And housing meant ticket sales. Rayners Lane, which had been a sleepy Metropolitan station with just sixty daily users in 1930, became a big interchange with 11,000 people using it every day a mere seven years later.

By then, several central London stations had been transformed from modest little entrances, often with poor transfer arrangements between lines, to magnificent modern interchanges. The most ambitious was at Piccadilly Circus, where the Piccadilly and the Bakerloo connect. Opened in 1928, this was designed by Holden, who created a huge circular tiled hall underneath the roundabout. In the centre were two banks of three escalators leading to and from the lines, all lit by the characteristic uplighters which created the welcoming glow that became a feature of the Underground system and its publicity material. Although there was a commercial element, with shop displays around the outer perimeter of what Holden called his 'ambulatory', the main theme was London as the centre of the world, an appropriate sentiment given that the British Empire was still at its height. On the wall above the top of the escalators were oil paintings featuring a map of the world, with side panels showing the objectives of Underground travelling: business and commerce, outdoor pleasure, shopping, and amusements of the town. Later, a world clock map was installed, showing the time at various places throughout the world. The self-confidence and panache of the whole station is still largely noticeable today, even though the uplighters have been removed and the numbers using the station, night and day, are so enormous that there is little chance of getting a perspective on Holden's great work. Not surprisingly, the station attracted widespread international recognition, and the Moscow Metro, built in the early 1930s as much to celebrate Soviet achievements as to provide the city with a transport system, incorporated many of the design features such as escalators with uplighters. Indeed, the design of the whole Moscow network, with a circle line and radial routes deep into the suburbs, owes a lot to the London Underground, which its designers spent many years studying. As O.S. Nock notes, 'the fact that the Moscow plan, conceived as a single entity, so closely resembled the complex that had been built up in London in nearly 70 years of unconnected private enterprise, many vicissitudes of fortune, and drastic changes of managerial policy is remarkable'.[8] In fact, by then the London system had gradually been melded together by twenty years of Lord Ashfield's guiding hand.

The Piccadilly was the first to benefit from the unified approach of London Transport. The next few years were to be the heyday of the network, a time when the London Underground was fêted around the world as the ideal transport organization. Before celebrating that period, a brief digression back to the Metropolitan, the line that was never part of the Combine and which did the most in stimulating the development of a whole section of London, even giving it a name: Metroland.

T W E L V E

METROLAND, THE

SUBURBAN PARADOX

Throughout the Edwardian and post-war period, one subterranean railway remained separate from the rest of the Underground – the Metropolitan. Indeed, it survived as a separate company until the creation of London Transport, despite various attempts by Ashfield to bring it within the Combine. The railway was able to remain independent after the war, despite perennial problems with its finances, because it had a great advantage over its rivals: the ability to exploit its land resources around its stations. The company also had an extensive ready-made railway and though it added a few minor extensions in the inter-war years, its survival depended on making good use of the huge stretches built deep into the countryside by Sir Edward Watkin.

As we have seen, developments of estates around new Underground stations started as early as the 1880s with the Bedford Park Estate in Turnham Green, and construction of Hampstead Garden Suburb started soon after the arrival of the Hampstead line in 1907. Metroland was to further that concept, but on a much greater scale.

The remote stretches of the Metropolitan built by Watkin in the 1880s were really a railway in search of a purpose. Indeed, in the early years of the twentieth century, the Metropolitan was heavily reliant on its goods and parcels traffic which, at its height in 1904, represented a fifth of the line's income, £153,000 out of £796,000. A nationwide parcels service from forty stations was actually advertised on posters right up until the 1930s. But this traffic was diminishing with the arrival of motor transport and clearly passenger usage had to be encouraged. The Metropolitan never realized Watkin's aspirations by becoming a major main-line railway, and to generate the suburban traffic that was essential to its economic viability large amounts of housing had to be built along its route.

There had been a handful of developments stimulated by the Metropolitan before the Great War, both on its own land and by other landowners who had sold to builders. For example, as soon as the line to Rickmansworth had opened in 1887, the Eastbury estate at one of the intermediate stations, Northwood, had been sold as fifty-three building plots for development, starting the town on its route to becoming an upper-middle-class residential area. The *Watford Observer*[1] waxed lyrical with the usual bucolic colour blended with commercial realism:

> A rare opportunity for small capitalists and speculators. Yet
> only a few minutes away is a charming landscape . . . tiny hills
> and hollows . . . pools of water, brambly wildernesses, where in
> spring nightingales sing and the air is sweet with the scent of
> violets, primroses and hawthorn, and in autumn the district is
> rich with crimson and gold leaves and hedges. This is the haunt
> of the nightingale. Let us hope that the delighted visitor will
> listen and let 'em alone.

Fat chance.

When the Uxbridge extension opened in 1904, Ruislip quickly expanded. King's College, Cambridge, the principal landowners, sold land near the High Street for luxury development while the local council, Ruislip-Northwood, became the first in the country to produce a town plan. This was a response to what the local councillors considered a worrying trend since the arrival of the Metropolitan. The British Freehold Land Company, which bought large areas of land and then sold off the plots, offering them locally for a mere £3 deposit and ten shillings weekly. The company tried to attract the sort of lowly clerks who had just enough money to aspire to home ownership, with advertising such as 'Try to own a suburban home; it will make you a better citizen and help your family. The suburbs have fresh air, sunlight, roomy houses, green lawns and social advantages.' This was advertising copy that could have been written by Charles Pearson half a century before.

In fact, though, many of the purchasers could not afford to complete their homes. It was not at all what the good burghers wanted for Ruislip, especially as the buyers were expected to find their own builder and architect and often they dispensed with the latter to save money, which resulted in a collection of ramshackle and partly built houses that was little better than a shanty town. Instead, the council set down rules in its town plan, ensuring that the houses would be of brick with access to proper services and linked by well-surfaced roads. A local company called Ruislip Manor Limited was formed and its vision was much more in keeping with that of the council. Its prospectus said that the company 'aims at introducing all classes into the community', but, of course, 'it is not intended to indiscriminately mix all classes and sizes of housing together'. Perish the thought. Ruislip Council had grand ideas for a garden city on the lines of Hampstead Garden Suburb or Letchworth but these were stymied by the advent of the First World War.

However, none of these developments were on the Metropolitan's own land and its extensive holdings were to be the real catalyst to the creation of Metroland. The company had been very fortunate – or possibly far-sighted – when in two Acts of Parliament during the mid 1880s it had separated off the finances of its land bank, accumulated as a result of deals with landowners. Normally, railway companies were precluded from developing surplus land they acquired and were required to dispose of it. However, the Metropolitan uniquely had the right to grant building leases and to sell ground rents, a concession the company had won during the early days of the Metropolitan in its negotiations with the City of London. The Metropolitan's holdings, acquired during the construction of the line deep out into the countryside, were substantial. Several landowners, rather than simply selling a strip for the railway under compulsory purchase powers, had come to a voluntary agreement to sell their whole holding, an easier transaction for both parties. Other chunks of land had been acquired for the path of the railway but had become redundant when opposition forced a change of route.

The first development by the Metropolitan itself, through its Surplus Lands Committee, was started at Cecil Park, Pinner, in 1900. The advertising copy was in the tone that was to become all too familiar over the next four decades as the flat and open lands of Middlesex were turned into the most developed of London's quadrants. The Committee's sales brochure read: 'Unique and tasteful, thoroughly well-built houses and also plots of land for a sale for the erection of houses of good class.' The brochure went on to extol the virtues of home ownership, arguing that it allayed the 'uneasy feeling' of tenants who might be given a notice to quit at any time: 'the owner occupier has the gratification of knowing that so long as the property belongs to him, all the improvements he may make to the house and garden are for his own benefit and that of his family – not for the landlord.' Indeed, owner occupation was pretty novel, with barely 10 per cent of the population living in homes they owned. One could argue, therefore, that these railways were changing the very way people lived by making them into owner occupiers, something they could never afford in central London. It was, in effect, the start of the 'property-owning democracy', the term coined by Sir Anthony Eden in the 1950s.

The name 'Metroland' was used initially as the title of a booklet first published in 1915 by the Metropolitan Railway to extol the virtues of taking a train out to the countryside for long healthy walks and cycle rides. But the real growth of Metroland itself was to come after the First World War, when the booklet's main focus became the marketing of property. It contained dozens of pages of advertising, interspersed with flowery editorial, which enabled the booklet to be sold for a mere twopence.

As well as rural suburban splendour – an oxymoron, of course, but one which clearly did not deter the purchasers – the very idea of modernity was being sold. The 1920 edition, for example, instructed readers to

> stake your claim at Edgware [on the soon to be built Hampstead extension, intriguingly, rather than on the Metropolitan]. Omar Khay-yam's recipe for turning the wilderness into paradise hardly fits an English climate, but provision has been made at Edgware of an alternative recipe which at least will convert pleasant, undulating fields into happy homes. The loaf of bread, the jug of wine and the book of verse may be got there cheaply and easily, and . . . a shelter which comprises all major labour-saving and sanitary conveniences. We moderns ask much more before we are content than the ancients, and Edgware is designed to give us that much more.

The *Metroland* booklets are replete with pictures and full colour drawings of what must have seemed another world to inner London residents: waterfalls, lakes, cows in fields and even farmers next to horse-drawn ploughs. Apart from the drawing on the front of the 1923 edition, there are barely any pictures of trains or stations. Rather, the covers display quaint rural scenes which would have not been out of place in William Morris's idyll. The world of Metroland is not cluttered with people: its suburban streets are empty, and its houses seem to sit alone, in their full grandeur, separate from any of their neighbours. There are, it seems, more farm animals than human beings in the wilds of Middlesex and Hertfordshire. The greater part of the books, apart from the advertisements, was taken up by 'a comprehensive description of the charming countryside served by the metropolitan railway'. Such places as Rickmansworth, Harrow, Uxbridge, Wembley Park, Ruislip, Amersham and Harrow on the Hill were invested with as much history as the anonymous authors could find by dredging up name origins and minor historical events that might give character to what were mostly villages with little claim to fame. In fact, possibly conscious of much of the area's banality and featurelessness, there is a slight air of defensiveness about some of the copy: 'Metroland is one of the most beautiful areas in the home counties; its share of the Buckinghamshire Chilterns is as picturesque and diversified as anything that Kent, Surrey or Sussex have to show.' The rural atmosphere described in *Metroland* pamphlets was perfectly accurate – in 1924 the Metropolitan railway was delivering eighty-seven milk churns per day from Harrow on the Hill station into London.

The central role of the Metropolitan's own property company was often highlighted, boasting by 1925 that 'the company is developing certain choice estates aggregating about 770 acres of which 200 acres have been disposed of and more than 400 houses erected'. Robert Selbie, the general manager of the Metropolitan, had seen beforehand the potential of using the Metropolitan's surplus land once the war had ended. Selbie was another of those talented and far-sighted pioneers who helped shape the Underground. He joined the Metropolitan in 1903 and became its general manager five years later, remaining in that position until his death in 1930. He was a great believer in the benefits of investment to improve the service and it was his commercial acumen that ensured the Metropolitan made use of its land. As early as 1912, Selbie had argued that Middlesex was 'daily growing in population' and suggested the Metropolitan should advertise its estates. The war had obviously interrupted the process, but now that it was over Selbie redoubled his efforts and created a separate company, Metropolitan

Railway Country Estates Limited, as the railway's development arm. He argued that railways were more likely 'to be trusted and are not open to the suspicion that often attaches to the speculative builder and estate developer',[2] which showed that the Victorian image of the railways as aggressive monopolists trampling over the rights of the people had been largely dispelled.

The Metropolitan, therefore, began to build its own estates at a variety of suburbs such as Kingsbury, Neasden and Wembley Park, and purchasers had the choice of either buying an off-the-peg home or arranging their own architect or builder to do the work. The Metropolitan became the trailblazer for opening up much of Middlesex and parts of neighbouring counties in the inter-war years. The sales literature became more and more seductive and sophisticated, always offering buyers a place in the country which their very purchase would help destroy, and often suggestive of the health benefits of the countryside compared with the polluted cities. Kingsbury was where 'peace and quiet prevail and the stretches of country around offer plenty of opportunity for invigorating exercise to those who are inclined to walking and cycling', while Chorley Estate, between Rickmansworth and Chorley Wood, was sold as 'an exceptionally attractive residential country estate comprising over 600 acres of beautiful undulating country rising to an altitude of 300 feet [with] detached residences of the country house type and of artistic design [served by] wide and well-made roads'. This was the largest estate developed by the Metropolitan itself and the houses, fitted with all modern and labour-saving devices (all mod cons, according to the expression used later), were a snip at between £975 and £2,150.[3] At Hillingdon, the station was opened in 1923 specifically to serve the new Hillingdon Mount Estate, which was advertised as 'only 15 miles from London in a delightful rural district . . . within easy reach of the quaint old market town of Uxbridge'.

Harrow Garden Village, an estate built for the Metropolitan by a council engineer turned developer, E.S. Reid, was described in his frequent advertisements in *Metroland* as having 'the particular advantage of being self-contained and where you choose a house on this estate, you may rest assured that you will be surrounded by other E.S. Reid houses'. In other words, don't worry about the riff-raff coming to spoil the estate – as Reid's advertising copy put it: 'you will not have a nasty cheap mass-production house anywhere near you to lower the value of the property'. In fact, Reid was making a rather fine class distinction. According to a history of Metroland, 'this was the first estate which was built with the lower middle-class house owner in mind'.[4] Reid was, of course, building mass production houses but, to be fair, they were of a good standard; even today estate agents sometimes use the term 'Met houses' in publicity blurbs.

Chalk Hill, Wembley Park, was said to be 'in a picturesque locality within close touch of London, yet in open country'. This was part of the largest area of development stimulated by the Metropolitan. Wembley, the site of Watkin's ill-fated tower (see Chapter 6), had not been the subject of much development during the Edwardian period but with the good transport links it was ripe for a major scheme. The catalyst was the Empire exhibition of 1924, which had been long in gestation. The idea for such an exhibition had been mooted as far back as in the early 1900s to use British pre-eminence in the world economy – which in reality was already waning – to market its wares in the face of increasing foreign competition.

The organizers of the exhibition chose Wembley as the site for much the same reason as, seventy-five years later, the Millennium Dome was built on derelict land well served by the Underground. The wider purpose of the exhibition was, as the organizers put it, 'to strengthen the bonds that bind the Mother Country to her Sister States and Daughter Nations . . . to enable all who owe allegiance to the British Flag to meet on common ground . . . it is a family party, to which every member of the Empire is invited, and at which every part of the Empire is represented'. Pavilions representing each colony were built at a cost of £10m. It was an imperial Disneyland, aiming to show Britain at the height of its global power with pavilions from every corner of the Empire which, at the time, encompassed a quarter of the world's population: Fiji to East Africa, New Zealand to Canada. Yet the very necessity of such an exhibition, intended to stimulate development of an ailing economy, showed that the Empire was already in decline.

The sports stadium was completed in 1923 in time for the famous 'white horse' cup final at which a crowd well exceeding the capacity of 100,000 – some estimates suggest twice that figure – turned up.[5] Over 100,000 people also, came to the opening by King George V of the main exhibition a year afterwards on 23 April 1924. Two days later on Whit Monday, despite an unofficial strike by Underground workers, almost three times that number visited the show, with each adult paying the quite substantial entrance fee of one shilling and sixpence. The Metropolitan not only catered for the sightseers visiting the exhibition – when its workforce was not on strike – but had played a key role in the building of the site, which used a staggering 200,000 tons of concrete in the construction of the pavilions. One of its electric locomotives was displayed in the Palace of Engineering, the most impressive of the pavilions, which was six and a half times the size of Trafalgar Square and at the time the largest concrete construction in the world. The Indian exhibits were housed in a replica of the Taj Mahal next to an artificial lake, Ceylon (now Sri Lanka) displayed a collection of pearl necklaces insured for a million pounds, and Canada produced a life-size statue of the Prince of Wales, made of butter. The most popular attraction was the Queen's Dolls' House, a complete mansion built to the scale of one inch to the foot.

The exhibition was so successful, with 17 million visitors in 1924, that it was kept open for a second year, during which it attracted about half that number. But as with the Millennium Dome, the exhibition was intended to be the catalyst for a long-term development of the area with both housing and industrial sites. As a result, Wembley became one of London's most successful areas in the inter-war years. The pavilions were dismantled,[6] leaving basic infrastructure on a site that was perfect for the type of lighter manufacturing business that was becoming the engine of the UK economy, replacing the declining coal and steel industries of the north. London had long been the largest manufacturing region in the country, despite the popular image of the north, but now the concentration was even greater, with two thirds of the jobs created between 1923 and the outbreak of the Second World War being sited in the capital.

Wembley and Metroland were thus part of a wider pattern which included both the transformation and expansion of London. The inner city was losing its population, partly as a result of better transport links which enabled people to live further out, but also because the growing number of offices pushed up rentals which made living in town uneconomic for most people. The suburbs had to accommodate both people moving from the city and the huge number of incomers attracted to London by its prosperity and rapid economic growth. While the population of inner London declined by almost half a million between 1901 and 1937, during that time the suburbs grew by 2.5 million. The population of the Greater London reached 8 million, representing its apogee in terms of the proportion of Britain's people living there. London became the engine of growth for the whole economy, and this was greatly facilitated by the Underground's incursions into the suburbs. Indeed, London as a whole fared much better than the rest of the country during the difficult years of the twenties and thirties, which explains why Metroland could keep expanding during that period with barely a break even at the height of the Depression.

Given that many of these newcomers were required for manual or blue collar jobs, they could not afford to buy their own homes and needed council housing which, for the first time, started to be built in large numbers. After the war the government had been panicked by social unrest and the demand for 'homes for heroes' into passing the Addison Act in 1919, which allowed local authorities to build housing subsidized by grants from central government. The London County

Council was at the forefront of building these homes, which were required to be of a high standard with indoor bathrooms and good space standards, and started work in 1920 on big estates in Roehampton, Catford and Becontree, the largest council development in Europe. The Addison Act itself was short-lived, but with the introduction of similar measures, the peak year for the construction of subsidized council housing was 1927.

After that, however, the private sector predominated as the LCC faced all kinds of opposition in its attempts to create further developments. The local authorities in the outlying districts were disinclined to give permission for houses to be built for these 'immigrants' from central London and, indeed, many of these potential tenants could not afford to move outside the central area because they were unable to pay the fares into central London where they had to work. Because of this problem, the LCC specified that this housing should be allocated only to more affluent tenants who could afford the relatively high rents as well as the travelling costs. The local authorities even refused to build sufficient schools, which meant hundreds of the new children from London roamed the streets when they should have been getting an education.

The focus towards private housing had been stimulated by government intervention, too. For a time, under a law introduced by Bonar Law's Conservative administration in 1923, a cash grant was available to house-builders amounting to £75 per house, about 15 per cent of the cost of a three-bedroom house with a bathroom. Therefore, not only did government subsidies smooth the way for the construction of the tube extensions (as we saw in Chapter 11), but they also helped accelerate the growth of the housing around them.

The other catalyst for the growth of owner occupation and the related spread of Metroland was the burgeoning building societies. Helped by a favourable taxation policy which gave building society accounts an advantage over other forms of investment, from the early 1920s the societies began to overflow with money available to lend for mortgages, and mass house-builders emerged, ready to use this source of finance. The two worked together to underwrite the initial cost of acquiring homes so that the first-time buyer was able to obtain a house through a down payment of a mere 5 per cent, rather than the previous 20 per cent. That partly explains how, even through the long Depression that followed the 1929 economic collapse, Metroland was able to continue to grow.

After the Empire Exhibition, Wembley and the area around the next station on the line, Preston Road, were soon transformed. According to a history of the suburbs, the land around Wembley Park had been largely rural before the Exhibition but now, once it had ended, 'housing estates began to grow along the roads and up the slopes of Barn Hill and Chalk Hill to the north of the Metropolitan Line'.[7] The 1926 *Metroland* pamphlet lauded the merits of Wembley Park, which, 'after its blaze of fame, has now settled down to the everyday activities of a residential suburb. It grows fast and the look of newness is very noticeable as one passes through on the railway.'

Preston Road station had a rather colourful history. It had first opened as a halt to cater for the competitors in the shooting events of the 1908 Olympics Games, because in the nearby hamlet of Preston were the grounds of the Uxendon Shooting Club. The club, together with the twenty-seven local inhabitants, had successfully petitioned the Metropolitan Railway to build the station which, on the other side, also served the Harrow Golf Course. In 1926, visitors could consider buying a house costing between £1,025 and £1,185 on 'a self-contained estate in the best part of Preston [which clearly had already grown somewhat] only eight minutes from the station'. As ever, the houses were 'carefully planned and soundly constructed' and 'of artistic merit and varied design, in an orchard setting of particular charm'. Harrow Golf Course, which in 1928 had 400 members, soon gave way to masses of smaller houses, while the north side of the line became the Woodcock Hill and Woodcock Dell estates, with much higher class accommodation.

The attractions of golf were a recurring theme for luring people onto the Metropolitan. In the aftermath of the war, the advertising stressed that the railway was 'the short cut to the nearest golf course. From his office he can step in at any of the Met stations close by, and be taken in a few minutes by electric train to the links without a change. The train service is rapid, inexpensive and luxurious.' Later, the game was an important part of selling Metroland. The 1926 *Metroland* booklet, for example, said of Wembley Park: 'Golf is plentiful at the very doors of Wembley park. There is a very good course on the pleasant slopes of Uxendon Hill; within five minutes by rail, two or three other courses can be reached.'

And so on went the development. There are countless such tales of estates springing up as much of the Middlesex countryside – including some more of its golf courses – disappeared under tarmac and housing. The most ambitious development was on the open fields between Pinner and Northwood where, in 1930, two developers proposed building a completely new suburb. The name for the station, Northwood Hills, was chosen from entries to a competition run by a local paper and it was designed by Charles Clark in the 'suburban villa' style used for all the new Metropolitan stations of that period. Northwood Hills opened in December 1933 but it was still a huge building site according to one new commuter: 'I arrived at the station and stepped into mud of the most adhesive quality I have seen or felt.'[8] But clearly he had no regrets: 'Yet, I was to find that residing in a suburb adds a thrill and a zest to life. It is an experience in having no traditions to live up to.'

The Metropolitan's most prestigious development was not in its suburban heartland but in the heart of London. In 1925, Selbie gave the go-ahead for the construction of Chiltern Court over Baker Street station, consisting of half a million square feet of shops and luxury flats. This was not really a development with any railway connection but, for form's sake, Selbie had told the board that the wealthy tenants of the 180 flats (there were thirty maids' rooms, too) would be able to use the railway to travel to their City offices during the week, and at weekends they could travel on the Metropolitan to their golf clubs (golf again!) and country homes. Designed by Clark, the building was so celebrated that initially Harrods showed an interest in the commercial space on the lower three floors, while on the ground floor the splendid Chiltern Court restaurant had room for 250 diners. Opened in 1929, the building quickly filled up with early tenants, including the likes of the writers Arnold Bennett and H.G. Wells, and the Metropolitan must have been delighted at the £40,000 in annual rental income for an outlay of £500,000, which, as one history notes, 'was a far higher rate of return than could be made from running the railway'.[9] Even today, Chiltern Court remains one of the most luxurious blocks in that part of London.

The most exclusive of the developments out in Metroland was at Moor Park. This was formerly known as Sandy Lodge, a little halt opened in 1910 which the Metropolitan provided for the eponymous golf club built by Francis Markes, a businessman attracted to the site by the sandy soil. The basic halt, with no facilities, had been put up for just £555 using old sleepers, on the basis that the golfers would provide revenue of at least £350 per annum in ticket sales, but it is not clear whether that target was ever reached. After the war, Lord Leverhulme, the founder of the massive Lever Brothers, detergent and food manufacturers, bought Moor Park, the nearby classical mansion completed in 1679, and sought to encourage tasteful development in the distant parts of the estate furthest away from the house. This exclusive housing 'combining the facilities of London with rural amenities' was Britain's first gated development, with barriers across the approach roads to discourage passers-by from entering the estate. The housing was much grander than any other in Metroland, sitting in huge plots reached by long tree-lined drives and tennis courts. It was sold as an estate 'where City men could live a life of luxury in the grounds of an historic old English Park and yet be just 40 minutes away from Baker Street by fast electric expresses'.

For this type of affluent commuter, there was the Pullman service still offered by the Metropolitan. It had been introduced in 1910 and continued to provide its passengers with meals served by obsequious waiters:

> For an extra charge of sixpence from Rickmansworth or a
> shilling from more distant stations, travellers could journey to
> work in morocco armchairs set in a drawing room panelled in
> fine fiddleback mahogany. Chaste electric lamps sat on the
> tables, and for privacy there were blinds of green silk damask.
> Nothing was spared from the carpet on which the tycoon's feet
> rested to the ormolu rack with finely traced panels of brass
> treillage upon which he deposited his despatch case.[10]

Although the Pullmans lost money and were really just a flagship service to attract publicity, they survived on the Metropolitan until the outbreak of the Second World War.

Moor Park was turned into a full-scale station when it became the junction for the Watford branch, one of two extensions built by the Metropolitan between the wars, neither of which was particularly successful in attracting passengers. The Watford branch had been on the drawing board for a long time, having first been the subject of a petition from residents as far back as 1906. A whole swathe of land had been acquired from Gonville and Caius College, Cambridge, just before the Great War, but the war's outbreak halted progress. The Bill enabling the construction of the line was passed in 1912, and a station – used temporarily as a restaurant – had even been built in Watford High Street. Opposition from the local council meant that the Metropolitan was reluctant to revive the project after the war. Various other alternatives for new branches, some much more ambitious and drawn up with development potential in mind, were considered and rejected. Therefore it was not until 1923 that work finally started on the line, which had an intermediate station at

Croxley and a terminus rather distant from the town centre at the edge of Cassiobury Park.

The construction of the line was hampered by difficult conditions near the River Gade and the Grand Union Canal, which pushed the cost of the two and a half mile extension to more than £300,000. The usual dignitaries attended the opening on 2 November 1925 and the *Watford Observer* commented: 'The Metropolitan Railway to Watford is likely to have a much greater effect on the development of the town than is at present realized. Just as trade follows the flag, so population follows the railway.'

Not always. The *Observer* was wrong and the line has always been something of a white elephant. Even though the Metropolitan's trains on the Watford branch were comfortable new electric stock with compartments – much better than the Bakerloo tube or the rival London Midland & Scottish suburban services from Watford Junction – the siting of the station on the outskirts of the town limited its usefulness. The service was initially run jointly with the London & North Eastern Railway, which operated steam trains on the line in contrast to the Metropolitan's state-of-the-art electric trains, but the LNER pulled out after the 1926 General Strike because of the poor patronage. The line had the feel of a rural branch line leading to nowhere – and indeed still does today, with a poorly used and sleepy station. Despite the Metropolitan providing buses to the centre of town, the seventy services on weekdays attracted just 2,000 passengers daily. There were a few football specials, too, and while passenger numbers picked up gradually with development in Cassiobury, the line's relative failure deterred the Metropolitan from pursuing other extension plans except for the four-mile-long Wembley Park to Stanmore branch. This line opened on 10 December 1932. Its construction had been made possible by cash provided by the government for capital schemes as part of attempts to recover from the Depression.

This last incursion of the Metropolitan into the countryside was also largely unsuccessful. There was little development on the route of the line, which had three intermediate stations – Kingsbury, Queensbury (which opened later and was another name chosen by newspaper competition) and Canons Park – all designed by Clark who always incorporated a few new shops into his design. While perfectly serviceable, compared with Holden's efforts on the Piccadilly they were banal and conservative, blending in with the red-brick environment rather than standing out as a prominent feature of the area. It was hardly surprising that the extension was not well patronized, given that, as a history of the Metropolitan puts it, 'the 72 trains per day, 37 of which went direct to Baker Street, were a good service for the wooded fields and uninhabited building plots'.[11] The line ended close to a golf course, well short of Stanmore village. There were so few potential passengers that outside peak hours the service was operated by a single-carriage electric car with cabs at each end. Oddly, the Metropolitan focused much of its early advertising of the line on the fact that its passengers could get to the greyhound racing at Wembley Stadium by taking a train to 'Wembley Park at which point a bus service connects with the stadium'. Not really all that convenient, then.

In the late 1930s the suburb of Queensbury, designed to provide homes for 50,000 people and some light industry, 'became the most rapidly developed estate in the north-west [of London]. The landscape was more or less devoid of natural features. Even the few elms were cut down along Honeypot Lane'[12] (the Honey was probably a reference to the stickiness of the Middlesex mud). Houses were cheaper there than in other parts of Metroland, going for as little as £600–£800, and therefore many lower-middle-class families, who had not been able to afford a home of their own, were drawn to the area. Despite the modesty of the houses, they still fulfilled the dream of Pearson and all the successive Underground pioneers by providing good homes for the masses. Each house had a hot-water boiler in the kitchen, a small garden and even space for a garage. Shopping parades around the station and cinemas soon provided people with all they needed for a self-contained suburban life. Nevertheless, despite this rapid development along the extension to Stanmore, passenger numbers were slow to pick up, not least because fares were charged at main line rates (i.e. based on distance), rather than being cross-subsidized like those on the Edgware and Piccadilly extensions.

The Stanmore branch was not only the Metropolitan's swan song, but the end of the haphazard process of planning – or rather lack of it – through which the private sector had created the Underground. From then on, new lines and extensions would be designed by committees in the hope that public money would be used to build them. The reluctance of the British government to recognize the importance of the Underground ensured that such funds were rarely available to finance such schemes, and consequently there were to be only minor additions to the network until well after the Second World War.

As well as attracting little custom, the Stanmore branch had another negative result. The extra trains on the line, created to improve development opportunities for the Metropolitan rather than to meet any transport need, worsened the bottleneck on the Finchley Road to Baker Street section, a problem that was left to London Transport to sort out. Eventually, in 1939, the Metropolitan trains out to Stanmore were replaced by much more modest tube trains and the line became part of the Bakerloo, thereby avoiding the most intensely used part of the Metropolitan.

Perhaps the relative failure of the Metropolitan's inter-war extensions was merely a reflection of geography. After all, there is a limit to how long most people are prepared to spend travelling to work and therefore Metroland had a natural limit. Frank Pick had long believed that this maximum was about half an hour plus a walk at either end, but this was being proved wrong as commuters seemed to be willing to take on much longer journeys, possibly up to an hour. In a paper presented in 1931,[13] Pick argued that the size of the city was determined by what area could be reached within that time. As average train speeds had increased gradually from fourteen to twenty-five mph, so the potential area got larger, too. But watching the growth of Metroland and other London suburbs, he began to be concerned that this 'natural' limit to the size of London was, in fact, much greater, so much so in fact that the city might destroy itself by becoming too large. Hence he began to develop and support the idea of a green girdle around London, an idea which during the 1930s gathered momentum as it was supported by the London County Council and became the basis of the Green Belt planning policies for the capital after the Second World War.

Houses were becoming more difficult to sell. The developers offered all kinds of inducements such as free tickets on the Underground to visit the growing number of houses, some of which now had 'fitted kitchens' (a novel concept), or even free furniture. Taking a trip out to see the houses with their newfangled radios and bedrooms entirely fitted out by Waring & Gillow became a fun thing to do on a day off. Most builders by the mid-1930s offered 'free' boilers, but refrigerators were still a rarity.

The Green Belt, the over-supply of housing and the war halted the spread of Metroland, which quickly became immortalized by John Betjeman. But there was a hint of ambivalence in his attitude towards the spread of the suburbs, an awareness that the development was killing the very England of small country churches which he loved. The first stanza of his poem 'Middlesex' reflects that contradiction:

Gaily into Ruislip Gardens
Runs the red electric train,
With a thousand Ta's and Pardon's
Daintily alights Elaine;
Hurries down the concrete station
With a frown of concentration,
Out into the outskirt's edges
Where a few surviving hedges
Keep alive our lost Elysium – rural Middlesex again.

In a 1973 BBC travelogue, Betjeman said of the encroaching urbanization of the 1930s: 'And over these mild, home county acres, soon there will be estate agent, coal merchant, post office, shops, and rows of neat dwellings; all within easy reach of charming countryside. Bucks, Herts and Middlesex yielded to Metroland, and city men for breakfast on the fast train to London town.'

The final edition of *Metroland* wistfully acknowledged the profound changes which more than a decade of massive housing development had brought about. Of Rayners Lane, where housing had once been sold with the slogan that life there would be 'all peace and quiet', the pamphlet admitted that its 'quiet rustic beauty' was 'now a thing of the past'.

Having given a whole quadrant of London its name, the Metropolitan as a separate entity was doomed. It had only survived as an independent concern because of its profits from housing. Selbie had approached Ashfield on several occasions to bring about a merger, but the terms offered were never to his satisfaction. Emboldened by this source of income, the railway tried to resist its inclusion into the new London Transport but inevitably that battle was to be lost. If only the rules had allowed the Metropolitan to benefit fully from all the development around its stations, then it might well have survived and, indeed, flourished. However, most of the property was developed by private concerns who often made enormous profits thanks, indirectly, to the provision by the public purse of the railway.

Frank Pick cited, for example, a developer called George Cross who bought seventy acres of farmland in Edgware for just £12,250 and had made a profit of nearly five times that amount within six years. Pick noted that if only the other lines had been able to capture some of that added value in order to pay for transport schemes, the Underground map would have many more colours and longer lines than it does today. He told the Barlow Commission, which examined the problem caused by urbanization and the possible need for new areas of development, the precursor to new towns, that in order for a public utility like London Transport to survive, it 'should receive its appropriate share of the land values it helps to create'. It is an argument which has raged ever since, but capturing that increased value through an equitable taxation system has, so far, proved an elusive Holy Grail – though it is being actively considered for the new Crossrail line underground tunnel between Paddington and Liverpool Street.

THIRTEEN

THE PERFECT
ORGANIZATION?

Even after twenty years of effort by Pick and Ashfield, London's transport system was still a haphazard mess at the end of the 1920s despite their achievements in extending the reach of the Combine. There had been a series of commissions and inquiries which recommended more coordination and cooperation between the various transport bodies in London, but little had changed apart from the steady growth in importance and dominance of the Underground Group of Companies. It was only with the advent of a Labour government, with the dynamic Herbert Morrison as transport minister, that London's transport system would be transformed by the creation of a powerful integrated organization, the London Passenger Transport Board, which, as mentioned before, immediately became known simply as London Transport.

The establishment of London Transport in 1933 was to mark the end of the era in which the private sector built and ran the capital's underground railways. It had been the pursuit of profit which had hitherto governed the shape and extent of the system and, as we have seen countless times, the private companies who had persuaded optimistic or gullible shareholders to part with their money for these scheme had an impossible task in trying to make a profit out of the enterprise of building lines. However, the importance of the new organization was not simply that the arrival of LT marked the beginning of much tighter state control over the capital's transport system, particularly its financing. It was much more than that. LT was the first example of how a public body could be invested with commercial as well as social responsibilities, and carry out both aspects successfully. It is almost impossible to exaggerate the high regard in which LT was held during its all too brief heyday, attracting official visitors from around the world eager to learn the lessons of its success and apply them in their own countries. London Transport was the right solution at the right moment, coming at a time when the Depression had alerted governments around the world to the limits of the free market. It represented the apogee of a type of confident public administration run by people imbued with a strong ethos of service to the public and with a reputation that any state organization today would envy. Its birth was a result of the vision and socialist drive of Herbert Morrison, but its success during the years leading up to the Second World War was only made possible by the brilliance of its two famous leaders, Ashfield and Pick, who became LT's first chairman and chief executive respectively.

It was a fortuitous and fruitful partnership whose legacy would survive well beyond both men. Ostensibly Pick was the junior of the pair, as Ashfield was technically his boss, but in many respects the latter was in awe of his colleague. Pick, the rather Spartan low-church northerner, was indeed a formidable figure, a mixture of shyness and arrogance, of self-confidence and timidity.

Shy he may have been, eating on his own in the staff restaurant, but Pick was very clear about who was boss. While he was the backroom boy, he was nevertheless confident of his own power, favouring a regime that was a benign dictatorship. He argued that it was a waste of time trying to draw up on paper the structure of the perfect organization, because its success would ultimately be the responsibility of the particular people who happened to be in charge. Pick wanted 'a single brain'[1] – presumably his – to be responsible for running the organization, rather than a disparate group of managers. He ran a series of committees which fed responsibility up to him but he saw his role as making decisions – endless strings of them, in fact. Pick described his job as 'day after day, [having] to find answers to a continuous stream of questions about staff, finance, traffic, engineering, publicity, supplies . . . In no sense am I an expert. I have and can obtain advice wherever I want it. I merely have to decide, but in deciding I become responsible for my decisions. And while they are all separate decisions, it is necessary for me to try and fit them together into a consistent whole.'[2] It is, probably, as good a job description for the role of chief executive in a public body as any, a blueprint for others to follow. Pick was tireless: '[He] oversaw and planned every detail of his public transport empire. He travelled it frequently, taking copious notes in his unexpectedly flamboyant green [he used green ink for all his correspondence so that the recipient knew immediately its provenance] handwriting, ensuring that no fire bucket was left unfilled, no escalator out of service for longer than absolutely necessary. He walked each bus route.' Remarkably, Pick met both Stalin, from whom he received a medal in 1932 for his help and advice on the Moscow Metro, and Hitler, to whom he was introduced at a major railway conference in Berlin in 1936, a measure of his peerless reputation at the time.

It was not only the brilliance of Pick's administrative abilities and his tremendous intellectual power which ensured that the creation of London Transport was perceived as such a success. There was also Ashfield, who ultimately was more crucial to the organization because of his political skills. Ashfield was dapper, a ladies' man, something of a playboy tycoon who was always smartly turned out and enjoyed moving in high society, in contrast to diffident Pick. As befitted his role as a non-executive chairman, Ashfield did not have the burdens of day-to-day management and decision-making, but could sit back and work out strategy. He was a skilled negotiator, and used that trick of feigned artlessness when unwilling to answer a difficult question. But artless Ashfield was not. 'He always seemed to be two or three moves ahead of the ordinary able person when it came to negotiation. When this faculty was associated with every appearance of bonhomie and charm, and an unfailing sense of humour, one can begin to understand why he was so successful in promoting and carrying through the long series of transactions which culminated in the unification of London's local transport agencies.'[3]

Ultimately it was the fortuitous combination of these two great talents on which the success of LT was founded: 'The two men seemed to work together like the blades of a pair of scissors. But there was a difference. Whereas neither blade of the scissors will cut without the other, it could not be said that Pick was indispensable to Ashfield as Ashfield was to him. The real dependence was all one way.'[4] Perhaps that is harsh, since capable administrators of such talent are a rarity. As the historians of London Transport put it: 'The combination of the experienced, far-sighted politically astute chairman, who was willing to adopt accommodations on the way to securing his objectives, with the brilliant chief of staff whose cast of mind did not so readily accept compromise, provided a balance of flexibility in approach with rigorous management methods which made the LPTB in its first years an object of (sometimes unwilling) admiration.'[5] It was a remarkable team, which worked together for a third of a century and does not appear to have fallen out significantly until late on, at the outbreak of the Second World War, in what was ostensibly a dispute over fares policy but in fact centred around the mundane issue of Pick's pension.

And London Transport nearly did not happen. Had it not been for a series of fortuitous events and remarkable political machinations, London would have got a semi-regulated private monopoly with none of the vision and creativity of London Transport. The need for a more integrated system had long been recognized by Ashfield. In a 1924 pamphlet,[6] he explained the fundamental problem with railway economics. Railways, he argued, were essential for the development of outer housing zones because to reach the centre by tramway or bus was too time-consuming. But there was a conflict between people's desire to live on estates laid out in spacious grounds and the needs for density required by mass transport systems. At twelve houses per acre, the standard generally applied in the 1920s, Ashfield calculated that there would be only 6,000 houses within a half-mile radius – walking distance – and at 500 railway journeys per year, which assumed the sole breadwinner went to work every day, the passenger traffic would be 3 million: not enough to 'yield a sufficient income to support a tube railway except at high fares'. Ashfield concluded that 'either the circuit covered by a station must be rendered wider or the traffic denser by some means; cheap auxiliary forms of transport such as the motor omnibus may be developed to concentrate traffic on the railway stations . . . A measure of coordination among the transport facilities in a district is thus unavoidable for success.' As he later pointed out, 'it may be a surprise . . . to know that the Underground railways in London have never been, in their whole career, a financial success. In other words, they have failed to earn a reasonable rate of return on capital invested in them.'[7]

Instead of integration, from the mid-1920s the system became more fragmented, with the outbreak of bus wars in the capital. The Underground Group, which since its takeover of London General had run the majority of buses in the capital, found itself up against countless small companies – often consisting of just one man and a bus – who were able to cream off passengers on well-used routes at busy times. The Group was short of buses for several years after the Great War because many had not been returned by the War Office, and it was powerless to prevent these independent operators, dubbed 'pirates', from causing chaos on the streets. The pirates, sold cheap new buses by manufacturers eager to push their wares, would try to run just ahead of a General service to maximize the number of passengers, and they frequently raced each other because the income of the drivers – who were often exceptionally skilled – depended on speed. Pirates were even known to do a U-turn, rapidly dumping any passengers if the driver noticed more potential customers waiting on the other side of the road. Passengers may have enjoyed the occasional low fare or quicker ride, but the pirates were more prone to accidents and breakdowns than were the more conventional operators. It was a risky business, as one passenger recalls: 'If there was an accident, they never used to wait for the police or anything like that, unless it was serious, but in a smaller accident, they'd just pat the bloke on the head and most likely slip him a quid and away they went.'[8] By 1924, there were nearly 500 such pirates on the roads; it may have only been 10 per cent of the number run by the General, but it was enough to dent the larger company's profit margins, which were used to subsidize the Underground system.

A fundamental difference of opinion over how to deal with this unruly situation led to a five-year battle between Ashfield and Herbert Morrison, who was already a strong local political force in London. Morrison's vision for London transport's system had been set out in a pamphlet published in 1916, *The People's Roads*,[9] in which he argued that 'the answer [to the lack of coordination between tram and bus routes] was the municipalization of the entire London passenger traffic'. Coordination, rationalization and equalization of burdens could, he said, all be achieved by common public ownership and control.

Ashfield wanted much the same, with one major difference: the word 'public' was not on his agenda. Of course he wanted control and a monopoly, but he sought to ensure that it was a private one, protected by regulation which would keep the pirates off his back and allow his company to make enough profits to pay its way. He also had his eye on taking over the tramways run by the London County Council and local boroughs, and which therefore were not coordinated with either the Underground Group's buses or its trains. Ashfield's vision clearly fitted in with the ideology of the ruling Conservatives and, in a

Parliamentary Bill, they backed his idea, setting out a scheme through which the Ministry of Transport, advised by local interests, would regulate routes. Morrison, by then an MP, was aghast. He organized the opposition and devised a striking poster showing a London County Council tram menaced by the grabbing hand of the Combine (Underground Group).

However, the Conservative government fell before the Bill could become law, and was replaced by the minority Labour administration of 1923. Morrison, who had hoped to become the Minister of Transport, thought the legislation would be dropped. However, he was passed over in favour of Harry Gosling, and as the result of a shadowy deal between Gosling and Morrison's lifelong enemy, Ernest Bevin, the Tory Bill was pushed through virtually unchanged. Although recognizing that the legislation was weak, the ministers argued that the chaos on the streets demanded urgent action. Morrison was so incensed that he even voted against his own government. The new Act created a limited amount of regulation – such as specifying routes for buses for the first time – but while it moderated the behaviour of the pirates, they were still able to operate on a significant part of the network. Moreover, the legislation did nothing to address the fundamental problem of the absence of integration between the various transport concerns. This lack of coordination meant that the trams and the buses were often rivals to the Underground trains, rather than complementary, and passengers still faced all sorts of difficulties in buying tickets which could take them right across London.

As a result of the new law, Ashfield managed to incorporate some of the smaller rivals into the Combine, but his main target was the LCC tram network. The new Traffic Advisory Committee, set up by the 1924 Act, recommended such a merger in a report of 1927 and early the following year the Underground Group, together with the LCC, prepared Bills which would coordinate their services and pool their income, while falling short of an outright merger. The Tories were back in government but Morrison fought a successful rearguard action to stop the Bill.

Morrison, reviving the potent symbol of the LCC tram being grabbed by the capitalist Combine, argued that the Bill was 'common theft, a capitalist counter offensive against public property'.[10] He managed to delay the progress of the Bill by organizing a lengthy filibuster at the London County Council and through fervent opposition in Parliament held up the Bill's progress sufficiently to prevent its third reading by the time the government went to the country in May 1929. With Labour elected, and Morrison newly installed at the Ministry of Transport, the Bill was effectively dead. Morrison had seen off Ashfield, but at the end of the bloody battle through the previous six years, the two were like a pair of tired gladiators, only strong enough to shake hands.

Morrison was clear about what he did not want, but he had failed to prepare an alternative plan, apart from a vague notion for a publicly controlled transport system. After some deliberation, he decided that the best option was a public corporation, a body which was state-owned but which had a commercial remit and consequently would not require any subsidy. That was a shift away from his previous notion of municipal socialism, whereby transport would have been under the direct control of the local authority, as the tramways already were. That change was an illustration of an enduring feature of Morrison's political career, his fundamental pragmatism. While he always fought his corner hard, he was nevertheless ready to compromise if he could achieve most of what he wanted, which the creation of London Transport undoubtedly did. Morrison had realized that a London Transport based on local authority boundaries was a pipe dream, at least in the short term. The LCC at that time covered only central London, while the transport authority would have to stretch out in a much wider circle, at least twenty-five miles from the centre. Extending the LCC's boundaries that far would have required a major reorganization of local government, but this was not on the agenda – indeed it would take another three decades before the expanded Greater London Council was born. Therefore Morrison accepted the inevitable compromise, despite derision from his left-wing colleagues. As his biographers put it, 'the public corporation was the logical extension of Morrison's previous attitude to socialism which he always stressed had to stand the tests of being both ethically and economically sound'.[11] There is no doubt that, much to the benefit of Londoners, London Transport passed those tests.

Morrison began the difficult task of selling his Bill. He was part of a minority government and had to try to keep the other parties on board. Like all brilliant politicians, Morrison was able to face different ways depending on his audience. To the Labour left, he had to show that this was a great socialist enterprise, talking up his plan by telling them it was the 'greatest socialist scheme ever put before the House' and that 'real coordination means a single consolidated ownership'[12] which could not be achieved in any other way. To Ashfield, and indeed the Tories, he had to downplay the socialist element and stress that a public corporation was the most efficient way of running the capital's transport system and that the board would not be a ministerial poodle but would have genuine independence.

The strongest weapon in Morrison's armoury was the threat – mostly implied but sometimes stated explicitly – that in the future, a more left-wing Labour would create a much stronger model of state control. While the idea of creating a public corporation might have seemed socialistic to some of the old Tory duffers sitting on the backbenches, it was similar to the measures introduced by their own governments in creating organizations such as the BBC and the Central Electricity Board. Public opinion towards such public–private enterprises had changed from hostility to acquiescence; the *Financial News* commented that a proposal to nationalize a group of private business undertakings, which not long previously might have been treated as a 'mild flight of collectivist fancy', now 'arouses very little excitement indeed'.[13] It was, after all, the era of Keynesian economics. In any case, the creation of a London-wide body responsible for transport was long overdue. The concept of unifying London's passenger transport facilities stretched back to the recommendation of a select committee of the House of Lords which had reported in 1863, the year the Metropolitan first opened for business, and therefore it could hardly be seen as a revolutionary measure.

Morrison's key objective, as his biographers succinctly put it, 'was to nationalize Ashfield'.[14] Morrison quickly came to admire Ashfield, immediately thinking of him as the future chairman of the board because of his spirit of public service and his friendly relations with the unions. Ashfield, the consummate charmer, clearly won over Morrison and, for his part, began to realize that the public corporation was not such a bad compromise. It delivered the unified management that was essential and stopped fruitless competition.

Morrison also needed to 'nationalize' Pick in order to ensure that his project was successful. Pick, though, was a tougher nut to crack. Morrison found him prickly, as indeed did much of the rest of the world. Morrison said of him – rather unfairly – that to Pick, London was just a market for transport: 'he is without social conscience, the business is everything'. That was to misunderstand Pick's great commitment to providing the best for Londoners, irrespective of class or status. As a London architectural historian put it, 'whether you hailed from Stepney or South Kensington, Arnos Grove or Amersham, Pick believed you should be treated equally and well. So superb custom-designed and engineered buses and trains met Londoners and took them about their business and off to play.'[15] That, in a way, was just as socialist as anything Morrison believed.

Pick and Ashfield played a Mutt and Jeff double act in their negotiations with the wily politician, whereby Pick would set out the most radical alternatives to Morrison's plans, which would be fiercely resisted, and Ashfield would come in to thrash out a compromise. Morrison, in fact, became so impressed by Pick that he eventually recommended him to be deputy chairman of the board.

There was one big concession when the Bill was published in March 1931 (after some clever footwork by Morrison who even managed to irritate the Prime Minister, Ramsay MacDonald, in his haste to introduce the Bill). Originally, the plan was to have included the London suburban rail services, at the time controlled by the Big Four private railway companies; but, to the long-term detriment of Londoners, that part of the scheme was considered to be over-ambitious and was shelved. Later, Pick would describe that as the main 'flaw' in the arrangements for London's transport system and therefore was a historic missed opportunity.[16]

Once he was on side, Ashfield played a vital role in winning over two pockets of potential opposition – the House of Lords and the shareholders. Ashfield had to gain the support of the owners of the Underground Group and in May 1931, at a mass meeting of the company's investors, he made one of the great speeches of his life in order to persuade them that amalgamation and integration were the only way forward. The shareholders had been very hostile but just before the vote was about to be taken, Ashfield made a personal appeal for them to support him. It was the kind of 'back me or sack me' speech favoured by today's politicans. And they backed him. As one of the audience put it, 'it was the power of his personality that turned the scales and secured a favourable vote'.[17]

The main issue had been over the compensation terms for the shareholders and Morrison had made sufficient concessions for Ashfield to win them over. Morrison had agreed a scheme to give them new, redeemable stock without voting rights but which paid a rate of interest partly dependent on the success of the new enterprise. The amount varied between the different concerns that were incorporated into the new organization but the Underground Group shareholders received the most, which included a small amount of cash. Pick later thought that the deal had been too generous, thus lumbering the new organization with a level of debt that meant it soon got into financial difficulties.

The most difficult negotiation was with the most powerful company being taken over, the Metropolitan. The death of Robert Selbie, the general manager of the Metropolitan, in 1930 had weakened the position of the Metropolitan but the company still put up a fight, managing to increase the offer for £100 nominal of its stock from £57 10 shillings to £67 10 shillings. Most importantly, the highly profitable property interests largely stayed with the shareholders; however the valuable Chiltern Court did go to the new board because it was directly controlled by the railway, unlike most of the rest of the property which was run by the Metropolitan's subsidiaries.

After the shareholders, it was the turn of the Lords. The following year, Ashfield – in his only speech ever to the House of Lords – played a key role in convincing peers of the benefits of the creation of London Transport. By then Morrison had gone, swept away in Labour's humiliating performance at the 1931 election, but the Bill survived. Indeed, after Morrison's amazing political victory over the coordination Bills, another near miracle was needed to salvage the Bill once the government collapsed. Normally, Bills automatically fall between Parliaments but this was a hybrid Bill – affecting both private and public interests – and therefore not only survived the general election, at which the Conservatives gained by far the most seats, but was also accepted by the incoming government, which was a national all-party administration. Morrison could only watch from the sidelines, having lost his seat at the election.

Ashfield used the old canard that worse might ensue from a later Labour government. His main aim was to convince his fellow Lordships that the Bill was *not* a socialistic measure and he argued, rather disingenuously, that there was little difference between the 1929 Bills which Morrison had blocked and the measure before them. Ashfield was also called upon to defend the arrangements for the shareholders. The Tory Lord Chancellor, Lord Hailsham,[18] closed for the government with a remarkably sanguine statement commending the Bill to the House: 'This measure is one which is conservative in structure, which is financially sound in its basis, which is urgently needed for the traffic of London, which is supported by the vast majority of those persons whose business is to look after the traffic of London'.[19]

There had been a final significant change to Morrison's Bill, one that ultimately benefited the nascent LT by giving it greater independence. Instead of board members being appointed by the Minister of Transport, they were to be independently selected by a committee of the great and the good, a motley collection of VIPs, including the respective chairmen of the Institute of Chartered Accountants, the BBC, the Law Society and the Committee of the London Clearing Banks. Only a decade earlier, Morrison had inveighed against boards with such indirect representation – calling such organizations 'Hole and Corner Boards';[20] but clearly he had become more emollient since subsequently he was always ready to lay claim to having given birth to a highly successful concept. Indeed, despite being separate from government in this way, London Transport would be able to benefit from the favourable borrowing terms which only state bodies, with their 100 per cent guarantee of solvency, can enjoy. London Transport was, therefore, one of the first big quangos – quasi-autonomous non-governmental organizations – long before the term was invented. Apart from Ashfield and Pick, the other five board members were part-timers: they included the assistant general secretary of the Transport & General Workers Union, a director of the Bank of England and a couple of men with local government experience, but they were all, effectively, independent of any outside interests.

London Transport formally came into being on 1 July 1933. As seemed inevitable, Lord Ashfield became Chairman of the Board, while Pick was appointed chief executive. Melding the disparate bits it inherited was to take the next two years. Although that task was a continuation of the work of Ashfield and Pick over the past two decades, the situation was, by the early 1930s, still very confused. Pick had the task of sorting out five railway companies (the suburban services of the four mainline companies had a complex pooling arrangement with LT), fourteen council-owned tramways, three private tram companies, sixty-six omnibus and coach companies and parts of sixty-nine others. There was much kerfuffle over compensation terms, and the smaller companies had recourse to an independent three-man tribunal to determine their entitlement.

A measure of the high feelings over the issue of what many saw as nationalization is demonstrated by a curious incident involving Pick being sued for slander by a group of independent bus companies. He had said that these companies' selfishness was 'unmoderated and undisguised, the only object was to secure as much profit as possible in order to stake a claim which might eventually lead to compensation'.[21] That was actually a perfectly reasonable and fair statement, but it led to a lengthy legal wrangle and though this was eventually settled out of court, Pick had to agree to pay some of the bus companies' costs.

Ultimately, Pick was relaxed about having being 'nationalized'. As his biographer puts it, 'Pick had always been willing to accept the principle of public control, not as a good thing in itself, but as an evil necessary to check and restrain another and greater evil – the rapacity of a profit-hungry business enjoying monopolistic power. He saw the LPTB as an experiment in monopoly power which might give London better forms of public administration ... "It is a new start in life. All that I have done in the past may be forgotten."'[22] In his letter accepting the job at LT, he wrote: 'Now begins the tussle to show that the board of public character can conduct its business on strictly commercial lines.'[23]

It was, like so much of the Underground's history, a great experiment. And it was a big organization. At its establishment LT employed over 70,500 staff, which rose to almost 100,000 by 1947. LT did everything. It encompassed the whole supply chain in a way that is unheard of today when outsourcing is the norm. LT designed its own trains and buses, ran a myriad of support services such as food production and engineering shops, and looked after its employees in a benevolent way. Indeed, LT was seen as a good employer, offering relatively high wages, staff messrooms, sports associations and the prospect of a retirement home. The job was secure, too, during a period when unemployment was an ever-present fear. The wages of the disparate organizations which made up LT were harmonized, largely upwards, to give the staff a sense of belonging. It was a uniform service, run to some extent, like the railways, on militaristic lines, and promotion was on a 'Buggins's turn' basis, through longevity rather than ability. The good conditions were partly a result of Pick's policy of paying fair wages with the expectation of high standards in return, but the staff were also very strongly unionized. The ability to go on strike has always been a powerful weapon for transport workers, since they are in a strong position to wreck the economics of their employer. Train drivers were relatively well paid, getting ninety-three shillings (around forty times more in today's money, say £186) per week after six years' service while a guard with a similar length of service received sixty-eight shillings. Booking clerks were paid something in between those two. Pick himself did all right, earning £10,000 per year, an enormous sum equivalent to £400,000 today, which was surprisingly uncontroversial.

Despite the glowing reputation of London Transport in this period, there was never a clear notion of how best to run the organization. There were frequent changes in structure, ranging from lumping all the operations under one head to creating separate divisions for the various modes of travel. Indeed, the success of London Transport during this period owes more to the individuals who were in charge than to the structures they managed. Pick was in no doubt about this.

The London Underground was, by the time of the inauguration of London Transport, at its historic best in terms of service, with many of the central stations refurbished and some of the extensions that now stretched deep into the suburbs beginning to be well used. It had expanded further in the east with the District reaching Upminster in 1932. Overcrowding, which had often been the source of complaint in the 1920s, remained, but there was more capacity in the network and, with a lot of new rolling stock, many passengers' perception of the system was a favourable one. However, much investment was still needed but the scheme devised by Ashfield and Pick, the New Works Programme, could not be started until 1935 when, again, government terms were favourable and the structure of London Transport had begun to settle down. In the meantime, there were growing numbers of passengers – 416 million in 1934 – and the organization's confidence in its own status was shown by its occupation of the Charles Holden-designed building at 55 Broadway over St James's Park station as its headquarters. That stark modern temple was the tallest office building in London when it opened in 1929, though its height was somewhat disguised by its bulk and the way that the floors are broken up in rectangular sections. The Broadway block had caused a furore when it was first built because of the two statues of nudes by Jacob Epstein overlooking the street. One displayed the male organ in all its splendour, but fortunately they were at first-floor level, making them vandal- (or rather philistine-) proof, and they survived, remaining largely unnoticed by the public today.

The hiatus from the lengthy birth pangs of London Transport created a backlog of investment in the existing system, and the need for various long-discussed extensions had become more pressing. Again, as had become the pattern, the investment plans had to wait for the government to initiate yet another Keynesian-style programme to bring down unemployment. This happened in 1935 and Ashfield and Pick were, as ever, ready with a whole host of schemes and plans which they dusted down with great haste to present to the government. The overall scheme was a joint plan with the railways of which the main elements for the Underground were extensions both eastwards and westwards to the Central; taking the Highgate section of the Northern out to East Finchley and, eventually, High Barnet, Bushey and Alexandra Palace (sadly the latter two were dropped); sorting out the bottleneck between Baker Street and Waterloo; reconstructing several stations including King's Cross; and various other important ancillary works such as improving the power supply. The total estimate of the cost was £40m, later increased to £45m, financed by money raised with government backing, which meant it cost £330,000 less in interest annually than if it had been borrowed at commercial rates. It was an arrangement under which, as one historian put it, 'Pick and Ashfield were able to run a public corporation raising funds where they saw fit, with little day to day interference from government and none from the private sector. They worked exclusively in the public interest but without their hands tied by political or economic dogma.'[24]

Apart from not including the suburban railways, the other flaw in the design of London Transport – as Pick had foreseen – was that it had been burdened with debt rather than given the clean financial slate it needed. In a speech in November 1936, Ashfield warned that the financial prospect was not a cheerful one. Rising cost of wages and pensions, demand for provision for renewals, stock redemption arrangements and the cost of financing extensions into the suburbs would mean that LT would be running a £3m deficit annually by the mid-1940s. As the war intervened, changing completely the finances of the organization and blocking the last part of the investment programme, Ashfield's prediction was never put to the test.

London Transport may have enjoyed a heyday during this period but it never really had time to settle down. Within six brief years of its creation, Britain was at war, and in between the organization had to bed itself in, implement a massive investment programme and cope with a growing financial crisis. It was, indeed, a successful organization, but it is remembered as such largely because of its brilliant public relations, notably its huge range of memorable posters, and the sheer consistency of design, policed so carefully by Pick.

By the time of the creation of London Transport, the Underground's tradition of innovative design had been in place for twenty years. Pick was a great pioneer in that respect, understanding right from the beginning the importance of good design in conveying the objectives of an organization. In 1909 Pick, who had frequently complained about the poor quality of the Underground Company's promotional material, was appointed traffic development officer with a remit to take responsibility for the design of its publicity literature; a task, incidentally, for which he was totally unqualified given that he was a solicitor by profession. What he did have, though, was a tremendous eye for design, and he can lay claim for establishing the image of London Transport as we know it. Every poster had a message to convey which was part of a wider purpose, that of convincing the public that the Underground system was an easy, convenient, fast, reliable and safe form of transport. The legacy of London Underground in commissioning art works is unique among transport organizations or, probably, among commercial business of any kind. As Pick's biographer puts it:

> For anybody who was strange to London, uncertain of the way,
> uncertain of the time it would take to get there, the posters were
> there to say: walk this way, the Underground will take care of
> you. An underground liftman standing beside his open gate calls
> 'let us give you a lift'; the underground stations are chessmen on
> a board beneath which is printed 'your next move'; another
> time the mood switches to the poetical but it is tongue in cheek:
> the underground railways are soaring female figures that bear
> above their heads a crepuscular London skyline gathered under
> the ball and cross of St Paul's.[25]

One of the earliest posters commissioned by Pick shows his ability to use design to wider effect. The poster depicts a stylized idyllic family scene, a cunningly disguised semi-detached house, with no other housing anywhere to be seen as even the other half of the building is cut off by the edge. Produced in 1908 soon after the opening of the Hampstead railway, the poster simply says 'Golders Green A place of delightful prospects'. The railway terminated there at the time and it is the weekend, probably a Saturday. The man is busy watering his sunflowers while the woman is sitting in a chair rolling a ball of wool, a three-year-old straight out of a Pears soap advertisement at her feet. You can almost feel the balmy air, and, just to make sure, there is a poem stressing the quietness of the scene and its distance from the hubbub of the metropolis.

The posters selected by Pick reflect his personality and those designed in the early days of London Transport very much reflect the Zeitgeist. They show a self-confidence with a slightly patronizing do-gooder tone but their artistry and elegance make one forget that. They exhort Londoners to travel by the Underground: perhaps to go to the Wimbledon tennis or a walk in the Chiltern Hills, using one of the three books of walks published by London Underground. Fresh air was certainly a common theme. But Pick and the others who commissioned the artists were not scared of posters with an elliptical message. For example, one by Graham Sutherland shows no people, just a desk with a typewriter and a torn newspaper cutting that starts: 'Go out in the country. The spring days which come in mid-winter are always the best of the year . . .' Several posters from the 1930s have a Soviet feel, with heavy-set workers toiling and powerful images of tools or engines.

There are not many organizations which can lay claim to having commissioned their own typeface in order to establish their identity. In 1915, Pick asked Edward Johnston, a leading calligrapher, to develop a typeface for station signage and posters. The result, Johnston, is familiar to all Londoners and still in use today; Johnston worked with the Underground and then London Transport for the rest of his life. Yet although the script was widely adopted for notices and posters, Pick did not require his designers always to use Johnston. There are many examples of other typefaces, but somehow there is a unity of image that marks out printed material for London Transport produced during Pick's tenure. One strange exception to the overall excellence was the tickets, whose format has been circumscribed more by what the automatic dispensers, first used in 1908, were able to issue cheaply – particularly after self-printing ticket machines were introduced in 1930 – than by any design considerations.

As a demonstration of just how far Pick went in maintaining high design standards, in the Acton depot of the London Transport museum there is a beautiful 1930s style oval table, covered in green baize with an embossed fleur-de-lis pattern around the rim, on which he held meetings in his office. The eight chairs around the table are also stylish, simple and armless, covered in a pleasing mauve woollen material speckled with blue and red which appears so durable that the whole set looks as if it is being offered for sale as new. The cupboard, which appears to have been standard, is even more solid. It is a miniature of the front of the 55 Broadway building, square with flat two-inch bevelled edges and the three slightly raised square panels that make it unmistakably 1930s. Pick had selected all this furniture as a way of emphasizing the unity of image and purpose of London Transport.

The consistent quality of the posters commissioned by Pick was not happenstance. For Pick, good design was good business and he put enormous amount of energy and thought into it. While the quality of the work had already attracted widespread admiration by the early 1930s, the establishment of LT with its corporate strength and financial stability gave Pick a wonderful platform to pursue his interest in showing how design could establish the image of an organization and be used for marketing its services, convincing the public that every care had been taken in providing them with the best possible service. Unlike the Underground Company, which had been one among many competing organizations, London Transport represented the whole of the capital; and given this single public authority responsible for bus, tram and underground railway operations, Pick saw it as essential to develop a design ethic for the whole organization. The board backed him in these efforts not only because they recognized that establishing such an identity was important in presenting a good face to the public but also, as the historians of LT design put it, because 'the new board saw immediately that if the group was to function effectively, it must replace that loyalty [to their previous employers] with an allegiance to the new organization'.[26]

Consequently, the new identity was used as a business tool both to display to the public the integrated transport system and also to unite the workforce. This corporate image, a novel concept expressed particularly through the logo,[27] was immediately displayed everywhere in the capital – on liveries, uniforms, signage and printed material. Indeed, because Pick and Ashfield sought to widen their organization's services as far as possible to what, today, would be known as the 'travel to work area', the logo and LT's neat liveries could be seen on country buses and Green Line coaches in towns and villages as far as fifty miles from the centre of the capital.

Even today, very few companies communicate their purpose as clearly as LT did in the 1930s:

> The remarkable thing about this early exercise in corporate identity is not that it existed, but that it was so sophisticated and stylish. Not for Pick the monoculture of the carefully controlled image, the proscriptive rules, the single voice. The images that emerged were witty and cultured, and promoted the idea of a progressive, efficient, caring and style-conscious organization . . . The use of good design became a tradition but was never 'traditional'. The main characteristics were a willingness to seek new ideas and solutions, to experiment with new methods and materials, unrestricted by the past.[28]

Pick's philosophy is best summed up in his own words: 'The test of the goodness of a thing is its fitness for use. If it fails on this first test, no amount of ornamentation or finish will make it any better; it will only make it more expensive, more foolish.'[29]

The influence of LT design went well beyond the passengers. As Nikolaus Pevsner put it, 'no exhibition of modern painting, no lecturing, no school teaching, can have had anything like so wide an effect on the educatable masses as the unceasing production and display of [Underground] posters over the years 1930–1940'.[30] It was free art for the masses.

The most enduring image of the Underground, also introduced by Pick, is, of course, the famous schematic Underground map conceived by Harry Beck. Along with the roundel, it typifies how London Transport wanted to be perceived – modern, clean, forward-looking and elegant.

Like London Transport itself, the map nearly did not happen. Its designer, Harry Beck, had been a junior draughtsman for the Underground but had been made redundant by the time he sketched out the first draft of the famous map. Beck had worked in the signal engineers' department for six years and the original map was based on an electric circuit diagram. The brilliant aspect of its innovation is the idea that conventional maps can be too accurate, and thereby unnecessarily complex. It is, of course, based on a simple bit of cheating. Instead of trying to portray the real distance between stations, and the correct angles at which lines intersect, the map provides a schematic display, suggesting that virtually every station is equidistant and that lines only meet or change direction at neat 45° or 90° angles.

When he first presented the map to Frank Pick's publicity committee in 1931, it was rejected. But he tried again the following year, by which time he was back working for the Underground, and although the original did not have the bright colours which later become an essential part of the distinctive design, the committee agreed that a test run should be commissioned. According to differing accounts, Beck was paid a mere five or ten guineas for his design but, after the trial proved successful, some 750,000 were produced in January 1933 and distributed free to Londoners. Certainly from London Transport's point of view it was a great bargain, since the design has brought in millions of pounds in licence fees for a veritable A to Z of items ranging from alarm clocks and boxer shorts to oven gloves and quizzes.

Beck's schematic design has been followed both for other underground maps, such as those of New York and Berlin, and for other modes of transport, such as main line trains and airlines. Even the French, with their latest Parisian Métro and RER (suburban rail services) map, now follow Beck's essential rules on angles and station distances.

The cleverness and durability of Beck's work is demonstrated by the ease with which nine lines became fourteen[31] but still retained the same look. Beck's stroke of genius was to look at the problem of the map from the passengers' point of view, rather than in the way that those running the Underground perceived it. The map tidies up the chaos of the city, giving the impression that the city is of a size and design that is comprehensible to both its inhabitants and visitors.[32] The Beck map, along with the roundel and the typeface, is the third part of the iconography of the London Underground which has done so much to establish the image of London across the world. Uniquely among transport systems, London Underground typifies the city itself.

The timing of the creation of a strong, state-run London Transport was perfect in historic terms. The 1930s were the point at which the Underground was probably most crucial as a means of transport to the widest range of social classes and it enjoyed its highest ever modal share[33] of journeys in London. The capital's population peaked at 8.6 million just before the Second World War. Mass car ownership was only beginning to take off, but would soon turn the centre of London into a permanent traffic jam and cream off some of the Underground's custom. Although the number of passengers rose to 488 million in 1938, the last full year before the outbreak of the war, the car was beginning to take its toll on certain types of journey.[34]

Ashfield had already realized that the Underground would no longer have a monopoly on the medium-distance journeys that were essential to its economics. Prescient as ever, he had pointed out in his speech to shareholders that 'the motor car has grown to be an important feature . . . they carry not only the family, but also neighbours and friends, and therefore withdraw more people from the public means of conveyance than at first sight would seem possible'.[35] In particular, the theatre traffic had been lost to cars and Ashfield predicted that it would be increasingly difficult for public transport to compete. He argued, too, that the quality of services, both in buses and trains, had to be improved in order to meet the competition. He was completely right, but all these developing trends, as well as the Underground's expansion programme, were about to be interrupted.

FOURTEEN

THE BEST
SHELTERS OF ALL

The Underground at war was not just about people in shelters, the most enduring image of the system. The trains, by and large, kept going throughout the conflict, playing a vital part in ensuring the capital still functioned. There had been, well before the outbreak of the war, a debate within government circles about the use of the system as a shelter and that would continue well after the commencement of hostilities. As far back as 1924, the Orwellian-sounding Air Raid Precautions Sub-committee of the Committee of Imperial Defence concluded that the tube lines would be needed for transport purposes and therefore should not be used as shelters. That view was partly informed by the widespread feeling among officialdom that allowing people to go underground would create a 'deep shelter mentality', fostering a subterranean population who would refuse to come up once the bombers had gone. Those fears were in sharp contrast to the attitude of the local politicians in Barcelona, bombed by Franco, who created a network of deep tube shelters able to accommodate much of the population.

The importance of the Underground in the event of an attack was recognized with the installation of anti-gas measures at new stations and the Post Office's plans for an emergency communications system.

More strangely, in the days running up to Neville Chamberlain's infamous visit for talks with Hitler in Munich, Londoners found that several stations close to the river had been closed and that trains could no longer travel under the Thames. The reason was that the panicking London Transport Board had ordered the construction of enormous concrete plugs at each end of the tunnels under the river because they feared an attack with bombs would breach them and cause disastrous flooding of the system. Following Chamberlain's return from Munich, clutching his peace pledge, the tunnels were restored two weeks after their closure. Instead, vast electrically operated iron floodgates were built to allow trains to continue running under the Thames. These were interlocked with the signalling so that they could not be closed with a train in the sealed part of the tunnel. However, by the time war broke out on 3 September, only the gates on the Bakerloo had been completed and for a time the Northern was, again, blocked by concrete plugs which were also used to seal off various passageways at nineteen stations deemed at risk of flooding from broken mains. Eventually, twenty-five floodgates, each weighing nearly six tons and electrically operated from a control centre at Leicester Square, were completed by October 1940, just after the start of the Blitz.

LT carried over half a million evacuees in the first four days of September 1939, a scheme organized by Frank Pick, but the long period of the 'phoney war' meant that many had drifted back to their parents by the time the Blitz started a year later. During the time of the phoney war, the authorities tried to hold the line on their non-shelter policy as announced by the government on the day the war broke out. Posters throughout the system stated baldly in Johnston capitals: 'The tube stations are required for traffic purposes and the tube stations are not available as air raid shelters'.

But banning people from seeking protection was always going to be a difficult policy to maintain. Had the authorities built a series of deep shelters elsewhere in the capital, perhaps that line could have held. But they had done little to protect their citizens – brick shelters had been built in the streets but these were clearly vulnerable to a direct hit and were highly unpopular. The tubes, in contrast, were perceived as safe havens. They were easily accessible and provided companionship and warmth, in what appeared to be a completely safe environment away from much of the noise of aircraft and their bombs, which could only occasionally be heard even underground.

Moreover, there was a popular movement of resistance to the ban on the use of shelters, spearheaded by the Communist Party, which ran a sustained media campaign throughout 1940 pressing for a proper policy on air raid protection which would include the widespread provision of deep-level shelters. As attacks began to intensify in the summer of 1940, the authorities were finding it harder to defend their stations. London Transport officials were instructed to turn away people who were not considered to be bona fide travellers, but this was an impossible task. The first heavy raids were on the night of 7 September 1940 when docks and gas works in the East End were targeted. That first big raid claimed the lives of 430 people and gave fuel to the Communist Party's campaign. It was not just the masses of the East End who were affected. A *Daily Telegraph* reader wrote to complain of being 'directed to a street shelter after being refused re-admission to a station I had left during a raid'.[1]

The Communist Party, inevitably, saw it as part of the class war against the workers. Its newspaper, the *Daily Worker*, argued predictably: 'The shelter policy of the Government is not just a history of incompetence and neglect. It is a calculated class policy, a determination not to provide protection because of profits being placed before human lives.'[2] The paper spoke of 'the ruling classes' in their 'luxury shelters' and to highlight this, on 14 September, a group of Stepney CP activists occupied the luxury shelter built for the guests of the Savoy where they partook of tea and other refreshments served on silver trays. This little bit of direct action attracted enormous press publicity and helped make the government's shelter policy untenable.

By then, it was already crumbling. People had quickly cottoned on to the notion that they could buy a cheap penny ticket for travel to the next station but could not get on a train. Shelterers had also started using, with official approval, the disused section of the City & South London line to its original terminus at King William Street. Within a couple of days of that first big raid, 4,000 people who had presented themselves at Old Street station to seek shelter had been allowed in by policemen too scared to resist them. Londoners, therefore, swarmed into the tube system. The *Daily Worker* cheered, celebrating its victory, which it claimed was a result of the efforts of the Communist Party. This was undoubtedly partly true, but once the bombs started raining down, it seems unlikely that the authorities could have stopped people going down below. Indeed, unless the authorities had been prepared to resort to using soldiers with fixed bayonets, the sheer intensity of the bombing ensured that nothing could stop the people taking to the tubes.

Herbert Morrison, who had been appointed Home Secretary in October 1940, quickly made clear that no attempt should be made by the police to prevent orderly access, provided that services were allowed to keep operating. The Labour Party had long argued for more shelters and Londoners welcomed the appointment of Morrison, expecting him to bring about rapid improvements. They were not to be disappointed. He announced a series of deep shelters to be built under tube stations, but also set about improving the lot of the shelterers in the Underground system. While those shelters would take too long to build to protect the citizens from the brunt of the Blitz, which reduced in intensity during the summer of 1941 when the Germans turned their attention eastwards, the announcement of their construction was a big morale boost for Londoners who felt that something was at least being done for them.

By 22 September, the *Sunday Dispatch* was reporting that '30,000 spent last night in the Tubes'. This was a gross understatement. The authorities leaned on the press to curtail enthusiasm for the use of the tubes as shelter. According to a history of the shelterers, 'four times that number had actually sheltered in the Tubes the previous evening'.[3] Indeed, the *Dispatch* rather gave the game away by reporting that 'by 6 p.m. there seemed no vacant space from St Paul's to Notting Hill, from Hampstead to Leicester Squares'. And who were these shelterers? The *Dispatch* said 'types varied much, from the trousered, lipsticked Kensington girls to the cockneys at Camden Town; but all were alike in their uncomplaining, patient cheerfulness'.

The *South London Press* was less impressed. The reporter told how it took him a quarter of an hour to reach the station entrance from the platform:

> I stumbled over huddled bodies, bodies which were no safer
> from bombs than if they had lain in the gutters of the streets
> outside . . . Little girls and boys lay across their parents' bodies
> because there was no room on the winding stairs. Hundreds of
> men and women were partially undressed, while small boys and
> girls slumbered in the foetid atmosphere absolutely naked . . .
> On the platform, when a train came in, it had to be stopped in
> the tunnel while police and porters went along pushing in the
> feet and the arms which overhung the line.[4]

It was, apparently, the same all along the line, a driver told the reporter.

At the beginning, life in the tubes was rough. The stench must have been horrific, as there were no toilets and urinating over the tracks or in corners was the norm. Moreover, through fear of a gas attack, the ventilation fans were switched to a minimum; and, more important, the trains, whose action through the tunnel has always been the tube lines' primary form of ventilation, did not run at night.

Spaces were, at first, reserved on a free-for-all basis, often by spivs with time on their hands who queued for hours before the warning sounded and then sold on the pitch. The spivs charged as much as half a crown (two shillings and sixpence), which, given that the wage of a station worker was a mere £3 per week at the time, is a measure of how much value Londoners placed on getting a good night's sleep in safety. The police tried to create some order by instructing people at overcrowded stations to go further down the line, but the early days in the shelters were chaotic.

Rules began to emerge quite quickly. At the beginning of October, white lines were painted at four and eight feet from the edge, allowing passengers a free passage along the platform and ensuring that no limbs overhung the rails (there was at least one report of a man plunging into the pit and being killed by a train). No reservations were allowed before 4 p.m. and then spaces could be taken up to the eight-foot line, and after 7.30 p.m., up to the four-foot one. By November, London Transport started to introduce a system of tickets, which were distributed to the shelterers by local authority marshals. This guaranteed people their allocated space and avoided the hassle of having to spend much of the afternoon queuing and scrambling for places, which occasionally led to fights. Some people took to bringing little brushes to sweep their space.

The sanitation problem, too, began to be addressed. Chemical toilets started to arrive late in September and by November a much more sophisticated sanitation system was introduced, involving the use of compressors to pump up sewage to ground level. Conditions were still not pleasant, however. The system was plagued by a variety of mosquito, *culex molestus*, which had led a relatively spartan existence until suddenly the massive influx of night dwellers provided a seemingly endless supply of blood. The population of the pest increased exponentially. Fortunately, though its bite caused itching, it did not carry any disease and the plague of insects was eventually brought under control, but not wiped out, by the spraying of its breeding grounds, mostly pools of water under platforms, with disinfectant and paraffin. Bedbugs also preyed on the shelterers, with outbreaks at various stations throughout the war caused by people bringing in their own infested blankets. Although LT said it would ban verminous-looking people, and those found with bugs were referred to the medical centres and subjected to the indignity of a home visit, according to the history of the shelterers: 'happily no shelterer had their reservation tickets cancelled on account of being carriers of vermin as suspects invariably submitted to the cleansing treatment'. The worst reported infestation was the discovery of a large group of rats at the Bethnal Green station shelter, which led to fears of a plague epidemic, but fortunately that never materialized.

Food was the other major task for the authorities. Refreshment trains began running by the end of October, delivering supplies to stations. The water for tea had to be heated using electric ovens, since gas flames were banned from the system. London Transport used 1,000 of its women workers, dressed in a kind of uniform with green frocks and red kerchiefs on their heads, to take the supplies to the public in baskets and specially constructed two-gallon teapots. A cup of tea or cocoa was a penny, as were buns (the favourite) and pieces of cake. Meat pies, packets of biscuits, apples and sandwiches were also available. Shelterers were, however, expected to bring their own utensils and cups.

The most telling evidence of LT's change in attitude from hostility towards the shelterers to acceptance that it had a duty to provide for them was, perhaps, a little sign put up at the depots where food was assembled for dispatch. It read: 'Tube refreshments. This depot supplies service points, stations and feeds people. They rely on us for food and drink night and morning. We must not let them down.' The Blitz spirit had clearly percolated upwards.

For a long time, the authorities tried to keep 'able-bodied' men out of the tubes, implying that sheltering there was an act of cowardice which took up space that could be occupied by women and children. London Transport put up bills stressing the need to keep services running and exclaiming: 'Be a man and leave it to them' because of the limited space. It was a theme quickly picked up by several newspapers, which greatly exaggerated the issue, even though the shelterers themselves do not seem to have been hostile to the presence of men. Indeed, many of the adult males were key workers in the war effort, who could work more efficiently during the day after a good night's kip in the Tube. The newspapers accused them of being aliens and pacifists, the same accusations as had been laid on *all* shelterers in the First World War.

By Christmas 1940, life started to become routine. As the authorities had now accepted the situation, a lot more amenities were available, thanks largely due to the efforts of a retired London Transport Manager, J.P. Thomas, who had been recalled from retirement to coordinate the organization's work. The refreshment trains carrying eleven tons of food nightly had become standard throughout; beds were installed with accommodation for 22,800 people, which LT proudly proclaimed represented eight and half miles of three-tier bunks; and medical teams provided by local authorities were installed at every station. Each medical post was a brilliant compact design with a consulting space, an isolation bay with five bunks for infectious cases, electric heating for sterilizing instruments, various cupboards and bunks for the nurses, all tucked into a space of 18½ft by 7½ft.

There were libraries at several stations and others were fitted with amplifiers which played records. Some groups of shelterers even produced their own newsletters. These may have been short-lived but they were lively records of life in the stations. The bulletins contained useful advice, such as recommending that children be inoculated against diphtheria, but also quite a lot of political messages. One issue of the Belsize Park newsletter,[5] for example, warned 'it has become more obvious lately that there is being created a definite anti-Semitic and anti-foreign feeling. We regret to have to remind some people that this is one of the things we are fighting against.' It recommended that everyone should see the new Chaplin film on fascism, *The Great Dictator*. The Swiss Cottage paper, the most expertly produced, as demonstrated by its witty name of *De Profundis*, announced that a committee of shelterers was to be formed to negotiate with London Transport. There was, too, a request for a penny from every shelterer 'for the porters to buy First Aid equipment for the users of the station'. It reported that 1,503 people slept there one night, '1,650 of whom seemed to be snoring'. One fellow found his romantic notions quickly thwarted: 'Last night, not six inches from me, lay the most beautiful girl. Then she began to snore, and her loveliness faded.'

By the middle of the Blitz, all seventy-nine tube stations were in use as shelters. There were, too, various redundant or partly built sections of the Underground which had been turned over to the shelterers with official blessing, such as the disused stations at South Kentish Town, British Museum and City Road, and the unfinished section of lines at Bethnal Green, the largest in the capital with accommodation for 5,000, and Highgate.

The deep shelters announced by Morrison were not available for use during the Blitz of 1940–41 and they were kept in reserve, as numbers in the shelters dwindled during the subsequent lull. Five of them finally found use as shelters briefly in the summer of 1944 during the assault by V1 and V2 rockets, but in terms of protection from the bombs they were too little, too late. They were later used to house returning evacuees made homeless by the bombing.

The elite of shelters was probably Aldwych. The whole little-used branch line to Holborn was given over for the use of thousands of shelterers soon after the onset of the Blitz, by Lord Ashfield. Westminster council provided generous facilities, including a library of two thousand books and educational lectures. Various feature films and Shakespeare plays were shown and there was even a performance by George Formby.

There are many myths about the tube shelterers. While it is undoubtedly true that they were a very visible expression of the Blitz spirit, contrary to the impression given by many accounts of London in the war, seeking protection in the underground from the air raids was a minority activity. The numbers were significant but not massive.

In the first year, London Transport reported that a total of 16 million nights had been spent in the shelters. On the first night on which a count was taken, 27 September 1940, 177,500 people were estimated to be in the tube stations, and the average throughout October was 138,000. A survey of all shelters at the end of November showed that 9 per cent of the population were in public shelters, 27 per cent in household ones, principally Anderson shelters at the bottom of their gardens (later many used the indoor shelter devised partly by Morrison), and only 4 per cent in the tube stations.

The nightly numbers dropped markedly during 1941, from the average of 70,000 in May to around 10,000 by November. The low point was in December 1942 when there were just 5,000, a number that rose rapidly to 150,000 per night when the 'little Blitz' of early 1944 started. About half the stations had been closed to shelterers during the long lull and, as the history of the shelterers puts it, 'although the unique communal existence of 1940/1 was never revisited after the closures . . . a significant number of people still retained an attachment to the security of the station shelters'.[6] Amazingly, in Islington and Southwark over half the shelterers still using the tubes in 1943 had been living there since the raids began three years previously. The concerns by the authorities about a deep shelter mentality developing may not have been entirely correct, but certainly a small minority clearly became attached to their troglodytic existence. Many of these were elderly people who liked the companionship and the hubbub, rather like those old ladies who sit in the street to watch the world go by in Mediterranean countries.

Other uses were found for sections of the Tube during the war. As in the First World War, some art treasures were taken there for safekeeping, including the Elgin Marbles from the British Museum, which were housed in the Aldwych tunnel. The disused station at Down Street became the HQ of the Railway Executive; it also served to accommodate Winston Churchill, and his war cabinet often met there. Most notably, two miles of the unfinished Central Line at

Wanstead and Ilford were converted into a factory making aircraft components for Plessey, which employed shifts of 2,000 workers, both day and night, with a little railway to ferry components.

The instincts of the shelterers to take refuge in the tube stations were right. The average tube station, sixty feet below the surface, proved to be 100 per cent safe during the war. All the major disasters where bombs penetrated stations involved those less than thirty-five feet below the surface. There were surprisingly few serious incidents, though the handful that did occur were among the most widely remembered of the war. The worst, in fact, was kept secret for several months and was not caused directly by enemy action. At half past eight on 3 March 1943 a salvo of anti-aircraft rockets were fired, prompting people to rush into the Bethnal Green shelter. The stairs were poorly lit and had no handrail, and people were groping their way down the stairs when a woman carrying a baby tripped and fell on the third step from the bottom. Suddenly, dozens of other people tumbled on each other and the people at the top of the stairs, unaware of the impending catastrophe, pushed down, fearing that the platform doors had been closed against them. The shoving continued for a horrible fifteen minutes, by which time twenty-seven men, eighty-four women and sixty-two children – 173 people – were crushed to death. The tunnel had filled with bodies from the floor to the ceiling but miraculously the woman and her baby survived the disaster.

The Bethnal Green shelter had been ordered to be open by Morrison during his first days as Home Secretary and he immediately launched an inquiry that, controversially, was held in secret. It concluded that while there had been defects with the shelter, which despite its size only had one entrance, the main cause of the disaster was that several people had lost their self-control and panicked. It even suggested that had there been a better design, the same result might have occurred. The report and details of the accident were not published until nearly two years later because of fears that it would damage morale. But observant Londoners would have noticed that stairwell entrances on several underground stations were hooded to enable better lighting, and handrails were fitted on the stairs. This incident is also the reason why nowadays throughout the system there are no long series of steps without breaks.

The most serious bombing disaster was at Balham where, on 14 October 1940, a device penetrated the northbound tunnel and ruptured a water main and sewers. The explosion filled the tunnel with an alarming sludge of water and gravel which, together with escaping gas, took the lives of sixty-eight people. Nineteen others, mostly Belgian refugees, had been killed the day before at Bounds Green on the Piccadilly. Since they are in the suburbs, both these stations are nearer the surface than those of the tube lines in central London and therefore offered less protection.

At Bank, on 11 January 1941, fifty-six people were killed by a bomb which cut through the concourse just below the street and exploded in the escalator machine room just beneath it. The blast penetrated deep enough to damage two trains but most of the dead had been relatively near the surface. Otherwise, there were no incidents in which more than seven people were killed and, in total, 152 shelterers and railway employees died in tube stations from the attacks.

On the vast majority of lines the services kept running throughout the war because even when there was bomb damage, reinstatement was impressively fast. Both the Balham and Bank bombs, for example, caused a closure of those sections of the Northern line for just three months. Overall, the damage to the system was severe but never crippling although 181 LT staff were killed while on duty during the war. In terms of disruption, the worst night was 10 May 1941 when the Underground was hit in twenty different places, resulting in the closure of ten sections. Nevertheless, most services were back on track within ten days except for sections of the Northern and Circle lines. Except when services were disrupted by such bomb damage, trains ran normally throughout the system, though travelling in the trains was a grim experience since at first trains ran without internal lights in the open sections; later, special

'Osglim' – a corruption of Osram – light bulbs, which emitted a cheerless blue glimmer, were fitted. Eventually, LT managed to design a light which beamed a small ray downwards to the seats and which it hoped could not be seen by the planes above even at stations when the sliding doors were open. The windows were covered by a sticky netting, designed to hold the glass if it shattered, but it meant that there was no view of the outside until, belatedly, small rectangular shapes were cut into the centre in order to allow some visibility.

Probably the most irritating experience for the passengers was having to read the advertisements featuring the awful cartoon goody-goody, Billy Brown of London Town, who advised them on how to behave in ghastly rhyming couplets. Notably, he warned them not to rip off the netting: 'I'll trust you'll pardon my correction, that stuff is there for your protection'.

Not surprisingly, the newspapers were wont to mimic Billy and the *Daily Mail* responded to the injunction about netting by saying

> *. . . But you chronic putter-righter*
> *Interfering little blighter,*
> *Some day very soon by heck,*
> *Billy Brown – I'll wring your neck.*

The Underground suffered a severe dip in passenger numbers in the early stages of the war, carrying just 333 million in 1941. But this decline was reversed as the attacks reduced and soon the system was being used by more people than ever before, as soldiers, including many from the US service, flooded onto the trains. By 1944 there were nearly 500 million passengers annually and in 1945 this leapt to 543 million. One result of the influx of all these non-Londoners was the erection of huge 'Please stand on the right' banners in escalator shafts and 'pass along the platform' flashing lights at busy stations. Londoners, of course, knew the rules without being told.

Another change brought by the war was the employment of women again. As in the First World War, women took over many of the jobs required to run the Underground. At first they were made to wear ghastly white dust coats and grey kepi hats, but later they were given proper uniforms with berets. However, unlike after the First World War, many remained in their jobs when hostilities ended.

The war came at just the wrong time for the Underground, not only halting its investment programme but cutting short its heyday. Had Ashfield and Pick been in control for a few more years of peacetime, they might have created such a robust structure that it could not have been dismantled although financially LT was hamstrung by the arrangements created at its birth and would have needed refinancing had the war not intervened. As it was, within a very short time after the conflict ended, the brilliant reign of Ashfield and Pick would be a distant memory and the system would be in seemingly terminal decline.

FIFTEEN

DECLINE –
AND REVIVAL?[1]

There is a paradox about the Underground. The miraculous system created by the pioneers is largely disliked and reviled by today's regular users. Few notice the elegant architecture or the brilliant simplicity of what has been called the 'turbine grinding out human beings on all sides'[2] at Piccadilly Circus. Instead, all most of them experience is the horrendous overcrowding which means that up to 800 people can be crammed into a train at peak times, their heads bowed as the doors crunch shut behind them. They see, too, the grime and squalor that is only half hidden behind the glossy advertisement displays and they notice, often admiringly, the little black mice gambolling under the tracks, which are well on their way to become a subspecies, presumably to be called *mus Metropolitanus*.[3] The trains are, on the whole, reasonably modern – though the newer they are, the fewer seats they have, which is hardly a measure of progress – and the service is generally reliable, even though it may not be as good as in the heyday.

So what is the big problem? There are fundamentally two issues: the lack of investment for much of the past fifty years, and overcrowding, with record numbers now using the system. The story of the Underground since the Second World War is a sad tale of missed opportunities, displaying a lack of foresight over the need for new lines and based on the mistaken notion that usage of the system would decline as a result of the nearly universal ownership of the motor car. There was the failure to build on the brilliant platform created by Ashfield and Pick, not just the system they left in such good shape but also the successful administrative structure they had created. And, above all, there was a complete lack of investment for much of the first three decades after the war. Nevertheless, half a century of neglect and muddle later, the London Underground remains the very life force of the capital; arguably, given the record number of travellers, even more so than during its heyday.

The post-war period started with a disastrous administrative change which appeared technical and innocuous but proved to be entirely negative. It was not so much the physical damage and neglect during the war, or even the overuse of the system, that caused the long-term deterioration, but London Transport's loss of independence. Instead of its quasi-autonomous status as a board controlled only remotely by the government, London Transport was nationalized in 1948, becoming part of the huge British Transport Commission (BTC) which, as its name implies, ran virtually all aspects of transport on the British mainland.

On the face of it, this seemed a logical step. This was the era in which state ownership was seen as the optimum way to provide key services and London Transport was just one of several industries over which the government now assumed total control. However, it was a slightly odd decision to include London Transport within the BTC since, in a way, it was renationalizing an organization that was already in the public sector. Pick, who died in 1941, would undoubtedly have warned against the plan, recognizing the dangers of merging LT into a much larger organization with national prerogatives. Ashfield too had become a peripheral figure and, having retired as chairman of LT in 1947, he died the following year. Pick's view that an organization is more dependent on its leaders than on its structure proved prescient. With the occasional exception, LT was to be led by a series of nonentities and placemen for the next fifty years.

LT, therefore, became just one arm of the British Transport Commission, which in turn was in the iron grip of the Treasury. London's needs for investment were bound to lose out to those of the country as a whole, given the massive requirements of health, electricity and housebuilding; and the small amount of money – and resources such as steel – made available for transport went to the main line railways which were in a dire state. The Underground consistently lost out in competition for investment because, as we have seen, it had benefited from successive government-funded improvement schemes between the wars, and therefore was in a relatively good state, compared with the railways. The contrast between its clean electric-powered trains and the grimy dirty steam engines which were still to be seen throughout the rail network was not helpful to the Underground cause. Moreover, far from being free to invest with no government interference, as London Transport had been able to do before the war, the new London Transport Executive was subject to a requirement of referring any item above £50,000 – not a lot of money even in those days – to the BTC. Inevitably under such constraints, buses, which were cheaper to buy and operate, absorbed what money London Transport could obtain. Improvement schemes to the Underground could never be justified on purely economic grounds but there was no money to subsidize them. Inevitably, planned extensions, such as the Central's connection to Denham and the connection between the Northern line's two ends through Mill Hill and continuing to Bushey Park, were scrapped – hence the existence of the funny little single-track spur to Mill Hill East, a real 'middle of nowhere destination' – as was its branch to Alexandra Palace. It was something of a miracle that the partly built extensions of the Central, both eastward (to Epping) and westwards (to West Ruislip), were completed by the end of the 1940s, thanks to a decision made by the board of LT on the orders of the government before its takeover by the BTC. These extensions aside, the system that was lauded as the best in the world started its long, slow process of decline.

After an initial increase in usage, once the war had ended passenger numbers were broadly stable, though in the long term the trend was clearly downwards. In 1948, when LT came under the wing of the British Transport Commission, there were 720 million passengers[4] annually, a number that would not be bettered until the late 1980s. Between 1950 and 1965 the number of cars registered in London quadrupled, from under 500,000 to nearly 2 million and, as Ashfield had predicted, this had a major impact on the Underground. In the 1950s, the annual passenger totals on the Underground hovered around 670 million, as those taking to their cars were replaced by new workers since London was enjoying virtually full employment. Then, despite the advent of the new Victoria line, numbers went into a decline – partly because TV ownership was becoming universal and proving more of an attraction than the cinema or theatre which often involved a trip up to town on the Underground.

The other social factor which affected the Underground was a tremendous labour shortage caused by the huge upsurge of jobs in the peripheral areas of the capital, notably on the Great West Road and the North Circular, as well as Heathrow Airport. Demand for the largely semi-skilled employment on the Underground and buses is highly dependent on the availability of jobs elsewhere which, since they require a higher level of skills, are usually better paid and therefore attract more potential employees at times of economic boom.

London Transport's solution was to attract labour from overseas. Employing immigrants from the Commonwealth was encouraged by the Tory government in the 1950s – a fact which seems extraordinary in these days of obsession with the problems caused by 'asylum seekers' – and London Transport was to play a key role in attracting immigrants, leading the way by opening an office in Barbados. LT's motives were hardly altruistic. With the post-war boom in full flow there was full employment, which meant that bus and Underground staff, whose wages had slipped behind those of many other similar jobs, were in desperately short supply. This had been partly alleviated by the employment of women, who had started being taken on as bus conductors at equal wages from 1951, but there was still a shortage and London Transport begun to cast widely for staff first within Britain, then Ireland and eventually the West Indies. There was a deliberate initiative by the Barbadian government to encourage its citizens to work for London Transport and it set up a Barbados Migrants Liaison service in 1955. The following year, LT's personnel director, Charles Gomm, went to Barbados and recruited seventy station men and seventy bus conductors, twenty of whom were women. It was the start of a huge influx. Between 1956 and 1965, LT recruited 4,000 Barbadians. Direct recruitment from Jamaica and Trinidad did not start until 1966 and numbers were much smaller.

Many West Indians only intended to stay a short time but remained for the rest of their working lives, often returning on retirement. The Barbadians were given an interest-free loan from their government to pay the fare to London.[5] Many of the new arrivals, though, found life difficult. They tended to come from the more affluent groups in their society and were often well educated but seeking higher wages in the 'mother country'. They were not, though, treated in keeping with this status and were given menial jobs for which they were overqualified. Some were housed in LT hostels but others had to cram into overcrowded accommodation where they had to share rooms, something they were not used to back home. But their experience was by no means all bad. Many reported not finding Britain racist, and although rising up the career ladder was harder for black people than their white equivalents, many did eventually get promoted. By recruiting so many West Indians, LT made a considerable contribution to the creation of a multi-cultural society; and while LT was by no means a perfect employer in terms of race relations, it was a lot better than many others. One recruit, Lloyd Ellis, who later became a high court judge back in Jamaica, said that while it was made harder for black people to climb the ladder, 'on the other hand, I must give credit to London Transport because it was one of the first corporate bodies in England to reduce the barrier. People eventually became supervisors and all sorts of thing in London Transport.'[6]

In the twenty years between the takeover by the BTC and the opening of the first section of the Victoria line, the Underground had lost its cachet as a pioneering organization. It was still setting high standards in technical and engineering development, but was clearly in decline. Even Ashfield and Pick would have struggled to have maintained standards in the face of its new structure. Indeed, they would have tendered their resignations long before rather than work in such a constrained context.

In terms of investment, the 1950s were the leanest years in the history of the Underground, causing long-term damage from which, arguably, the system has never been able to recover. The levels of spending on re-equipping the system were quite remarkably low. The modest pocket-sized London Transport annual reports of that period show the extent to which the system was being run down. Most tellingly, none of the reports of this period contains any sign of planned maintenance programmes or assessments of future needs. The 1953 report, for example, records that 'capital expenditure on the railways, on station reconstruction and other works including signalling ,modernization amounted to £0.3m during the year', a staggeringly low sum. The following year mentions £276,000 spent 'on the provision of passing loops at Wembley Park, to improve the running of the Metropolitan and Bakerloo services and to improvements in signalling' and 'other capital expenditure on stations, tracks and other non-depreciated assets' amounted to just £126,000. These were minor works; clearly major overhauls or replacements of big assets such as lifts or escalators were simply not on the agenda.[7]

Part of the reason why the Underground had less money available for investment was because it could no longer rely on cross-subsidizing from the profitable bus services. LT's bus services had been something of a cash cow for the Underground ever since the First World War when Ashfield created the Common Fund, pooling the resources of the

Combine. Now buses were becoming less profitable because of the growing number of cars, a damaging bus strike in 1957 and the resulting congestion. The business sense of the management at the time also seems questionable. In 1957, the little-used extension from Epping to Ongar, operated as a shuttle by steam trains, was electrified at a cost of £100,000, a large proportion of the investment funds available that year. Not only did few people live in these wilder parts of Essex, but even after electrification the service was still run as a shuttle, necessitating a change at Epping, and a journey into central London would normally take over an hour. Not surprisingly, there were few regular users.[8]

The 1960s were something of an improvement but still little was spent on the existing network. There were more funds but few went on refurbishing the system of tunnels and track, parts of which were now entering their second century. Instead, the purchase of much-needed new rolling stock took up most of the available cash. The rest went into preparations for the first new tube line under central London since the opening of the Yerkes tubes – the Victoria line – which was originally known as Route C. The historians of London's transport sum up the decision-making process over the new line with well-merited sarcasm:

> The story of the development of the Victoria from its appearance as Route C in the London Plan Working Party's report of 1948 to the opening of the main stem from Walthamstow to Victoria in March 1969, shows characteristic features of public handling of investment projects in mid-twentieth century Britain: general acceptance of the intention as desirable; delay for argument on constantly changing bases; final approval under temporary pressures which were largely irrelevant to the arguments.[9]

They could have added: constant rows over financing and cost overruns during construction.

But here again, London Underground was breaking new ground in that this was the first time that cost–benefit analysis methods were used. This is a methodology which attempts to assess the wider costs and benefits of a project, rather than merely examining the costs and making a crude judgement about whether these are likely to be paid back by the profits from the scheme in the long term. It is, in short, a way of trying to calculate the overall benefit to society of a project by including factors such as time saved by passengers (and even road users) and the savings from reduced bus services in the overall equation. The notion, then, is that the government should put money into schemes for these social benefits, because they are not paid for through the fare box. If such a method had been available to the Underground pioneers, it would have ensured that London had a much bigger system – except, of course, Victorian governments were not ready to step in to pay for these non-monetary benefits. Even now governments are reluctant to pursue the logic of this methodology and fund such projects, as witnessed by the number of highly beneficial schemes which have been decades in gestation, such as Crossrail, the proposed tunnel connection between Liverpool Street and Paddington. It was only through using the cost–benefit analysis method, now standard on all major transport infrastructure schemes, that the project was given the go-ahead in 1962.

Bizarrely, the fear of growing unemployment was the other spur that persuaded the government to give the final go-ahead to the building of the Victoria line, even though by the time work started in earnest a severe labour shortage was developing. The main purpose of the line was to relieve congestion on the underground system in central London, which had been recognized as far back as the 1930s. The line which was extended to Brixton in 1971 took twenty-three years to build, from its acceptance as a worthwhile project to the opening of the full line at a cost of £90m, rather than the £38m first estimated for a railway that would have gone four miles further south to Croydon.

The Victoria line was pioneering in one key respect: the trains are driven automatically from a control centre. The person at the front is really a guard with the ability to make emergency stops. This major technological advance was made possible by one of the little-known heroes of the development of London Underground, Robert Dell.[10] He had first joined the Metropolitan District in 1916 at the age of sixteen and his career was a glittering, albeit unsung one. He was a signal engineer who invented a host of devices to make installation easier and to automate more and more parts of the process. Gradually, thanks to Dell's work, signal boxes were dispensed with, to be replaced by control centres, one or two per line. But the height of his achievement was, as chief signal engineer, to introduce automatically operated trains onto the Victoria line, run remotely from a control centre. Not only did this do away with half the staff of the train but it made operation far more reliable.[11] Sadly, Dell's achievement has not been built upon as the Jubilee Line Extension completed thirty years later requires drivers; though Docklands Light Railway trains, now part of Transport for London, are automatic and run on a far more complex system than the Victoria line, and so is the Central.

Under the new regime of direct control by the Ministry, which started when the BTC was abolished in 1963, there was still little money available for refurbishment. That year, for example, a paltry £1.1m was made available for improving stations, track, signalling and depots as most of the £17.6m in the budget went on preparations for the Victoria line and new rolling stock. The level of capital spending available for refurbishing the existing system improved little during the construction of the Victoria line and no attention was being paid to the gradually declining system. The answer to the mystery of why today's Underground is in such a dilapidated state gradually becomes apparent.

In 1970 there was another change of structure for London Transport, which now for the first time became part of the local authority: the Greater London Council, the expanded version of the LCC. It was the realization of Morrison's original dream of having the transport system under the direct control of local politicians. Given that nothing much had been spent since the New Works Programme of the late 1930s, by then the Underground had suffered from a full three decades of neglect. Over that time, LT had become burdened by a massive debt – £270m – much of it the legacy of the 1930s investment programme. Therefore, in 1970 the Tory leader of the GLC, Desmond Plummer, successfully insisted that the debt should be written off before he would take on the burden of running the system.

Local control brought some immediate benefits. With the annual burden of having to service the debt lifted from the GLC, and grants available from central government under the new legislation to pay for capital expenditure, LT faced a rosier future than it had under its two previous regimes. Indeed, the recognition by the GLC that there was an enormous backlog of investment led to the drawing-up of a plan to spend £275m over the following twenty years – representing more than a tenfold increase in annual spending on essential renewal – to bring the system back to a reasonable physical state. It was basic stuff with most of the money going on trains – as ever – escalators and lifts rather than the total refurbishment which many stations, now well into middle age, needed. The public did get a few improvements, as the 1972 annual report said: 'The importance of station lighting as a means of updating the appearance of stations is fully recognized and authority has been given for a major increase in expenditure on lighting improvements in 1972 and in subsequent years.'[12] The plan was largely although not very coherently implemented, and investment expenditure increased steadily but patchily over the fourteen years of GLC control. Again much was absorbed in expansion: the Heathrow extension, and the creation of the Jubilee line hewn out of one branch of the Bakerloo.

The GLC was often ruled by the opposite party to the one in control at Westminster, and, moreover, swung between Tory and Labour at virtually every four-yearly election. With the rapid succession of changes in political control at both national and local level, the decade and a half of GLC control over London Transport was a volatile one characterized by rapid shifts in policy. The merger of London

Transport into the Greater London Council had, however, made the capital's local government too strong. There was always a difficult relationship between the government and County Hall, just across the Thames from Parliament, and this came to the fore over a radical attempt to reverse the long-term decline of Underground usage. The annual number of passengers had fallen below half a billion a year for the first time since the aftermath of the war, a result of the outflow of jobs from central London (a government body seeking to encourage office relocation outside London advertised prominently on the Underground in the sixties and seventies, not a clever tactic by the advertising department of London Transport had it thought through the consequences!), greater use of the car, the rundown of the system, the economic recession and a policy of increasing fares above the rate of inflation. The Underground was at its lowest ebb, being no longer perceived as the backbone of the capital. The motor car was king.

That was the mitigating factor for this lack of investment. The contemporary view of most transport and planning 'experts' was that the use of public transport would continue to decline in the face of competition from the car. It was only with the rejection of the proposed motorway rings by Londoners who elected Labour (which had stood on an explicit platform of abandoning plans for the new roads) at the 1973 GLC elections that policy-makers began to recognize that cars had to be restrained and not encouraged in city centres.

Nevertheless, it is on the whole inexcusable that the system was neglected for so long. Once the decline in passenger numbers was reversed in the mid 1980s, and the limitations of road transport became clear, it should have been obvious to London's planners and to its politicians, both local and national, that a thriving city was dependent on its lifeblood, the Underground. It should not have been difficult to predict that the usage of the system would increase as London attracted more and more jobs and office blocks sprouted up like mushrooms on a rotting log.

The new Labour administration at the GLC intended to reverse the decline. In May 1981, Labour won the GLC election and the Labour councillors quickly ousted the right-wing leader, Andrew McIntosh, and replaced him with the charismatic left-winger, Ken Livingstone. After flirting with the notion of abolishing fares entirely, the councillors imposed a cut of a third and gave their policy the catchy slogan of 'Fares Fair'. The long-mooted zonal system of fares was introduced, a move that was to prove more significant in the long term because it allowed for Travelcards, now the routine way for Londoners to travel around the capital. The concept had first been proposed by Yerkes but rejected by successive LT managements on the basis that it would lose revenue, but in fact it was to help generate substantial increases in usage.

The 'Fares Fair' policy led to an incredible three-way tussle between the government, the GLC and London Transport (which was often at odds with its political masters – even, at one point, being on the opposite side of a court case with the GLC), with regular interventions from the judiciary, which saw fares yo-yo and ended, through an astonishing act of vindictiveness by the then Prime Minister, Margaret Thatcher, in the abolition of the GLC. Fares Fair may have been controversial, but it revitalized the Underground, turning it into a popular political cause as well as increasing passenger numbers. The fall in fares, which covered both buses and the Underground, had an immediate impact, boosting the number of passengers using London Transport each day from 5.5 million to 6 million and reducing the number of cars coming into central London. It was too good to last.

Bromley, a Conservative-controlled outer south London borough with no Underground station, challenged the GLC's right to impose such a dramatic cut in fares because the move had increased the level of subsidy raised from London ratepayers by £125m per year. Why, Bromley asked, should our residents be forced to subsidize a system which they do not use? This omitted two key arguments: that many Bromley residents did travel into central London and use the facilities, and that even those who did not were likely to benefit from the reduction in traffic congestion. Judges, not noted for the frequency with which they use public transport, ruled against the GLC both at the Appeal Court and in the House of Lords.

Livingstone complained that the judgement was political but, after taking legal advice, decided that the only way of complying with the law was to virtually double the fares, leaving fares a third higher than when Labour had won control of the GLC. Passenger numbers on London Transport quickly fell to 5 million per day and traffic congestion worsened. It was, in effect, a gigantic experiment in testing what economists call the elasticity of demand for public transport – the effect that a change in price has on demand for a product.

Clearly the fares were now too high, a fact recognized even by the Tory government, which promptly asked the GLC to consult the public over ways that they could be reduced. In late 1982, the GLC put forward a 'Balanced Plan' for a 25 per cent reduction in fares which aimed to strike a compromise between London's transport needs and the ratepayers who had to subsidize the system. After a court case to test its validity, the cut was implemented by London Transport in May 1983, pretty much restoring fares to the level of two years previously when Livingstone had taken over. Mrs Thatcher, though, never forgave the man Londoners perceived as the cheeky chappie across the Thames and, boosted by her second election victory, promptly announced legislation to abolish the GLC which came into effect in 1986. This meant another administrative change for London Underground as it became the responsibility of London Regional Transport, which, as before, was the responsibility of the Ministry of Transport. Mrs Thatcher, the great architect of privatization, had effectively renationalized London Transport, a strange irony that was a side product of the Fares Fair battle.

Throughout this battle over fares, investment and the long-term needs of the system yet again took a back seat. However, the fourteen-year rule of the GLC had by no means been all bad. Local control has a positive side as it means that politicians can be held to account for the poor state of the infrastructure. The GLC helped bring about the Heathrow extension, the Jubilee Line and the long-deferred modernization of lifts and escalators, and, as mentioned, enabled the introduction of Travelcards. Ironically, in 2003 control of the Underground was handed back to local government in the form of the Mayor of London, who was none other than Ken Livingstone.

The Conservative government created a new organization, named London Regional Transport, though still known to the public as London Transport, to run the Underground and the buses. It suffered, as ever, from interference from central government, and now that Thatcherism was in full flow the ethos had to change too. The era of 'London Transport does everything', from making its own pies at its factory in Croydon and designing special caps for its Rasta staff to the heavy engineering of its trains, was, at last, beginning to be challenged. The role of the Acton Works, where trains had undergone both minor and major servicing, was re-evaluated as a study found that most of the work was overpriced when compared with outside contractors. This led, eventually, to much of the work being spread out to individual line depots. Engineering was divided into 'client' and 'contractor' functions so that contracts could be let out competitively to the private sector. For the first time, under the Act which created LRT, London Underground had to seek competitive tenders for all major work.

Again, the funding situation for London Underground looked bad, with little attention being paid to its investment needs. A pattern developed by which every year there would be a lengthy process of negotiation between the LT management and the Treasury, which would be resolved late in the autumn when the chairman would be called in to be told how much money London Underground would have to invest in the following financial year. Some years there would be adequate amounts (even, very occasionally, more than expected), but most years there was not enough. That was no way to run an organization which needed a long-term planning framework in order to ensure that the system was in a reasonable state. The worst two disasters on the Underground system, at Moorgate and King's Cross, occurred during this period when underinvestment and short-term political interference had almost brought the system to its knees.[13] While that may have been a coincidence in the case of Moorgate, it certainly was not at King's Cross.

Apart from these two catastrophes there has been no Underground accident in peacetime in which more than a dozen people have been killed, a remarkable and proud record for the system during its 140 years. Moorgate was a strange disaster in that the underlying cause has never been explained. The facts are simple. Moorgate was the terminal stop of that odd little stub of a line, the Great Northern & City, which at the time was a branch of the Northern line, although now it is no longer part of the Underground as it is served by National Rail trains. A train packed with commuters at quarter to nine in the morning of 28 February 1975 did not slow down as it approached the station and instead continued through and slammed into the wall twenty-two yards beyond the platform end at an estimated speed of forty mph. The results were horrific with the front carriages being concertinaed into each other. Some of the victims were found dead but still standing and clutching the straps or sitting and holding newspapers, killed by the impact or impaled by twisted metal and broken glass. Others survived thanks to the heavily upholstered seats which fell on them. Forty-three people were killed and seventy injured, the high proportion of deaths being a result of the fast speed of the crash. It took five days to get all the dead out, including the driver who was clearly the focus of the investigation. Had he been drunk? There was evidence of alcohol in his blood but this was probably an irrelevance because the production of alcohol is part of the natural decaying process. Or depressed as a result of his marital problems and therefore suicidal? Or in some kind of trance state induced, perhaps, by a medical condition? We will never know. The investigators found that previously he had had a good record and was known to be conscientious.

Although there was no obvious technical fault, perhaps the automatic train stop system used throughout the network at other signals should have been introduced at a potentially disastrous dead end such as the tunnel at the station. Apart from that, Moorgate was just bad luck; but King's Cross[14] was a disaster that illustrated everything that had gone wrong with the system in the previous forty years since nationalization. Not only was it eminently preventable, there was a certain inevitability about the disaster. At 7.45 p.m. on 18 November 1987 a fire that had been smouldering for half an hour under the Piccadilly line escalator suddenly erupted into a fireball that killed thirty-one people. The accident and subsequent report by Desmond Fennell[15] revealed a shocking state of affairs in the Underground, symptomatic of an organization in decline. There was a long catalogue of reasons why the fire, probably started by a lighted match from a smoker, spread so quickly: junk, much of it inflammable, had been left under the escalator for years; station employees were allowed to 'bunk off' work, either simply not turning up or having extended meal breaks, leaving the concourse severely understaffed; fires were treated as an unavoidable routine hazard rather than as preventable; there had been no training in emergency procedures; and the management was sloppy and remote.

It was, perhaps, not surprising to find that London Underground was in such a mess after years of neglect; still, it was an amazing testimony to the legacy of Ashfield and Pick that it had taken so long for its decline to reach crisis point. King's Cross forced London Underground into a complete reappraisal of the way it was run. Following the accident, the management system was reorganized and modernized. No longer was promotion based solely on longevity, and more managers were recruited from outside the organization.

The welcome rush of investment funds which became available to London Underground after the King's Cross disaster was, within a couple of years, cut back as the recession of the early 1990s hit hard. Again, money for routine maintenance and refurbishment was in short supply because most of the capital spending went on the creation of a new line, the Jubilee Line Extension. The Jubilee line itself, running from Charing Cross to Stanmore, had been opened in 1979 after lengthy delays and a name change from Fleet line. The only new section was a tunnel between Baker Street and Charing Cross, since the rest had been hived off from the Bakerloo and the primary purpose had been to relieve congestion on the older line.

Terminating at Charing Cross was clearly an interim solution, and it was always intended to continue the line through central London and out the other side. But where? The original name suggested that it would run to Fleet Street, an area ill-served by the Underground, but the Tory government's obsession with regenerating Docklands, supposedly a private sector enterprise but funded by considerable amounts of taxpayers' money, determined that the route should go through south-east London and back across the Thames to Canary Wharf and thence to Stratford. The developers of Canary Wharf, Olympia & York, had lobbied hard to ensure that their massive site – which included the highest building in Britain – should be linked into the Underground system, and had promised to pay part of the cost. In the event, the company went bust and the conditions under which they were supposed to pay over the money were never entirely fulfilled; therefore their contribution has been minute – less than 5 per cent – in relation to the eventual £3.5bn cost of the scheme. Yet, because of the concentration on Docklands, another long-mooted scheme, Chelsea to Hackney, which showed far greater community benefits, remains on the drawing board, with no possibility of being built before 2015. Fortunately, at the insistence of local politicians and the managing director of the Underground at the time, Denis Tunnicliffe – and despite the opposition of Olympia & York which wanted the trains to reach Canary Wharf from central London as quickly as possible – intermediate stations at Southwark, Bermondsey and Canada Water were built, contributing greatly to the regeneration of those areas. Nevertheless, the Jubilee Line Extension is unique in being an underground line designed primarily to satisfy the needs of a private developer rather than London and Londoners as a whole, although it did create several useful interchanges in East London.

In some ways, the Jubilee Line Extension was a return to the heyday of Pick and Ashfield in terms of the grandeur of the stations and the 'no expense spared' feel of the scheme. The stations, all designed by different architects, are one of the most innovative and exciting modern developments in the capital – and there are platform doors, which add to safety by preventing people falling on the track. Yet, paradoxically, a late change to an older form of signalling, after a new method proved unreliable, means that insufficient numbers of trains can be run to cope at rush hours and the whole signalling system will soon have to be replaced at a cost of hundreds of millions of pounds.

The cutback of funds during the early 1990s was precisely the kind of 'stop-go' policy that made it impossible for the London Underground management to plan ahead. For example, a scheme to upgrade the Northern Line had to be postponed when the money was cut back, even though it had been dubbed London's 'misery line' by the *Evening Standard*.

The Treasury's inability to understand the long-term investment needs of the system was the main driving force which led London Transport's management to accept the Labour government's proposal of a public private partnership (PPP)[16] to bring investment into the Underground after its victory in the 1997 general election. While capital spending did, broadly, rise during the 1990s, there was still a substantial backlog but the incoming government had promised to stick to its predecessor's spending plans. Private money was seen as the only solution by John Prescott, who was transport secretary and deputy prime minister, and the plan for the PPP was announced in March 1998. That involved the breaking up of London Underground into an operator, which remained in the public sector, and three infrastructure companies, responsible for three or four lines each, which were to be privatized. The operator was initially under the direct control of the government but the intention, achieved in July 2003, was to pass it on to Transport for London, part of the new system of governance in the capital which involved the creation of a mayor.

It was an incredibly complicated scheme, a novel type of contract. Instead of paying a set amount for an improvement such as a new signalling system, the cost will be based on the amount of time that passengers will save as a result of the investment. Therefore contractors will be rewarded mainly as a result of their performance in terms of reducing delays and improving the capacity of the service through large-scale investments. As well as shortage of money, the government was tempted by this solution because the PPP was a way of bypassing inefficient public sector management which, it felt, was not up to the task of managing the massive funding required to bring the Underground up to standard. In particular, ministers used the Jubilee Line Extension cost overrun of over £1bn to argue that the private sector had to be given responsibility for such major schemes. It was a somewhat disingenuous argument since much of the overrun was the result of the need to finish the scheme in time to meet the target opening date of 1 January 2000 to coincide with the inauguration of the ill-fated Millennium Dome.

The PPP deal led to a four-year controversy that delayed any major investment into the system, which, as a result, continued to deteriorate. And during those negotiations, it emerged that far from being self-funded, as had been promised initially, the PPP would require a massive annual £1bn in subsidy from the government, more than the management of London Underground had sought during the 1990s, to modernize the whole network under a ten-year plan.

The complexities of the system are such that it cost £500m to create the contracts. The deals were eventually signed in 2003 and the thirty-year schemes are now under way, but it is far too early to judge their efficacy. It would be comforting to believe that the PPP will return the system to its former grandeur. At worst, there will be some improvements, albeit at a high cost. Michael Cassidy, a former chairman of the City of London's policy and resources committee, has even suggested that the PPP is not unlike Yerkes's way of funding investment in the Underground. Bearing in mind Yerkes's crookedness, that is hardly a compliment to its architects.

Yet again London Underground is being revolutionary, in a way which appears even more incredible than Pearson's notion that trains could run under cities. It will be several years before Londoners notice any difference and there are severe doubts whether these very expensive contracts will prove value for money. In June 2004, the National Audit Office published two reports which suggested there was only 'limited assurance' that the price of the contracts was reasonable or that improvements would be delivered. The NAO confirmed that nearly £500 million had been paid, in consultants' fees and other costs, to set up the PPP. In other words, the whole PPP scheme is an experiment being tested out on London's Underground passengers for the next thirty years.[17]

The Underground is still a wonder, a fantastic achievement that is a credit to its pioneers, but it is set to remain undervalued as it has done throughout its 140-year history. Perhaps its subterranean nature means it will never get the credit and the money it needs. Thanks to the dithering over the Victoria line, followed by equally damaging delays over the Jubilee Line Extension, Thameslink 2000, the East London line and Crossrail, London is effectively two lines behind what would be a sensible rate of growth on rational economic grounds given the growth of employment and housing in the city. The PPP, sadly, is only about improving the existing infrastructure, rather than building any new lines to increase capacity. And, unfortunately, all the major schemes to improve the system are, at the time of writing, in the balance. The extended East London line, which would make better use of Brunel's tunnel by running services through it both north and south of the river, has been stalled even though clearance work on part of the scheme started in 2001. A bill to build Crossrail was finally announced, after much delay, in July 2004 but there are still doubts as to whether it will ever be built. New methods of funding the scheme, possibly by a special business rate are to be explored. There have even been some exciting suggestions about tapping into the increased land values, as Pick had suggested, in order to pay for it but, as ever, the politicians are too timid and refuse to recognize the importance of the scheme to London, or the urgency of the situation. The whole process is very slow and the ever-cautious Labour government refuses to commit itself, because it has no grand vision for using Pearson's magnificent invention to make a radical improvement to transport in London and, consequently, to the lives of London's inhabitants. The great pioneers of the subterranean railway are all long dead, and no one has taken on their mantle.

NOTES

Introduction: THE PHANTOM RAILWAY

1 Peter Ackroyd's picaresque *London,* an 800-page book, has barely half a dozen references to the system. Even Roy Porter's superb *A Social History of London*, for example, only gives a brief history of the construction of the Underground railways and mentions their stimulus on the growth of the city, and does not really dwell on the long-term effects or successes or put the scale of the achievement in context.

Chapter One: MIDWIFE TO THE UNDERGROUND

1 Quoted in T.C. Barker and Michael Robbins, *A History of London Transport*, Vol. 1, George Allen & Unwin, 1963, p. 102.

2 While there are some claims that the line which opened in Budapest in 1896 was an underground railway, in fact it was little more than a tunnel for part of a tramway system.

3 Simon Jenkins, *Landlords to London*, Constable, 1975, p. 100.

4 Hugh Douglas, *The Underground Story*, Robert Hale, 1963, p. 13.

5 The term became current in the US in the 1840s, taken from the custom of people who 'commuted' their daily fares into a season ticket, but was not used in Britain until a century later.

6 F.M.L. Thompson, *Victorian England, The horse drawn society*, pamphlet.

7 Gavin Weightman and Steve Humphries, *The Making of Modern London, 1815–1914*, Sidgwick & Jackson, 1983, p. 99.

8 Jenkins, pp. 100–102.

9 John Kellett, *The Impact of Railways on Victorian Cities*, Routledge & Kegan Paul, 1969, p. 25.

10 Ibid., p. 26.

11 House of Commons, *Royal Commission on Metropolis Railway Termini*, 1846, Q 2192, p. 283.

12 Ibid., p. 5.

13 Quoted in Kellett, p. 5.

14 Commons Select Committee on Metropolitan Communications, 1854–5, question 1345.

15 Kellett, p. 48.

16 The best description is to be found in B.G. Wilson and J.R. Day, *Unusual Railways*, Muller, 1958, pp. 58–61.

17 Henry Mayhew, *The Shops and Companies of London and the trades and manufactories of Great Britain*, Strand, 1865, p. 144.

18 Ibid., p. 145.

Chapter Two: THE UNDERGROUND ARRIVES

1 The terminus was originally called Farringdon Street, and did not assume its present name, Farringdon, until 1936.

2 Jack Simmons, *The Railway in Town and Country, 1830–1914*, David & Charles, 1986, p. 32.

3 At the time it was known as New Road, as its construction started in 1756 to appease City dwellers because, even as early as the mid eighteenth century, traffic had began to be a source of annoyance. It was effectively London's first bypass.

4 It was not until 1874 that railway companies were obliged to rehouse displaced residents.

5 George Godwin, *Another blow for life*, 1864.

6 Reverend William Denton, *Observations on the displacement of the poor by Metropolitan railways and other public improvements*, quoted in Richard Trench and Ellis Hillman, *London under London*, John Murray, 1985, p. 139.

7 Nicholas Faith, *The world the railways made*, Bodley Head, 1990, p. 89.

8 He posted out this letter to prospective shareholders with a stamp for subscribers to reply, a very early example of such direct mail marketing given that the first stamp had only been introduced in 1840.

9 F.S. Williams, *Our Iron Roads*, Bemrose and Son, 1884.

10 The Metropolitan Board of Works was the first and only London-wide administrative body and it was a very new concept. Created in 1855, it was indirectly elected by parish vestries and other local authorities, and it was

principally concerned with roads, bridges and sewers. The absence of a London-wide authority, until the creation of the London County Council in 1889, was a constant problem for those seeking to provide infrastructure like the Underground.

11 *London Journal*, January 1862.

12 Trench and Hillman, p. 132.

13 As an aside, a small atmospheric 'tube' narrowly missed being London's first underground railway, albeit passengerless. A 2ft 6ins diameter tunnel was built by the London Pneumatic Despatch Company (chaired by the Duke of Buckingham) from under Euston station to a post office sorting unit half a mile away in Eversholt Street. The little piston-shaped trucks were powered by compressed air in one direction and pulled through by a vacuum in the other. The line started operating on 20 February 1863, just a few weeks after the Metropolitan opened, and carried up to thirty-five mailbags twice as fast as they could be transported on the surface. The plan was to demonstrate the viability of the concept and then extend it to a series of stations around London underneath railway termini, post offices and market places, to transport general freight and, eventually, passengers. The system was extended to Holborn, with a bigger, 4ft 6ins diameter, tunnel through which the capsules averaged an impressive seventeen mph. But the Post Office was never quite convinced about the idea and in 1874 stopped using it, forcing the London Pneumatic Despatch Company into liquidation. Half a century later the Post Office built a system of driverless trains to carry mailbags under London using rather large tunnels, which kept running until 2003.

14 It may well, however, have served the Metropolitan's purpose. The company's promise of smokeless locomotives had, after all, ensured the successful passage of the Bill through Parliament.

15 Quoted in Trench and Hillman, p. 138.

Chapter Three: LONDON GOES UNDERGROUND

1 *The Times*, 30 November 1861.

2 *Illustrated London News*, 17 January 1863.

3 At the time, Great Western trains operated on a wider gauge, 7ft 0¼ins rather than the standard 4ft 8½ins, and the Metropolitan was originally built to accommodate both types of train.

4 *Daily Telegraph*, 12 January 1863.

5 *Morning Advertiser*, 12 January 1863.

6 *Daily Telegraph*, 16 January 1863.

7 William J. Pinks, *History of Clerkenwell*, London, 1865.

8 A name normally associated with the Waterloo & City line built more than thirty years later.

9 S.M. Ellis, *A mid-Victorian Pepys*, 1923, p. 246.

10 As reported to Henry Mayhew in *The Shops and Companies of London and the trades and manufactories of Great Britain*, Strand, 1865, p. 146.

11 E.L. Ahrons, quoted in O.S. Nock, *Underground Railways of the World*, A. & C. Black, 1973, p. 113.

12 *The Times*, 14 October 1879.

13 The Great Northern locomotives operated on the smaller standard gauge, using the hitherto redundant middle rail, and on the first day there were six derailments due to misalignment of the track.

14 Quoted in Hugh Douglas, *The Underground Story*, Robert Hale, 1963, p. 115.

15 Mayhew, p. 146.

16 Quoted in Alan A. Jackson, *London's Metropolitan Railway*, David & Charles, 1986, p. 53.

17 Pinks.

18 T.C. Barker and Michael Robbins, *A History of London Transport*, Vol. 1, George Allen & Unwin, 1963, p. 135.

19 This method of train control had recently, in August 1861, caused an accident resulting in twenty-one deaths and 176 injured in the Clayton tunnel on the Brighton line when a stalled train was hit by the following one.

20 Barker and Robbins, p. 118.

21 The powers were extended in 1864. Nevertheless, this shows that the Metropolitan was already thinking of expansion even before the first section had been completed.

22 This quote and all the following are taken from Mayhew, pp. 144–9.

23 Douglas, 1963, p. 111.

24 J.M. Wilson, *The Imperial Gazetteer of England and Wales*, 1869, ii, p. 167, quoted in Jack Simmons, *The Victorian Railway*, Thames & Hudson, 1991, p. 165.

25 Commercially, it was probably a nonsense, illustrative of the railway companies' tendency to run trains for the sake of them.

26 Nock, p. 27.

27 Ibid.

28 The excavated soil was used to reduce the depth of the lake in nearby Regent's Park for safety reasons as forty skaters had drowned there in January 1867 when the thin ice gave way.

29 Roy Porter, *London: a social history*, Penguin, 1994, p. 216.

30 Quoted in Barker and Robbins, p. 127.

Chapter Four: THE LINE TO NOWHERE

1 Piers Connor, *The District Line*, Capital Transport, 1993, p. 10.

2 *The Times*, 24 August 1866.

3 Where it can still be heard on a rainy day.

4 Most of these examples are cited in Simon Jenkins, *Landlords to London*, Constable, 1975, p. 107.

5 *The Times*, 24 August 1866.

6 Now the site of the headquarters of London Underground and St James's Park station.

7 *The Times*, 24 August 1866.

8 Ibid.

9 Connor, p. 12.

10 *Illustrated London News*, 18 June 1870.

11 O.S. Nock, *The Railway Enthusiast's Encyclopedia*, Hutchinson, 1968, p. 288.

12 At which the famous accident that caused the death of the statesman William Huskisson took place.

13 Clive Foxell, *The story of the Met and the GC joint line*, self-published, 2001, p. 19.

14 Stephen Halliday, *Making the Metropolis, Creators of Victoria's London*, Breedon Books, 2003, p. 42.

15 Both railways were, therefore, built somewhat on the cheap, a legacy which still affects passengers today, especially those in East Kent. The poor reputation of the two railways for feuding was legendary, as was their rotten service. *The Times* recalled, 'The little overlapping companies were always good for a laugh, ribald every now and then and sardonic. The

London, Chatham & Dover became the Undone, Smash'em and Turn'em over. The South Eastern & Chatham main line was the scene of the fictitious tragedy in which a would-be suicide laid his neck on the line and died of starvation.'

16 The result of this folly can be seen at South Kensington today where only the central platforms are in use, leaving the two outside ones redundant.

17 The track layout was also developed so that trains could connect from Earls Court with the putative Circle line, both eastwards and westwards.

18 Something which today would be illegal, and even at the time various court cases tried to put a stop to the practice.

19 T.C. Barker and Michael Robbins, *A History of London Transport*, Vol. 1, George Allen & Unwin, 1963, p. 159.

20 While conversions are necessarily vague, that sum would be worth around seventy times that figure today, i.e. almost £11m, more than today's fat cats even dream of.

21 From the company minutes, 23 October 1872, quoted in Barker and Robbins, p. 161.

22 From the company minutes, 23 October 1872, quoted in Barker and Robbins, p. 162.

23 Barker and Robbins, p. 165.

24 Hugh Douglas, *The Underground Story*, Robert Hale, 1963, p. 100.

25 Benjamin Baker, *The Metropolitan and Metropolitan District Railway*, The Institution of Civil Engineers, 1885.

26 The Metropolitan was, in fact, according to a deal reached in November 1884, allowed a couple of trains in that direction because of its greater original investment.

27 This was a problem which, interestingly, was to be repeated over a century later when Railtrack was privatized in 1996 and found itself under an obligation to allow trains onto its network without the capacity to cope with them.

28 *The Times*, 7 October 1884.

29 *The Times*, 16 October 1884.

30 At least they did not have to cope with the electrified third rail which would make such action far more dangerous today.

31 *West London Advertiser*, 30 August 1884, quoted in Barker and Robbins, p. 232.

32 O.S. Nock, *Underground Railways of the World*, A & C Black, 1973, p. 33.

33 Quoted from *Herapath's Railway Journal* in Barker and Robbins, p. 237.

34 *Railway Times*, 18 October 1884.

Chapter Five: SPREADING OUT

1 Charles E. Lee, *The Metropolitan Line, a brief history*, London Transport, 1972, p. 22.

2 Parliamentary Papers, *Correspondence with reference to the proposed construction of a Channel Tunnel*, C3358, Accounts and papers, 17 (1882).

3 Clive Foxell, *The story of the Met and GC joint line*, Clive Foxell, 2000, p. 22.

4 Except at stations where there were two tracks.

5 Quoted in Dennis Edwards and Ron Pigram, *The Romance of Metroland*, Baton Transport, 1986, p. 16.

6 Now called Harrow on the Hill.

7 Quoted in Edwards and Pigram, p. 16.

8 Quoted in ibid., p. 18.

9 Quoted in ibid., p. 18.

10 Quoted in Foxell, p. 32.

11 Indeed, a century later, a similar idea was put forward to build a cheap version of Crossrail, the proposed new underground railway between Paddington and Liverpool, using that same section of line. This was briefly and foolishly considered by the Labour government of 1997 but quickly rejected as unworkable as there are too many trains using it.

12 In fact, work started on extending the line both north and southwards in 2003, after a lengthy delay over planning difficulties, and along with several developments on the route this may finally transform what has been a Cinderella line into a major cross-London route; although funding for the whole scheme is still not confirmed. This has stimulated development in Shoreditch which is possibly becoming, at last, the trendy district which its geography suggests it should be.

13 While that still remains true today, the development in London of many major shopping centres, often with associated leisure facilities, on the fringe of the metropolis means that the major source of traffic growth now is of such radial journeys. Croydon Tramlink, for example, a light railway which skirts around

the fringes of south London from Wimbledon to Beckenham via Croydon, has been highly successful in terms of attracting large numbers of passengers; and many new bus routes have been introduced to serve this market.

14 Hugh Douglas, *The Underground Story*, Robert Hale, 1963, p. 98.

15 These are the modern names – all three, curiously, started off with different ones: Acton Green, Mill Hill Park and Ealing Common & West Acton.

Chapter Six: THE SEWER RATS

1 Fred T. Jane, 'Round the Underground on an Engine', *English Illustrated Magazine*, August 1893.

2 R.D. Blumenthal, *Diary 1887–1914*, Heinemann, 1930.

3 Quoted in Roy Porter, *London, a social history*, Penguin, 1994, p. 213, from a contemporary but unspecified source.

4 Porter, p. 225.

5 O.S. Nock, *Underground Railways of the World*, A & C Black, 1973, p. 34.

6 The District briefly later tried a parcels service in East London using tricycles to carry the goods off the train to their final destination, but it was not a success as it did not really have a competitive edge over rival road services.

7 *The Times*, 14 December 1904.

8 For example, the Strategic Rail Authority estimated in 2002 that it would cost a staggering £154m to electrify, using the same third rail method, the twenty-five mile stretch of line between Ashford and Hastings.

Chapter Seven: DEEP UNDER LONDON

1 T.C. Barker and Michael Robbins, *A History of London Transport*, Vol. 1, George Allen & Unwin, 1963, p. 307.

2 Widened in the 1920s to 11ft 8½in, later adopted as the standard tube tunnel size which is still too small for London's needs.

3 *Daily News*, 5 November 1890.

4 *The Times*, 4 November 1890.

5 *Railway Times*, 8 November 1890, p. 545.

6 Conversation with author.

7 Barker and Robbins, p. 313.

8   The City & South London carried 5.1 million passengers in 1891, the first full year of operation, compared with nearly twice that number when the Metropolitan, which was a similar length line, first opened. And numbers increased only slowly over the subsequent decade, reaching only 7 million by 1899.

9   Hugh Douglas, *The Underground Story*, Robert Hale, 1963, p. 139.

10 Where trains run either side of one central, quite narrow, platform. Most of them on the system have been replaced for safety reasons as the Underground has become busier.

11 Later Lord Cowdray, who built up the Pearson company which now owns the *Financial Times* and who, like so many of the developers of the Underground, had strong connections with the USA.

12 In 1975, shortly after the Underground's worst ever disaster, at Moorgate in which forty-one people died, the line transferred to British Rail. After a brief closure, it was converted back to take full-size trains and connected with the rest of the suburban network at Finsbury Park, achieving its original aim seventy years after opening.

13 Barker and Robbins, p. 42.

14 *Railway Times*, 10 November 1900.

15 J. Graeme Bruce and Desmond Croome, *The Twopenny Tube*, Capital Transport, 1996, p. 18.

16 O.S. Nock, *Underground Railways of the World*, A & C Black, 1973, p. 76.

17 Charles E. Lee, *The Central Line, a brief history*, London Transport, 1973, p. 17.

18 *The Times*, 29 August 1900.

19 *The Times*, 30 August 1900.

20 *The Times*, 1 August 1900.

21 *The Times*, 2 October 1900.

22 Richard Trench and Ellis Hillman, *London under London, a subterranean guide*, John Murray, 1985, p. 147.

23 *Daily Mail*, 30 July 1900.

24 *Railway Times*, 25 August 1900.

25 Nock, p. 82.

26 It is, today, the second busiest, after the Northern, of the tube lines with 600,000 users daily on weekdays.

27 *The Sun*, 30 July 1900.

28 From *San Toy* in *The Emperor's Own* by Sidney Jones, 1905.

29 As a result of the large amount of US capital used to fund the line, the locomotives and the electrical equipment, including the power station at Shepherd's Bush, were American-designed and built.

30 *The Times*, 29 September 1900.

31 *The Times*, 9 October 1900.

32 It was to be almost forty years before the name of Wood Lane station was officially changed to White City in recognition of the long-forgotten exhibition.

33 Lee.

Chapter Eight: THE DODGY AMERICAN

1 *Trilogy of Desire.*

2 From Tim Sherwood, a biography of Yerkes, unpublished, London Transport Museum.

3 Sidney I. Roberts, 'Portrait of a Robber Baron: Charles T. Yerkes', *Business History Review*, 1961, xxxv (3) pp. 344–71.

4 In the event he seems to have put in only $316,000, according to the University records.

5 Sherwood, op.cit.

6 Alan A. Jackson and Desmond F. Croome, *Rails through Clay*, George Allen & Unwin, 1962, p. 64.

7 Dennis Edwards and Ron Pigram, *London's Underground Suburbs*, Baton Transport, 1986, p. 10.

8 Mike Horne, *The Bakerloo Line*, Capital Transport, 2001, p. 7.

9 Ibid.

10 Detailed in David McKie, 'The fall of a Midas', *Guardian,* 2 February 2004.

11 A reasonable approximation of the financial figures in this chapter would be to multiply them by a factor of fifty to calculate what these sums are worth at 2004 prices.

12 T.C. Barker and Michael Robbins make an attempt to explain Yerkes's method of raising money in the second volume of their seminal work, *A History of London Transport*, George Allen & Unwin, 1974 (pp. 71–2), but it is only partial and, not surprisingly, convoluted.

13 Barker and Robbins, Vol. 2, p. 72.

14 Quoted in ibid., p. 71.

15 Edwards and Pigram, p. 10.

16 Barker and Robbins, Vol. 2, p. 74.

17 Horne, p. 11.

18 Jackson and Croome, p. 107.

19 The far-sighted nature of this innovation is demonstrated by the fact that though the system has long been installed on all underground lines, the overground railways resisted installing a similar system, resulting in many fatal crashes – most notably Ladbroke Grove in 1999. Only now, nearly a century later, has a similar device called Train Protection and Warning System been introduced on Britain's main lines, and even this is not 100 per cent effective at speeds above seventy mph.

20 An odd choice since there was no formal connection between the two bodies and, indeed, the LCC repeatedly refused to bail out the Underground in subsequent years.

21 Who wrote under the name Sekon, his name spelt backwards.

22 Daily Mail, 4 April 1906.

23 R.D. Blumenthal, Diary 1887–1914, Heinemann, 1930.

24 Jackson and Croome, p. 83.

25 Quoted in Barker and Robbins, Vol. 2, p. 82.

26 Quoted in ibid., p. 84.

27 House of Commons, Parliamentary Debates, 113, columns 1144–1154.

28 According to research by the London Transport Museum.

29 The Times, 2 October 1911.

30 Charles E. Lee, The Piccadilly Line, a brief history, London Transport, 1973.

31 By 1994, with only 600 daily users, the branch was doomed when the lifts needed replacing at an estimated cost of £5m and now it has a better role as the preferred location for any film requiring a scene in the Tube.

32 Although platforms under a pub called the Bull & Bush between Hampstead and Golders Green were built, they were never connected with the surface.

33 In one of those historical confusions, some contemporary reports say three.

34 Hampstead & Highgate Express, 22 June 1907.

35 Edwards and Pigram, p. 10.

36 In fact, the Suburb, as it is known locally, soon became a middle-class enclave, because after the war houses were only built for sale rather than

letting; but it still represents one of the best examples of early town planning and suburban domestic development with, today, 13,000 residents.

37 Jackson and Croome, p. 122.

38 Starting whistles were tried briefly on the Piccadilly in 1907 but were quickly rejected, probably because they made the noisy atmosphere even worse.

39 Quoted in Jackson and Croome, p. 121.

40 The practice continues today: there were massively over-optimistic projections of passenger numbers for both the Channel Tunnel and the high-speed link to the tunnel, without which they would not have been built. There have even been attempts to quantify the likely level of overestimate.

That does not mean these schemes do not benefit society but merely that the analytical tools to assess them are insufficiently developed. A financial assessment of the Victoria line made thirty years after the first section opened in 1968 still suggested that it was only a marginally worthwhile development even when taking into account the social benefits, such as savings on car journey times. Looked at purely financially, the Victoria line appeared to be a complete non-runner, destined for massive losses and with no hope of making a financial return. Yet the line is operating at virtually full capacity for much of the day and is a vital part of London's infrastructure. Thus, even with the benefit of hindsight, private investment would not pay its way and this strongly suggests that the dream of Yerkes and Speyer to make high returns out of building tube lines could never be realized, especially given that the technology at the time was so much more primitive than that available to the contractors on the Victoria line.

Chapter Nine: BEGINNING TO MAKE SENSE

1 Indeed, local politicians were not to gain control of London Transport until 1970, and, after losing it in 1986 with the abolition of the GLC, did not regain it until 2003, a measure of the instability of the complex relationship between central and local government over London's transport system.

2 A familiar complaint. Even today, London Transport receives around half the level of subsidy in relation to income compared with its counterparts in European cities – typically only 30 per cent of its money comes from subsidy, compared with twice that level in Paris or Berlin.

3 *The Times*, 24 June 1907.

4 By coincidence, both momentous years in the future history of London's transport system: the creation of London Transport and its nationalization.

5 The family was originally called Knattriess.

6 Stanley told this story, for which there is no contemporary evidence, much later in life.

7 Much was well designed, such as the folding card for the Hampstead, which, when opened, revealed a tube train emerging from a tunnel.

8 The early maps all fall into the trap of trying to represent the real path of the Underground rather than the schematic illustration which Beck introduced.

9 *The Times*, 7 October 1908.

10 Alan A. Jackson and Desmond F. Croome, *Rails through Clay*, George Allen & Unwin, 1962, p. 137.

11 Ibid., p. 149.

12 Ibid., p. 143.

13 John Betjeman, *London's Historic Railway Stations*, John Murray, 1972.

14 Piers Connor, *Going Green*, Capital Transport, 1993, p. 40.

Chapter Ten: THE UNDERGROUND IN THE FIRST WORLD WAR

1 Stephen Halliday, *Underground to Everywhere*, Sutton Publishing, 2001, p. 151.

2 *Railway Gazette*, 5 October 1917.

3 Cited in John Gregg, *The Shelter of the Tubes*, Capital Transport, 2001, p. 5.

4 Interestingly, work on that railway, with its little two-foot gauge trains and nine-foot diameter tunnels, continued despite the war until 1917, but it was not actually fully fitted out and opened for a further decade.

5 Alan A. Jackson and Desmond F. Croome, *Rails through Clay*, George Allen & Unwin, 1962, p. 155.

6 Stanley's talents had been spotted by the government which enlisted him in the war effort first as director-general of mechanical transport at the Ministry of Munitions in 1916 and then as President of the Board of Trade, a post which necessitated finding him a seat in the House of Commons and which he held until May 1919.

Chapter Eleven: REACHING OUT

1   He later became Lord Brabazon of Tara and had been a keen early aviator in his youth. His main claim to fame was that in 1909 he took a pig up in his aircraft in order to show that the saying about pigs not being able to fly was mistaken. The poor creature was strapped into a bucket on which the slogan 'I am the first pig to fly' had been written.

2   Alan A. Jackson and Desmond F. Croome, *Rails through Clay*, George Allen & Unwin, 1962, p. 186.

3   Read out at a public inquiry held by the London and Home Counties Traffic Advisory Committee.

4   Christian Barman, *The Man who built London Transport, a biography of Frank Pick*, David & Charles, 1979.

5   Jackson and Croome, p. 206.

6   Dennis Edwards and Ron Pigram, *London's Underground Suburbs*, Baton Transport, 1986, p. 38.

7   Desmond F. Croome, *The Piccadilly Line*, Capital Transport, 1998, p. 45.

8   O.S. Nock, *Underground Railways of the World*, A & C Black, 1973, p. 177.

Chapter Twelve: METROLAND, THE SUBURBAN PARADOX

1   Quoted in Dennis Edwards and Ron Pigram, *The Romance of Metroland*, Baton Transport, 1986, p. 24.

2   Quoted in Edwards and Pigram, *The Romance of Metroland*, p. 26.

3   Say, £30,000 to £65,000 today, but comparisons are difficult because house prices have risen much faster than the retail price index.

4   Edwards and Pigram, *The Romance of Metroland*, p. 26.

5   Thereafter, despite the annual cup final and a few other events, Wembley Stadium's mainstay was its greyhound track, which attracted large crowds travelling by the Underground.

6   Some survived in a different form: the Palestinian one became a Glasgow laundry and the New Zealand one a dance hall.

7   Dennis Edwards and Ron Pigram, *London's Underground Suburbs*, Baton Transport, 1986, p. 66.

8   Quote in Edwards and Pigram, *London's Underground Suburbs*, p. 71.

9   Stephen Halliday, *Underground to Everywhere*, Sutton Publishing, 2001, p. 114.

10 Hugh Douglas, *The Underground Story*, Robert Hale, 1963, p. 162.

11 Mike Horne, *The Jubilee Line*, Capital Transport, 2000, p. 16.

12 Edwards and Pigram, *London's Underground Suburbs*, p. 72.

13 Christian Barman, *The Man who built London Transport, a biography of Frank Pick*, David and Charles 1979, p. 247.

Chapter Thirteen: THE PERFECT ORGANIZATION?

1   T.C. Barker and Michael Robbins, *A History of London Transport*, Vol. 2, George Allen & Unwin, 1974, p. 287.

2   Christian Barman, *The man who built London Transport , a biography of Frank Pick*, David & Charles, 1979, p. 205.

3   F.A.A. Menzler, address to the Institute of Public Administration, *Lord Ashfield and the public corporation*, 1951.

4   Ibid.

5   Barker and Robbins, p. 285.

6   Lord Ashfield, 'London's Traffic Problem Reconsidered', *The 19th Century and After Review*, August 1924, p. 4.

7   John Glover, *London's Underground*, Ian Allan, 1999, p. 39.

8   Gavin Weightman and Steve Humphries, *The Making of Modern London, 1914–1939*, Sidgwick & Jackson, 1984.

9   It was originally published in the *Daily Herald* and is quoted in Bernard Donoghue and G.W. Jones, *Herbert Morrison, Portrait of a Politician*, Phoenix Press, 2001, p. 116.

10 Donoghue and Jones, p. 121.

11 Ibid., p. 145.

12 House of Commons, 31 March 1931.

13 *Financial News*, 14 March 1931.

14 Donoghue and Jones, p. 145.

15 Jonathan Glancey, *London bread and circuses*, Verso, 2001, p. 38.

16 Indeed, this lack of integration still causes problems today. When Transport for London introduced the Oyster card in 2004, it could not be used on much of the suburban rail network for individual journeys.

17 Menzler.

18 This was the first Lord Hailsham, the father of the one who was Lord Chancellor in the 1970s and 1980s.

19 House of Lords, 30 March 1933.

20 Donoghue and Jones, p. 114.

21 Barman, p. 155.

22 Ibid., p. 160.

23 Ibid., p. 155.

24 Glancey, p. 35. It was the financial framework which Ken Livingstone, the London Mayor, would seek, unsuccessfully, in his battle with the government during 2001–2 over the Public Private Partnership.

25 Barman, p. 26.

26 Oliver Green and Jeremy-Rewse Davies, *Designed for London: 150 years of transport design*, Laurence King Publications, 1995, p. 13.

27 A term not invented until the 1960s.

28 Green and Davies, p. 15.

29 Quoted in Ibid., p. 15.

30 Nikolaus Pevsner, *Studies in Art, Architecture & Design*, Vol. 2, Thames & Hudson,1968, p. 193.

31 It now includes other railways such as the Docklands Light Railway and the North London line. See Tim Demuth, *The Spread of London's Underground*, Capital Transport, 2003.

32 But visitors may be deceived, too. Bill Bryson points out in his book *Notes From a Small Island* that a tourist might use Beck's map to get from, say, Bank Station to Mansion House, which would involve a change and six stops, only to emerge 200 yards down the street from where he started.

33 A transport term to describe the share of each mode of transport – bus, rail, car, underground etc. – as a percentage of overall journeys.

34 To put this in perspective: even though there was for most people no alternative form of transport in those days, that total represents just half the numbers travelling on a system that is only slightly bigger, with two extra lines, today. Given that car journeys have soared, too, and that the population of the capital is now smaller, that reflects the massive increase in mobility today compared with sixty-five years ago.

35 Barker and Robbins, p. 282.

Chapter Fourteen: THE BEST SHELTERS OF ALL

1 *Daily Telegraph*, 2 September 1940. Some of the newspaper quotes in this chapter are taken from the very comprehensive book, *The Shelter of the Tubes* by John Gregg, published by Capital Transport, 2001.

2 *Daily Worker*, 7 September 1940.

3 Gregg, p. 24.

4 *South London Press*, 1 October 1940.

5 Quoted in the *Hampstead & Highgate Express*, 3 January 1941.

6 Gregg, p. 24.

Chapter Fifteen: DECLINE – AND REVIVAL?

1 Part of this chapter is based on Chapter 3 of my previous book, *Down the Tube*, Aurum Press, 2002.

2 Steen Eiler Rasmussen, *London, the Unique City*, MIT Press, 1934, p. 343.

3 There are, incidentally, also well-documented tales of pigeons deliberately hopping into a train for a stop or two, apparently knowing precisely their destination.

4 The figures are not entirely comparable with those in previous chapters because the BTC included those who had travelled on the Underground using British Railways tickets.

5 The first recruits came by boat but flying became the norm thereafter.

6 Interviewed by Felicity Premru at the London Transport Museum for the exhibition 'Sun-a-shine, rain-a-fall'.

7 As Stephen Halliday points out in *Underground to Everywhere*, in the five years '1954–9 the value of the Underground's fixed assets increased by less than 5 per cent before depreciation, which demonstrates that the assets were being run down rather than built up'. It was what economists call disinvestment. In 1955, the British Transport Commission launched a plan to modernize the national rail network and replace steam with diesel at a cost of £1.24bn (over £20bn at today's prices) in the ensuing fifteen years but made nothing available for London Transport.

8 After three failed attempts to shut it, the line was finally closed in 1994 when there were so few passengers – 100 per day – that the drivers reportedly said they knew most of them.

9 T.C. Barker and Michael Robbins, *A History of London Transport*, Vol. 2, George Allen & Unwin, 1974, p. 344.

10 A small pamphlet, *London Transport Railway Signalling, papers on the life and work of Robert Dell 1900–1992*, Nebulous Books, 1999, outlines his achievements.

11 Computers generally drive the trains in a more economical way, although the issue is quite complex. The frequent adjustments to the speed made automatically, compared with a human being who will make fewer changes, can increase the wear and tear on a train.

12 London Transport Executive, *Annual Report and Accounts for the year ended 31 December 1971*, p. 22.

13 The only other accident of note, the first major tube disaster, occurred on the Central line in April 1953 in a tunnel east of Stratford. There had been a signal failure and trains were being allowed through on a 'stop and proceed with caution' basis, but the driver clearly went too fast and slammed into the rear end of the train in front. Twelve people were killed and forty-six injured, and safety procedures following signal failures were tightened up.

14 See C. Wolmar, *Down the Tube*, Aurum Press, 2002, Chapter 4, for a detailed account of the King's Cross disaster.

15 Desmond Fennell, *Investigation into the King's Cross Fire*, HMSO, 1988, Cm 499.

16 My previous book, *Down the Tube*, is an account of how the PPP scheme came about.

17 National Audit Office, *London Underground: Are the Public Private Partnerships likely to work successfully* and *London Underground PPP: Were they good deals*, The Stationery Office, 2004.

FURTHER READING

This is a list of books to which I have referred and which are likely to be of interest to the general reader. It is by no means comprehensive.

Benjamin Baker, *The Metropolitan and Metropolitan District Railways*, Institution of Civil Engineers, 1885.

Felix Barker, *Edwardian London*, Laurence King, 1995.

T.C. Barker and Michael Robbins, *A History of London Transport*, Volumes 1 and 2, George Allen & Unwin, 1963 and 1974.

Christian Barman, *The Man who built London Transport*, David & Charles, 1979.

John Wolfe Barry, *The City lines and extensions (inner circle completion) of the Metropolitan and District railway*, Institution of Civil Engineers, 1885.

J. Graeme Bruce, *Tube Trains Under London*, London Transport, 1968.

J.E. Connor, *Abandoned stations on London's Underground*, Connor & Butler, 2000.

J.E. Connor, *Stepney's own railway, a history of the London & Blackwall system*, Connor & Butler, 1984.

Mark D'Arcy and Rory MacLean, *Nightmare, the race to become London's Mayor*, Politico's, 2000.

R. Davies and M.D. Grant, *London and its railways*, Book Club Associates and David & Charles, 1983.

John R. Day and John Reed, *The story of London's Underground*, Capital Transport, 2001.

Tim Demuth, *The Spread of London's Underground*, Capital Transport, 2003.

Bernard Donoghue and G.W. Jones, *Herbert Morrison, Portrait of a Politician*, Phoenix Press, 2001.

Hugh Douglas, *The Underground Story*, Robert Hale, 1963.

Dennis Edwards and Ron Pigram, *London's Underground Suburbs*, Baton Transport, 1986.

Dennis Edwards and Ron Pigram, *The Romance of Metroland*, Baton Transport, 1986.

Andrew Emmerson, *The Underground Pioneers*, Capital Transport, 2000.

Desmond Fennell, *Investigation into the King's Cross Fire*, HMSO 1988, Cm 499.

Clive Foxell, *The story of the Met and GC joint line*, self-published, 2001.

Jonathan Glancey, *London, bread and circuses*, Verso, 2001.

John Glover, *London's Underground, the world's premier underground system*, Ian Allan, 1999 (ninth edition).

John Glover, *Principles of London Underground Operations*, Ian Allan, 2000.

John Gregg, *The Shelter of the Tubes*, Capital Transport, 2001.

Stephen Halliday, *Making the Metropolis, creators of Victoria's London*, Breedon Books, 2003.

Stephen Halliday, *Underground to Everywhere*, Sutton Publishing, 2001.

H.F. Howson, *London's Underground*, Ian Allan, 1962.

Steve Humphries and Gavin Weightman, *The making of modern London, 1815–1914*, Sidgwick & Jackson, 1983.

Steve Humphries and Gavin Weightman, *The making of modern London, 1914–1939*, Sidgwick & Jackson, 1984.

Steve Humphries and Joanna Mack, *The making of modern London, 1939–1945, London at war*, Sidgwick & Jackson, 1985.

Alan A. Jackson, *London's local railways*, Capital Transport, 1999.

Alan A. Jackson, *London's Metropolitan Railway*, David & Charles, 1986.

Alan A. Jackson, *London's termini*, David & Charles, 1985.

Alan A. Jackson, *Semi-detached London*, second edition 1991, Wild Swan Publications.

Alan A. Jackson and Desmond F. Croome, *Rails through Clay*, George Allen & Unwin, 1962.

John Kellett, *The Impact of Railways on Victorian Cities*, Routledge & Kegan Paul, 1969.

Charles Klapper, *London's lost railways*, Routledge & Kegan Paul, 1976.

Peter Laurie, *Beneath the City Streets*, Penguin, 1972.

Henry Mayhew, *The shops and companies of London and the trades and manufactories of Great Britain*, Strand Printing and Publishing, 1865.

O.S. Nock, *Underground Railways of the World*, A & C Black, 1973.

Mark Ovenden, *Metro Maps of the World*, Capital Transport, 2003.

Ben Pimlott and Nirmala Rao, *Governing London*, Oxford University Press, 2002.

Roy Porter, *A Social History of London*, Penguin, 1994.

Steen Eiler Rasmussen, *London, the Unique City*, MIT Press, 1934.

Sheila Taylor (ed.), *The Moving Metropolis, a history of London's transport since 1800*, Laurence King, 2002.

Richard Trench and Ellis Hillman, *London under London, a subterranean guide*, John Murray, 1985.

H.P. White, *A regional history of the railways of Great Britain*, Vol. 3 *Greater London*, David St John Thomas, 1987.

John Withington, *Capital Disasters*, Sutton Publishing, 2003.

Christian Wolmar, *Down the Tube*, Aurum Press, 2002.

The line history pamphlets produced by Capital Transport and written by various authors are very useful. They now cover all the Underground lines and earlier versions for most were produced in the 1970s by London Transport.

Underground News is a monthly newsletter produced by the London Underground Railway Society with a wealth of information about the system.

INDEX

West Kensington
116–17
West London Advertiser
89
West London Air
Terminal 2
West London line 65,
67–8, 79, 103
West Ruislip station 294
Westbourne Park station
66
Westbourne River 72, 73
Westminster station 72,
74, 109
White City 159
Whitechapel & Bow
Railway 102
Whitechapel station 84,
101, 102
Whitehall 119
Wilhelm II, Kaiser 210
Willesden Green station
96
Willesden Junction 103,
208, 209
Williams, Watkin:
'The Underground
Railway' (comic song)
51
Willing, J 56
Wimbledon Common
106
Wimbledon station 106,
107, 224, 320n

Windsor station 49, 60,
68, 103, 106
Wire, David 31
Wolseley, Lieutenant
General Sir Garnet 94
women
employment during the
First World War
213–14, 291
employment during the
Second World War
290–91
Wood Green 118, 226
Wood Green station 63,
64, 65, 178
Wood Lane station (later
White City; closed)
153, 159, 322n
Worcester 94
workmen's trains 54–6,
118, 119, 142
Wright, Whitaker 168–9

Yerkes, Charles Tyson
123, 160, 195, 298,
303, 311, 324n
colourful early life in
America 161–5
takes control of the
District 123, 166
electrification issue 123
intention of uniting the
underground network
127, 176

promised increase in
traffic 128
and funding 147,
169–72, 192–3, 197
controls much of the
underground network
161
partnership with Perks
165, 166, 184
buys up the Baker
Street & Waterloo
169
creates the UERL 169
Charing Cross, Euston
& Hampstead line
172–3
replaced by Speyer as
chairman of UERL
174
design pattern on
Yerkes tubes 175–6
and flat fares 176, 197,
198
declared aim of 176–7
and Morgan 178–81
and Sellon 190–91
ensures that London
had a tube network
191
Yerkes Observatory,
University of Chicago
64